the
craft
of
advice

essays 1995-1998

D1571136

nick
murray

OTHER BOOKS BY NICK MURRAY:

The Excellent Investment Advisor
On Becoming A Great Wholesaler

AUDIOTAPE PROGRAM:

You Are What You Do

Library of Congress Catalog Card Number: 99-90006
ISBN: 0-9669763-0-4

This book is for my son
MARK PATRICK MURRAY
artist's eye, hero's heart

In the life of an artist, there comes
a moment when he realizes that
to pursue his talent he has to make
a commitment to his art that he must honor,
no matter what hardships he has to endure.

– Paul Alexander
Boulevard of Broken Dreams:
The Life, Times and Legend of James Dean

For every thing you have missed
you have gained something else ...

– Emerson
Compensation

Contents

Contents

Foreword To The Essays

This book contains 34 essays written for *Dow Jones Investment Advisor* magazine between December 1994 and December 1998. It also includes 10 book reviews published in *Dow Jones Asset Management* magazine in 1997 and 1998; these are the subject of their own foreword later on in the book.

By any reasonable standard, this was a brilliant period in the life of the world — a time of generalized (though not universal) peace, prosperity, rapidly expanding political freedom and property rights, and the continuing eclipse of big government.

For those of us who manage investments as well as the emotions of the people who own those investments, an unprecedented torrent of change was compressed into these four years.

First of all, markets were spectacularly volatile, surging upwards by thousands of Dow points in a matter of months, then correcting savagely in a few weeks late in 1997, roaring to new all-time highs again — and then putting on the fastest peak-to-trough-to-peak bear market in our lifetimes. For many investment advisors, the difficulty of keeping the markets in perspective was nothing compared to dealing with the euphoria/terror cycle of investor psychology.

And at the same time, the financial services profession itself was undergoing profound change — revolutionary rather than evolutionary in nature, and with several revolutions happening at once. In this brief period, we experienced (1) the accelerating conversion of our industry from commissions to fees, (2) immense technological advancement which multiplied our capacity to serve our clients but also metastasized their temptation to do "it" themselves, and (3) the *de facto* repeal of Glass-Steagall, promising a new dawn of comprehensive financial planning in which one family can finally have one advisor.

Yet if these essays have a single common theme — and I was somewhat startled to find that they do — it is not merely coping with

vii

change, or managing it, or even understanding it. The theme is rising above change — transcending that which varies, and rooting one's professional beliefs and behaviors in the things which do not change at all. And, of course, the thing above all things which does not change is human nature.

Economies, markets, investments, and technology are all subject to significant change; the immutability of human nature is not just *a* constant but *the* constant in our professional lives. And since financial independence proceeds not from investment performance but from investor behavior, human nature must be the first and final study of the Excellent Investment Advisor.

In the last great romantic novel of the 20th century, John Le Carré's *The Russia House*, the narrator says of the noblest of his colleagues, "In that sense he was the determined primitive, as people who deal in human nature have to be." The goal of these essays is to give aid and comfort to the determined primitives in our profession — those in quest of that simplicity which lies beyond sophistication.

This book is meant to be read in addition to — and certainly not instead of — *The Excellent Investment Advisor.* EIA is, above all, a system, and it demands to be read more or less systematically. But these pieces are as discontinuous as the events and emotions which occasioned them each month. Thus I hope the reader will enjoy dipping into them at random, and/or repairing to whichever of them resonates with the concerns of a particular moment.

And if you have even half as much fun reading these essays as I had writing them, we'll both be way ahead.

THE GHOST OF BUSINESS FUTURE ... THE GHOST OF BUSINESS PAST

Old centuries do not necessarily end in years numbered 99, nor do new centuries start in years that end in double zeros.

The 19th century really didn't end, nor the 20th century begin, until the summer of 1914, with the outbreak of The Great War. And the 20th century ended, I'm convinced, on November 9, 1989, the night the Berlin Wall came down. We have entered the 21st century not with the start of a war, but with the onset of a global capitalist revolution.

At the same time, our business has undergone almost a tectonic shift, and it bears virtually no resemblance to the business as it existed even five years ago. The nation's first mutual fund, Massachusetts Investors Trust, was started in 1924; on the night the Wall came down 65 years later, there were still fewer than $1 trillion in mutual funds. Just four years later, mutual fund assets hit $2 trillion, and nothing about the way Americans save and invest will ever be the same.

Similarly, not that many years ago, the bank handled an American's checking, savings, and home mortgage; a life insurance agent handled his life and health insurance; and a stockbroker sold him individual stocks and bonds. Today, all of those walls are falling; each of those three entities now provides virtually all of these products and services, and each offers complete financial planning/asset management.

As in every other area of our lives, from health care to technology, the pace of change has accelerated to a rate that is almost blinding. And it is axiomatic that those in the middle of such rapid change are often least able to see it for what it is. (Indeed, I do not think it's unfair to say that, on Election Day '94, there was an immense change — the kind you see maybe three times in a century — in our political landscape. And yet, in his public statements in the days following the election, the President of the United States gave no indication that he understood what it really meant.)

So, in this last column of the year, I'd like to set out what I see as the major elements of the sea change that's taken place in our industry. I'd encourage you to sit down and take stock of your business (as well as of your business plan) to assess, as cold-bloodedly as you can, whether you're looking backward or forward.

And even if you're doing a high level of business, you'd better realize that, if it's backward-looking business, it's moribund. You can be doing a whole lot of volume, and your business can still be dying: that's the nature of very rapid, total change.

For instance, have you been in a video store lately? Lots of people going in and out, you can't get new releases for weeks because they're always out, the cash register's firing ... looks like a great business, doesn't it? And yet, quite clearly, in a very few years this business will be dead. All the video stores — not many, not most, *all* — will be closed. Why? Because, on that great gettin' up morning when the information superhighway reaches your house — when your TV, PC, and phone have merged, and are interactive — the first thing you're going to be able to do is dial up every movie ever made, at any hour of the day or night.

And on that day, all the video stores will close. (No one sees this inevitability more clearly, or is repositioning his company more effectively in the face of it, than Wayne Huizenga of Blockbuster Video.)

So it is with our business. I don't care if you're running the biggest, most profitable transaction-oriented, commission-based financial services "video store" in your town. Your business is as good as dead; it's just waiting to fall over.

Here, then, is my take on the future and the past.

1. It used to be about commissions; it's going to be about fees. We are clearly going to get paid in the future to gather assets, deploy them advantageously to the client ... and keep them on the books, for a fee. We will, in other words, finally get paid to advise the client to do nothing, if nothing is the right thing for him to do.

"Wrap fee" was sort of the Bastille Day of this revolution; the explosive success of "wrap" showed the intense hunger of the investing public for fee-based asset management, rather than commissions with their inherent, insurmountable potential conflict of interest. (However, since all revolutions devour their children, "wrap" itself is, I believe, doomed; it's been consigned to the guillotine by "C" shares. And good riddance. Three points? Yuck.)

Fee arrangements will continue to develop through many more iterations (and the overall level of fees will continue to go down, as assets under management continue to explode). But the genie is out of the bottle, never to be put back. "A" shares will always have their place because they're cheaper for the client in the long run (though I do not accept that "cheaper" is always synonymous with "better"). But Americans hate 'em. Believe me: I have seen the future, and it is fees.

2. It used to be about transactions; it's going to be about relationships. Gathering, deploying, and retaining assets is (and ought to be) intensely relationship-oriented. The plan, the goals, the proper portfolio balance, the long-term focus — these are the watchwords of the 21st century, just as "Buy it now; it's hot" is a cry from the past.

You generally think — and not without justification — of wirehouses as being terminally transaction-oriented. So, when you see Merrill Lynch's brilliant new advertising campaign for financial planning, you have to know that the millennium is already here.

That's why it's so sad to see relationship-oriented investments sold in a transaction-oriented way. Virtually all "no-help" funds are advertised in this kind of "It's been shooting the lights out for the last three years so buy it now because it's hot" way, which sets the investor up to fail. (Nor, if the truth be told, are "help" funds insusceptible to this temptation. I recently saw an ad for a "help" fund that actually said that the kind of stocks it buys historically get a pop over the three months through January. In other words, buy this cornerstone of an intelligent long-term fund portfolio *right now* because you'll get a trade out of it. When are we going to learn?)

Look carefully at the way you present investments to people. Are you helping them achieve the great goals of life, or are you renting them a video?

3. It used to be about knowledge, it's going to be about trust. People don't begin to care what you know until they begin to know that you care. And, if they sense that you really care about 'em, they'll trust you with everything they've got. No amount of superior smarts induces that magic act of faith; indeed, quite the contrary, I've always said that people don't really want to know *how* it's going to be all right; they just want to know *that* it's going to be all right. Knowledge makes you a good financial advisor/investor on people's behalf, and therefore, makes you more confident that you can get the job done for people. But it's the confidence people respond to, and not the knowledge behind it.

Knowledge, almost by its nature, is insidiously transaction-oriented ("this annuity *will* outperform *because...*"). Knowledge, in other words, causes you to make an argument, so please don't be surprised if your prospective client argues back. And all arguments in the context of our business are the tar baby.

If a prospect believes I have his best interest at heart, and senses (rather than comprehends) the depth of my store of knowledge, he intuitively knows that I won't recommend second-rate investments. So, I don't really have anything to prove (which is good, because in our business you can't really prove anything). Try to think of knowledge as a wonderful secret that someone has entrusted to you: it wouldn't be polite to tell it to anyone else.

4. It used to be about the phone; it's going to be almost totally face-to-face. The phone is an excellent, highly efficient medium for transactions. Relationships are forged and initiated face-to-face. This is why people with life insurance sales training start the new century so far ahead of everybody else: They were always trained to get in front of the prospect, just the way stockbrokers are trained to get the prospect on the phone. (It also doesn't hurt the life insurance folks that the first truly 21st century product, variable universal life, comes from them, not from Wall Street.)

You might consider using the month of January to take a very scientific reading of how much of your business month you spend face-to-face with folks. If it's a whole lot less than a third, I'd say that's a really nice video store you've got there. (And please don't tell me you have a lot of service work to do in January, what with getting people year-end statements and all. That's busy work used as an avoidance behavior. Delegate it and go have lunch with a client.)

Oh, and by the way, if you apply the January test to your business and get a reading north of 60% (that is, 60% of your business month was spent face-to-face with folks), I'd say you've got it knocked.

5. It used to be about asset turnover; it's going to be about asset retention. Hey, what about asset *gathering*? Isn't that what the millennium is all about? Well, no, actually, asset gathering is an indispensable means to an end; it's not the end. Asset *retention* is the end (just as in the bad old days, turning the assets over was the end).

This ought to put "performance" in a whole new light for you. If you're selling only top-performing funds, you are probably selling funds that are taking maximum risk in order to get the top performance. (Does the word "derivatives" resonate anywhere in your consciousness?) Hanging your clients' assets over the edge so that you get to hide behind performance statistics is *very* yesterday.

Serious people, investing their (you should pardon the expression) serious money, are not trying primarily to make a killing; they are trying to keep from being killed … while earning solid, consistent returns over the long term. (Hint: the next time someone says to you, "The fund you put me in hasn't done anything all year; I'd have been better off in cash," fire him. If it happens more than six times in the next six months, fire yourself. You're running a video store. Get serious, so you can get serious accounts.)

The key to a 21st century business is asset retention. The key to asset retention is managing client expectations. Managing expectations is the antithesis of "performance" selling. If you're planning to be in the business for any length of time, don't sell the sizzle, sell the blackened redfish. (Steak? Who the hell eats red meat anymore?)

6. It used to be about the man; to a startling extent, it's going to be about the woman. If this comes off like some kind of reverse sexism, I'm sorry; I just call 'em as I see 'em. But through death, divorce, lifestyle choices, and their booming careers, women are going to control a vastly larger piece of the investable pie in the new millennium than they did in the old one. You're either incorporating this inescapable fact into every phase of your business plan, or you're very slowly tying one of your hands behind your back.

7. It used to be about stock price appreciation; for a while, anyway, it may be about dividends. The '80s were terrific, I guess, but I tend to agree with Putnam's Dr. Bob Goodman that the only people who really made money in the '80s were those who dollar-cost-averaged through the '70s.

At any rate, a long period of overperformance in returns from equities, such as we had from 1982 through 1993, is not usually followed by another long period of overperformance. *Au contraire.* So, if you think that we may be in for more than another six weeks of pretty bland returns from stocks (at least relative to what people — and "no-help" fund advertising departments — have gotten used to), you better pay a lot more attention to dividends. Because, in a pe-riod of below-trendline returns (that is, less than the long-term 10% to 11%), dividends become much more important, financially and psychologically.

And, in the long run, it's the dividends from their stock funds that clients are going to be living on; you can't take your NAV to the supermarket. Moreover, dividends are much more stable than stock prices, and that tends to have a calming effect on the panic-prone. So, if you're going to be stressing asset retention in your business plan, dividends are a platform that will get you elected (and re-elected) a lot more reliably than price appreciation (which becomes very difficult to talk about when prices are, in fact, depreciating).

I sincerely hope that you've found this column a BGO (that is, a Blinding Glimpse of the Obvious). In the spirit of the season — which is that it's better to give than to receive — I hope I don't get any credit for this column ... because every reader says, "Yup; got that; doing that already; no news here; this wasn't one of the old fella's better efforts, but thanks for the reality check."

If, on the other hand, you found anything here that was thought-provoking (and especially if you found a number of things thought-provoking), well, you just might want to close up the video store a little early today, and go on home ... and think about it.

And to you and everyone you love, I say with Tiny Tim: God bless us, every one!

EMERGING MARKET MELTDOWN: DCA DREAM

It was just about a year ago, while I was waiting to go on stage for a client seminar up in Canada, that I heard a mutual fund sponsor speak about what he called "the free lunch of international investing."

He had a bunch of charts and graphs that purported to show that international diversification raised your portfolio's long-term return, while reducing its volatility. And he referred to that phenomenon — not once, but twice — as "the free lunch of international investing."

At first, I thought it was some kind of gag — that he had to be doing some sort of self-parody, because everybody knows there's no such thing as a free lunch. But the second time he said it, I had to accept that he was making (to him) a serious point.

So I waited for the audience to rise in a body, carry this guy out into the public square, and burn him at the stake. It didn't happen. In fact, there were six product presentations at the seminar (which was an all-day-Saturday affair). And, as I watched with mounting horror, five of the six turned out to be about international/emerging market funds.

This was, as you can well imagine, an epiphany for me. You see, up until that time, I had been expecting a few of the more grotesquely overvalued markets (like Hong Kong — up 100% and more in '93) to collapse. But, as I watched sponsor after sponsor troop to the stage and talk as if Canada and the U.S. didn't exist, it began to dawn on me. The emerging markets were *all* going to get killed!

Even then, I doubted my instincts — for another month. That's when the guy who cuts my lawn in summer and plows out my driveway in winter — who had not said three complete sentences to me, all at once, in half a dozen years — stopped me and asked what I thought of emerging markets. It was then that I knew I had received a sell signal from God.

Over the ensuing year, these markets have blown up, one after another, culminating in last month's Mexican meltdown. (And, because everything that goes around comes around, I know that somehow, somewhere, that fund sponsor is choking to death on his free lunch.)

So what I'd like you to do right now is grab a blank piece of paper, and write on it, in big block letters:

EMERGING MARKETS

Have you done that? Okay, now draw a line through the word

~~EMERGING~~

and write above it, in even larger block letters,

TUNA

Now draw a line through the word

~~MARKETS~~

and write above it

FISH

So, you should now have a piece of paper in front of you that says:

TUNA FISH

~~EMERGING MARKETS~~

Am I getting through to you on this? If not, please go back and re-read my July '94 column, *The Great Value Rally of 1994.* In the meantime, just keep reciting your mantra: high prices, bad! low prices, good!

Try to think of all of those emerging markets as little cans of tuna fish, stacked up to the ceiling in the supermarket. Over the five years through the end of '93, every time you came into the supermarket, the price of tuna had been marked up a little more. First it was $1.00 a can, then three for $5.00, then $2.50 each ... then $5.00 ... and then it went totally crazy. ("I don't have to pay $25 a can for your lousy Argentinean tuna fish. Why, I can pay $37.50 all day long in Hong Kong!")

Now, of course, we're at the polar opposite of this tuna/tulip mania. It's now widely reported in the press that tuna is a known carcinogen. There is even a theory that you don't even have to eat the tuna to get cancer. If you just walk past it in the supermarket, it emits cancer-causing rays into your head, like a cellular phone ... .

TINSTAAFL. This word (which my wife pronounces "Tinschtaffel," with the accent on the first syllable) is an acronym that means, of course, "there is no such thing as a free lunch." With respect to emerging markets, I use it to express my core belief:

> Emerging markets will produce
> much higher long-term returns than
> will mature markets ... with much higher volatility.

The early stages of a free-market economy in a devastated country starting from ground zero are bound to be spectacular. Just look at Japan. When the Tokyo stock market opened in 1949, for the first time since the war, the Nikkei stock index stood at 179 ... which is right about where the Dow Jones Industrial Average was on the same day. Since then, the Dow's been to 4000, while the Nikkei's been to 40,000! (Higher returns!) The Dow subsequently declined about 10% from its all-time high (so far, anyway). The Nikkei fell 60% from its high, and remains just off those lows. (Higher volatility!)

Now, I'm not suggesting that Japan be thought of today as an emerging market. But, in the post-war period, I think Japan can fairly be viewed as a paradigm: The Mother of All Emerging Markets. (Nor do I think Japan is atypical because its devastation was war-related. Was Mexico in 1985 any less devastated economically than Japan in 1949? I think not.)

So the upside to emerging markets is decades of catch-up ball, where huge returns can and should be expected. And the downside is political instability, wildly fluctuating currency values, and shallow markets with no effective regulation (nor any particular commitment to even staying open; Hong Kong's stock exchange shut down for a week in the '87 crash). Much higher returns, *much* higher volatility.

Now, for what kind of an investor is a high-return, high-volatility scenario the very best of all possible worlds? Sure: the dollar-cost-averager.

Dollar-cost-averaging remains, to me, the Rodney Dangerfield of investing: No respect! It don't get no respect at all! Here's a technique that can make great investors out of everybody ... and almost nobody consistently does it. (Or maybe, in that sense, DCA might better be analogized to the weather: everybody talks about it, but nobody does anything about it!)

DCA is not only the optimum way to participate in the growth of emerging markets, it may be the only sane way to insulate the investor from the terrible greed/panic cycle that these markets bring out in everyone.

Certainly, DCA is to buy-and-hold in these markets as Dom Perignon is to Dr. Pepper. Where do you buy these markets, anyway, and until when do you hold 'em? How do you know what's fair value — without which you can identify neither undervaluation nor overvaluation? (If you sold Japan when its price/earnings ratio got as high as ours had ever been, for instance, you missed the last 20,000 points!)

Step back from the headlines for just a moment, and try to remember that daily journalism is — because it must be — the permanent, mortal enemy of all truth about investing. This is because today, journalism reports the consensus view today. ("Salinas is a combination of George Washington, FDR, and Keynes; the gallant Mexican people are committed to democracy and capitalism; the peso's as sound as a dollar and the Bolsa's going to the moon.") Then, tomorrow, it reports tomorrow's consensus. ("The lucky Presidential candidate got himself shot; now Zedillo wishes he did. Telmex missed the boat; AT&T is gonna eat their lunch. The peso is toilet paper; the whole country's a quagmire whose problems won't get solved in our lifetime.")

12

The problem here is twofold. (1) The consensus is already in the price. (2) In a volatile situation (which all emerging markets should be regarded as), today's consensus may very well be the diametric opposite of yesterday's. So, just by reporting the rapidly changing and often totally contradictory facts, journalism blinds you to the essential truth. Which is that you'd better have a very strong stomach, and be prepared to ride out some horrific jolts, in order to capture the tremendous potential returns. TINSTAAFL. Just make sure you go in with your eyes open, and that you're prepared to stay the course. And above all, don't buy 'em when they're hot.

These and many of the other "problems" of emerging-market investing are opportunities for the dollar-cost-averager. (Indeed, all investing problems are opportunities for somebody.) You see, the dollar-cost-averager reasons as follows:

1. I'm going to do better than the market(s) I'm investing in, by definition. Since the dollar-cost-averaging approach guarantees that I'll buy more shares at below-average prices, and fewer shares at above-average prices, I'm going to outperform the markets. And that's pretty terrific, because, as we've agreed, emerging markets are going to produce extremely high long-term returns to begin with.

2. I'm completely relieved of any need to know when these markets are overvalued or undervalued. Dollar-cost-averaging does that for me, forcing me to become more and more aggressive during panics and extremely cautious during booms.

3. But wait, it gets better. *The more volatile the markets become, the better I'll do.* Because, of course, volatility — higher highs and lower lows around a rising trendline — exaggerates the benefits of DCA. Once again: the crowd's "problem" is the smart investor's opportunity. "Volatility," the bane of most investors' existence, just makes the dollar-cost-averager even richer.

4. Now, suppose I can pick a fund (or a separate account inside an annuity) whose manager is smarter than the market averages. And go a step further: suppose — although this may be too much to hope for — that the fund I pick, in addition to having returns superior to its relevant index, *is also more volatile!* (Higher returns: good! Higher volatility: *even better!*)

Under these most happy circumstances, we observe the following quite wonderful outcome:

A. The investor far outperforms his own fund.
B. His fund outperforms the emerging market(s) it invests in.
C. Those emerging markets far outperform more mature markets in the long run.
D. The investor gets rich.

Most people ignore the simple beauty of the DCA approach, trying instead to figure out whether Chile's going to beat Peru, or whether this is the "right time" to get back into Hong Kong, or whether Gronsky's Cambodia Fund is going to outperform Gritsky's. (How sophisticated they are; how much smarter than the dumb, happy dollar-cost-averager who never got closer to Mexico than the inside of a Taco Bell. How distressing, then, that the DCA devotee runs rings around all of 'em. *In his sleep.*)

In a recent column, I suggested that you build your business plan for the next year or two around what I call megathemes: huge investment planning concepts that are essentially insensitive to what the markets are doing at any given time. I'd like to add one to that list: dollar-cost-averaging into devastated emerging markets over no less than the next 36 months.

You not only don't have to know when these markets are going to turn, but you can wear that ignorance like a badge of honor. Dollar-cost-averaging knows exactly when they're turning and always reacts appropriately. So you and I, Mr. Client, can bask in our ignorance. We'll let people much "smarter" than we are drill themselves into the ground trying to "time" markets that few people can understand in the first place.

If there's one critical thing I've learned in almost 28 years in the business, it's this: ALL VALUE IS BORN OUT OF CHAOS. And the greatest values — the lifestyle changers that come along once in a decade if you're lucky — are born out of the greatest chaos.

And in the greatest chaos, nobody, but nobody makes more money with less effort than the dollar-cost-averager. She doesn't just outperform the markets; she outperforms her own funds!

I guarantee it.

TIME TO CAPITALIZE ON "NO-HELP" DISILLUSIONMENT

"A period during which common stocks are returned to their rightful owners." That's how a very wise elder of Wall Street defined a bear market for me, when I timidly approached him during my first encounter with the bear in 1969-70.

I loved that definition the moment I heard it, and, as time goes by, I see how it applies to every aspect of the business. Because the principle is truly global: "good" markets favor the amateur, by making it look easy to achieve superior returns. "Bad" markets leave people adrift, feeling betrayed by the things they thought were "good."

In that vein, I think there is a well-nigh pandemic incidence of disillusionment with "no-help" funds (previously, and erroneously, known as "no-load" funds). And I believe that now is a golden time for the professional to begin to capitalize on that disillusionment.

(Please note that when I take the name of "no-help" funds in vain, I am only talking about "no-help" funds bought directly from the sponsor without professional advice, in such a way that the investor gets ... no help. "No-help" funds acquired pursuant to the advice of a fee-based financial planner are (a) just great, (b) actually "help" funds, and (c) excluded from the following discussion.)

If bear markets are when stocks are returned to their rightful owners, I believe the markets we've had over the last year are when accounts are returned to their rightful owners. And we — the investment professionals who render sound advice and are compensated (I care not how) for doing so — are the rightful owners. Make no mistake about it.

I'd be willing to bet that at least three out of four investors — and maybe as high as 85% — would honestly say right now that they need help with their investments. How could they not? Look at the numbers and the kinds of things that have blown up in their faces over the last year and a half.

First and foremost, of course, are bond funds. After the greatest secular bull market in bonds of all time, money cascaded out of CDs and into bond funds — right at the top. (I don't know what percentage of bond fund assets came in under 6.50% on the long bond, but I'll bet it's a very big number.) Investors were then greeted not by a mere correction, nor even by a normal bear attack, but by the biggest bear market in bonds since they've been keeping accurate records (circa 1927).

Utility funds — wildly popular because of their high yield and dividend growth — were also burned beyond recognition. While the broad market averages have never (yet) closed 10% off their all-time highs, utility funds posted 30% peak-to-trough hits.

And let us not forget emerging markets (the subject of last month's column). They were the investment equivalent of a state lottery ticket: the middle class's pipe dream of instant wealth — and everybody bought one. (Some folks bought more than one.)

People simply can't believe the magnitude of their NAV declines, and many of them got 1099'd for capital gains distributions even as they watched their account value melt down. They are seriously interested in understanding how they were double-whammied like that. And my guess is that the 22-year-old customer service rep at the "no-help" fund's 800 number isn't explaining things to their satisfaction.

Overhanging all of this is the generalized discomfort engendered by a whole year of flat-to-slightly-negative returns from nearly all stock funds. When large numbers of people are heard moaning, "I'd have been better off in cash," the professional's opportunity detector starts ringing, very loudly. It's very hard to move accounts when they're happy where they are. The converse is — delightfully — also true.

Now, of course, you yourself may have an account (or two) who's noticeably less than ecstatic. And you have the option to focus on that aspect of the current malaise, if you like. But, as I've said before in this column, you can obsess about how upset your clients are, and that'll paralyze you. Alternately, you can (and I would) obsess about how upset everybody else's clients are, and that'll get you enthused and energized as never before. You decide.

I just know that about 45% of all the fund dollars that came in over the last couple of years went into "no-help" funds. And all my years in the business tell me that the huge preponderance of those dollars bought the wrong things at the wrong time, and for the wrong reasons. And now the folks know something is awfully wrong. So, they might be open to an offer of help, if it's presented in the right way.

You won't make a lot of friends if your approach is any combination of (a) I told you so, (b) "help" funds are better than "no-help" funds, and (c) my funds are better than your funds. And you certainly can't take the attitude that, virtually sight unseen, people should sell their "no-help" funds — not least of all because many of them shouldn't. In many cases, people bought the right tool; they just didn't know how to use the tool when they got it home. (Journalists forgot to tell them that it doesn't matter how much you save on points and plugs at the AutoZone store, if you don't actually know how to change points and plugs.)

And the whole point is: the direct cost of acquiring the investment was never supposed to be the issue. It doesn't matter what your investments cost (or didn't cost). It doesn't even matter that much how your investments perform. What matters is what you do with your investments after you buy 'em. And that, in turn, is a pure function of the advice you're getting. Or, in the case of "no-help" funds, not getting.

Americans think that, when their utility fund is down 20%, they'd better sell, because somehow utilities are going (and I quote from a real investor in a real article in the real *Wall Street Journal*) "down the tubes." So they go in the den, turn on the electric light, run a pencil through the electric pencil sharpener, and write their redemption request. Then they go downstairs, turn on the electric light in

19

the kitchen, take a frozen pizza out of the electric refrigerator, pop it in the microwave, and turn on the electric TV to watch gloom-and-doom-today on CNBC. Left to their own (electric) devices, they just don't get it.

But if there's a professional investment adviser anywhere within the sound of the investor's voice, she says, "Not so fast. Let's take a vote on this. Which way is your electric bill going?" "Up," says America. "Yes, and which way is your dividend income going?" "Up." "Bingo. Now, which way is your NAV going?" "Down."

"By a vote of two to one," says the pro, "the Ups have it. It's just that they're having a 20%-off sale on NAV. How much more can you buy before the sale ends?"

The critical variable is your advice, the cost of which is literally the best money your clients ever spent. But if you don't believe that, why should anybody else? And, if you set the agenda in any other terms, why should anybody take you seriously?

All you really have to do is offer the critical ingredient — your professional help — in a non-argumentative way. Here are some suggestions:

1. Are you happy with the way your investments are being handled? This is something you can say (or write) to literally everyone with whom you come in contact. Please note that I did not say, "Are you happy with your investments?" because that's stressing the wrong variable. Ask that, and America says, "No, of course not, but is your utility fund down any less than mine?" And, in record time, you're at Game Over. Remember: the amateur is always selling investments; the professional is always selling himself.

When someone answers my question with "I handle my own investments," he's told me he only buys "no-help" funds. My response is a gentle, smiling, "Well, I guess my question still stands: are you happy with the way you're handling your investments? Or could you use a cup of coffee and a second opinion?"

I'm not looking for an intellectual victory, here; I don't want to reason or argue. I want the client to say, years from now, "I still don't know why I opened up to the investment professional; I guess I just had a feeling that he genuinely wanted to help." As a professional, you see, I don't need folks to know why they trust me. I just need 'em to trust me.

2. What we offer: A cup of coffee and a second opinion. This can be the headline of a prospecting letter (provided each and every letter is followed up with a phone call), or of an advertisement in a local newspaper. The text would read:

These days, a lot of people are a lot less than happy with their investments.

Sometimes, that's because people bought the wrong investments. And sometimes, it's because the investments were right, but the timing was wrong.

We at (fill in your firm's name) can usually tell the difference. That's why, in these difficult times, we've instituted what we call Second Opinion Hour. From 8:00 a.m. to 9:00 a.m. every business day, we'll offer to give you (or to get for you) an intelligent second opinion on the one investment you're holding that's causing you the most concern.

No cost. No obligation. You can call on the phone, and we'll try to help. But if you'll stop by our office, we'll also buy you a cup of coffee.

We don't have all the answers. But we may have the one answer you really need right now.

3. In no-load funds, you don't pay to get bad advice. Or good advice. This is also a letter/advertisement headline. You can go on to say something such as:

Maybe, like a lot of people over the last few years, you invested in no-load mutual funds. You didn't feel you needed any professional advice ... and so you didn't pay for it.

These days, you may be having second thoughts. Uncertain, unsettled markets have a way of generating lots of second thoughts.

We at (insert your firm's name) are professional investment advisors. And, we'd like to make you an interesting offer.

From 8:00 a.m. to 9:00 a.m. every morning, we offer a cup of coffee, and a second opinion. If you have an investment that really concerns you — and can't, or just don't want to, seek advice from the folks you bought the investment from — come in and see us.

If we can offer an intelligent opinion, we will. If not, we'll tell you that, too.

If we think you made a good investment, we'll tell you so, and send you on your way. If we think you'd be better advised to own something else, we'll tell you why.

No cost. No obligation. And the coffee's on us.

When you start thinking along these lines, you'll come up with ideas (and wording) of your own. The whole point is to put yourself very visibly out there, gently offering the one thing a "no-help" fund buyer doesn't get: help. Good, caring, professional help. Oh, incidentally, will you also get prospects who bought "help" funds from amateurs? Yes, of course, and I'm sure you'll rise to the challenge.

One final note: the current troubled (that is to say, wonderful) environment must be exactly what God was thinking of when She invented "C" shares. Yes, I know, "A" shares are "cheaper" in the long run, and every prospect should be clearly told that. But, as the great John Maynard Keynes said, in the long run we are all dead. And, to the crestfallen, wounded "no-help" fund refugee, "A" shares may be too much of a countercultural leap.

But "C" shares let you say, in effect: assume the difference between "help" and "no-help" funds is me. And assume the cost differential is 1% per year. In other words, my help costs you 1% per year. So, the only question, now that you've been through the reality check of the last 18 months, is: do you believe my counsel is worth 1% per year?

A guy who says no to that question doesn't actually need a financial advisor. He needs a psychiatrist.

THEY DON'T NEED YOU TO SELL 'EM WHAT THEY WANT TO BUY

Last month, I worked extensively with the retail investment division of a major bank. The bank started its program long before most banks did, staffed it with real professionals, and has run it like a business instead of like a tenth-grade chemistry experiment. Bright people, long-term focus ... just everything you'd want a bank program to be. So why, other than for entertainment value, did they need me?

Anecdotally, the answer was this: in February, the bank's deepest, most productive region had higher sales of Treasury securities than all other investments combined. Wounded by double-digit declines in bond funds, utility funds, and other "safe" CD "alternatives," the bank's customers were putting their heads in the sand *en masse* — and the reps were letting 'em do it.

The reps, in other words, were doing the one thing that will most reliably destroy both the client's real net worth and the rep's career: Selling Americans what they want to buy at the moment, rather than what they need to buy for the rest of their lives.

This story, with different characters and different products, is being played out all over the industry. I'm told that at a recent meeting of life insurance B/Ds, it was reported that the relationship of fixed annuity to variable annuity sales was running 80/20 in favor of fixed (from nearly 80/20 the other way two years ago). This can't be good, either for the folks or for us.

But, as one rep recently complained to me, "I'm the guy who sold them the utility fund that went down 20%. I led them into that bear trap. How do I tell them, with any credibility, that they're wrong to now want to get stability and a halfway decent yield from Treasuries for a couple of years?"

My answer is simple. It may not be easy (doing the right thing

23

rarely is), but it is simple. You tell them ix-nay on the Treasuries because it's true, and because it *is* best for them in the long run. (And how about adding some more money to that utility fund while the value/yield rally lasts, i.e. before the sale ends?)

In editing my new book *Gathering Assets* (a compilation of my 33 favorite columns from this magazine), I was pleased to note the relative consistency of the major themes with respect to clients. In no particular order, they are:

1. American portfolios today are highly appropriate for the early 1930s; unfortunately, this is the cusp of the 21st century. The primary reality of financial planning has to be 25 to 30 years of retirement, during which you can and should expect the price of a postage stamp — and everything else you need to buy — to triple. You can't be a loaner; you've got to be an owner. You have no choice but to own equities, and who, in the long run, would want a choice?

In July 1932, the Dow Jones Industrial Average hit 40; in March 1995, it cruised past 4140. The risk: not owning 'em. The ultimate wealth strategy: get on the train. Sit down. Read your paper. Look neither to the left nor to the right. Wait 'til the train gets to your station. The train *always* gets to your station.

2. Fluctuation isn't loss, it's oxygen. With it you live; without it, you die. Investments that can't fluctuate aren't investments, they're savings. And the long-term return on savings, net of inflation and taxes, is always zero or less.

The ability of an investment (e.g., a portfolio of The Great Companies in America) to decline 20% over the next 90 days is the key to its ability to appreciate 100% in the next five years or so. (And it's also the key to the portfolio's ability to quadruple its dividend in the next 20 years, as the S&P 500 did between '74 and '94.) Fluctuation only becomes loss if you panic and sell. Markets don't lose money for people, people lose money for themselves.

3. All generalized price declines are temporary, and all are buying opportunities, not occasions for panic selling. If Americans bought investments like they buy canned tuna fish and paper towels — stocking up when there's a big sale — we'd all be a lot richer. High prices, bad; low prices, good. It always *looks* like the wrong time to invest (Ecclesiastes 11, 4); it's always the right time to invest (DJIA 40, 4140).

So much for the major client-oriented themes, which, while they always bear repeating, aren't the focus of this column. I want to discuss the truth of what happens when you let Americans buy what they want instead of what they need.

1. Its next major move is south. You name it: when Americans want to buy it, its already got one of the front wheels over the cliff. And if enough of them want to buy it enthusiastically enough (Mexico at 3,000 on the Bolsa, utilities and long govvie funds at 5.79% on the 30-year bond), not only are both front wheels over the cliff, but one of the back wheels is already spinning in new-fallen snow.

Thus, selling folks what they want always involves diminishing your money line; doing it often enough takes your asset base to the vanishing point. (And, in the bargain, introduces you to the Wonderful World of Binding Arbitration, as folks blame you.)

Want to know why I'm convinced that Fed funds are going to 7.50% in '95? Well, sure: part of the reason is that my favorite Fed watcher, Wayne Angell of Bear Stearns, says they are. But the big reason, of course, is that so many Americans are buying two-year Treasuries!

2. They can buy what they want cheaper and easier away from you. The function of no-help funds is to give Americans an easy, cheap way to pour kerosene all over themselves and strike a match. (And then, magically, do it again tomorrow.)

When America dials 1-800-NO-HELP, and says, "Buy me that Jim K. Dandy no-load, low-expense-ratio, long government bond fund," in September '93, the Cardinal Hayes High School dropout on the other end of the phone says, "Yes, sir!" A year or so later, with rates up 50% and that fund's NAV tail-spinning toward the deck, America calls and says, "Sell me out of that carcinogenic bag of snakes before I lose all my money!" And the same kid goes (you guessed it): "Yes, sir!"

The point is: no one has to pay you to do that for them. And tomorrow, as electronic avenues for instantaneous, no-cost self-immolation multiply, you'll become ever more superfluous. (Just wait 'til they can buy a no-load Mexico fund at Bolsa 3000 through a street-corner ATM! Won't that be the millennium!)

You and I will never again be the low-cost provider of investments (thank God), so if people already know what they want to buy, what do they need to pay us for?

3. What people really want to buy are savings surrogates. And those don't pay us anything, now do they?

No, this isn't quite the same as the previous point. The issue here is that you have to sell about a gazillon two-year Treasuries in order to earn the price of a New York City subway token — because, like the passbook savings accounts for which Treasuries and CDs are a proxy, there's no production credit in 'em. (Nor should there be.)

4. We can — and should — get paid if, and to the extent that, we add value. And, when all is said and done, we add value only when we make people see that what they *want* to do (lend, for a short time) is the opposite of what they *need* to do (own, for a long time).

Or, that instead of buying when all value has been extinguished (Nikkei 39,000), you'd rather buy when headlines are bleak ("Kobe in Ruins") and values have rallied spectacularly (Nikkei 18,000).

Or, that lending Disney the money to make *The Lion King* at 8% isn't as good as owning a little piece of that classic film — and every other timeless gem in the Disney library — even if the current dividend yield is 1% ... something Americans will never see without our help. (God help them, they think 8% is *more* than 1%!)

Our value, in the end, is a pure function of our courage, in opposing (gently, therapeutically, non-argumentatively) what the investor wants to do, and championing the cause of what he needs to do. Will you lose some business? Sure. But, as I've been at pains to point out, it's business you really don't want, anyway. You don't want that kind of money because you don't want that kind of blood on your hands.

You won't think much of yourself if you take blood money. And if you don't think much of yourself, people will sense that. And they won't think much of you, either.

Do the right thing. Failing that, at least don't do the wrong thing. There are plenty of accounts out there waiting for a good person to call them and tell them what to do. And, when your conscience is clear, you have the energy it takes to make those calls.

It's not about your month. It's about your life.

RE-SET YOUR AGENDA; RE-START YOUR BUSINESS

These days, you're probably able to go a whole week without a complete stranger calling you up to do business with you.

Unlike the golden years 1991-1993, when the CD rate went from over 8% to under 3%, and the DJIA went from 2450 to 4000, last year was one of progressive, metastasizing disillusionment. As Martha and the Vandellas sang 30 years ago, there was "nowhere to run to, bay-bay, nowhere to hide." And the referral machine ground to a sickening halt.

In its own paradoxical way, this year has been even worse. Granted, some of people's devastated investments, like bond and utility funds, have recovered a little. So why isn't anybody happy? Because going from being down 28% to being down 16% is mighty cold comfort when you've watched the broad market averages march far into new high ground without you!

As I was at some pains to point out two months ago, the huge preponderance of the new money that disintermediated from savings to investments (without actually knowing the difference) in 1991-93 bought exactly the wrong things at exactly the wrong times for exactly the wrong reasons. You can beat yourself up because they did an infinitesimal fraction of that buying through you. Or you can ask, "What did I learn from this, and how can I use what I've learned to help my clients for the rest of my career?"

In our business, as in all of life, trying to figure out the answers is a complete waste of time until you're sure you've got the questions framed right. When you've framed the questions right, the answers become fairly obvious. But unless you get the questions framed right, no matter what answers you come up with, they're going to be wrong, and sooner rather than later.

Here are the four critical questions you've got to re-frame right now in order to salvage some of 1995, and to use the remaining months of this year to set you up for a record-breaking '96 — no matter what the markets do.

All professional business people have business plans. They set goals for their businesses, and then figure out precisely what activities they have to perform during the year in order to reach those goals. They do not, among many other things, sit around waiting and hoping for "the market" to bring business to them.

As I travel around the country, I ask a lot of reps what their business plans are. Very often, I get an answer like this:

"Well, our firm's economic research confirms the probability of a soft-landing scenario. We think you've seen the worst at the long end of the yield curve, and most, if not all, of the necessary Fed tightening at the short end. As the economy slows, rates will ultimately fall, and that will be good for stocks and bonds. We're recommending that investors concentrate on [fill in the blank]."

To my mind, there are a couple of little things — and one huge thing — wrong with that answer. The (relatively) little wrong things are: (1) it's the consensus viewpoint, which means it can't be right; and (2) it presumes that people should be buying investments because the next move is up.

People should be buying investments — every bloody month — because you have to be in the capital markets all your investing lifetime, if you're to have any hope of achieving the Great Goals of Life. "Invest because we're bullish" is just the worst thing our industry can say to America. We need to say, "Invest regularly pursuant to a long-term financial plan because you have no choice." The direction of the next 20% market move doesn't matter.

But the Really Big Thing Wrong with the aforementioned answer is that it is in no way responsive to the question. It isn't a business plan; it's a market outlook. If the critical variable in your business plan is the behavior of markets and/or the economy, you simply haven't got a business plan: you've got a bet on the markets. And that bet is either going to come home, or it's not. (And even if it does, rising markets do not automatically yield you an increase in business, as I'd have thought the last six months amply demonstrated.)

No good businessperson builds a business plan based primarily on a variable he/she cannot control. Moreover, the nature of our business is that there's no way materially to increase your assets under management or your income today. (Indeed, to materially increase your business today, you needed to increase your prospecting activity starting around eight months ago.)

My experience of this business is that it is a chain of events, and that my income is the last link in the chain. The chain is as follows: The more times I get rejected, the more prospects I get. The more prospects I get, the more accounts I open. The more accounts I open, the larger my money line becomes. And the larger my money line, the larger my income.

I have never, in 28 years, found a lasting way to intervene somewhere in the middle of that chain. So I no longer try to do so. If I want to materially increase my business, I need only materially increase the number of times I get rejected every day. This is a variable over which I have total control, so it is the variable in which I denominate my business plan.

My experience is that the incidence of rejection doesn't change much; no matter what I do, I still need to get rejected N number of times to get a prospect, and my N has long since become an irreducible number. So if I want to effect a 50% increase in my business somewhere down the road, I just have to increase the number of times I get rejected — today, tomorrow, and every day thereafter — by 50%. Increased business follows increased rejection, in Shakespeare's lovely phrase, as the night the day. And thus rejection has become, for me, not some ego-destroying corrosive acid, but the fuel my business plan runs on.

I've been talking a lot lately in this column about my enthusiasm for utility funds, now that utilities have gotten massacred. And the other day, a guy actually called me up and asked me what utility fund I recommend. He was saying, in effect, "Give me a magic talisman that will cause my acceptance to go up and my rejection to go down." As if acceptance were a function of the fund itself, rather than of the number of times each day that you present the fund to people. But that's ridiculous.

My advice is: stop trying to get rejected less. Try to get rejected more. All good things happen when you get rejected more. Increasing rejection is the ultimate business plan, in that it leads, with 100% reliability, to more business. And nothing else does.

Let's do this by the process of elimination: first, let me tell you a couple of things my job is not.

My job isn't to "outperform the market." I'll do that in the long run (I'm a dollar-cost-averager, so I'll always outperform in the long run), but I can't prove that. In the short-to-intermediate term, I haven't the foggiest notion whether or not I'll outperform and I don't care, because it doesn't matter.

Nor is it my job to pick mutual funds that outperform most or all other similar funds. Long-term, I can't find much evidence that fund performance is predictive (although I think *manager* performance is, if you see the distinction). And short-to-intermediate term, I'm quite convinced that performance is perversely predictive: that sector/style/discipline which overperformed in the last block of time will underperform in the next.

My job is to be a behavior modifier: I help people stop making the self-destructive mistakes that keep them from getting anything remotely close to "market" results.

If I can close the hideous gap between *investment* returns and *investor* returns — and I can — I've performed an immensely valuable service, and I deserve to be compensated with wealth and honors. The markets conspire to make Americans rich (e.g., the DJIA went from 40 to 4300 in a whole lot less than 63 years). Why is everybody talking about "beating" that, when not one in a thousand Americans does even that well?

Wealth, in America, comes by dint of the elimination of inappropriate behaviors (greed, panic, underdiversification, chasing the hot dot on the scattergram, etc., etc.). I'm the behavior modifier. My job is to help people set reasonable goals, to put a program in place for the achievement of those goals, and to make people stay with the program — regardless of today's tulip mania or tomorrow's apocalypse *du jour.*

I can, in other words, never be sure I'll "outperform the market." But I can always be sure of my ability to make my clients wealthy, as they define wealth. And I never have to do the former to accomplish the latter. How about you? What's your job?

A recent print ad from a prominent "no-help" fund group pictured an attractive, obviously successful professional woman, about 40 years old. She was saying that this year she was going to invest her bonus for her retirement. "How can I do it conservatively?" she asked.

The ad suggested she consider a U.S. government money market fund, which gives you a good insight into the evil that is "no-help" fund marketing. No-help funds vie with one another to sell Americans what they want to buy, even if it's wildly inappropriate for them — the way a money market fund is, as a long-term retirement investment.

Here's a woman with 20 years to work and 50 years to live. She'll spend upwards of 30 years in retirement, during which time I have every confidence that consumer prices in the U.S. will triple. Is this woman getting a wrong answer? Yes, but it goes far beyond that: she's framing the question — in this case, "How do you define conservatism?" — all wrong.

Her definition of conservatism is the same as her mother's and grandmother's: a conservative investment is one in which she is guaranteed to get back the same number of pictures of George Washington she invested. She has made the classic American mistake of confusing currency with money, when in fact (as she'll find out much too late) only purchasing power is really "money." Only equities are truly "conservative" for this woman, because only equities conserve (and, indeed, accrete) purchasing power (i.e., money) net of inflation and taxes.

But to make her see that, we must, first and foremost, decline to accept her agenda. ("No-help" funds neither can nor will do that. They'll sell her what she wants to buy, and doom her financially in the process.)

So the third of my four questions becomes, "Who's setting the agenda?" Accept America's agenda, and you are guaranteed to sell it the wrong thing (or, at the very least, the right thing at the wrong time). Re-set the agenda (gently, non-argumentatively) and you can save lives.

There's no need to spend a lot of time on this issue here, because it was really the subject of last month's whole column *(They Don't Need You To Sell 'Em What They Want To Buy)*. And I don't want you to think that I'm being redundant ... that I'm repeating myself ... that I'm saying the same thing over and over again.

But re-setting the agenda, in every way, is vital to your long-term success. For instance, since America mistakes journalism for thought, it will always ask you journalistic questions, such as, "Which Way Will the Market Go Next?" Now, you and I know perfectly well which way the market will *ultimately* go: first, to DJIA 8000, then 12,000, then 16,000, and so on. (Go ahead, ask me when, and I'll smack you one.) But we cannot know which way it will go *next* — no one can, and great investors like Warren Buffett and Peter Lynch proudly tell us that every chance they get. So just re-set the agenda from "next" to "ultimately."

Business that you do in accordance with the client's agenda is almost always business you end up regretting (e.g., selling bond funds, instead of systematic withdrawal from equity funds, to newly retired 62-year-olds). To make people really happy in the long run — so the referral machine stays in overdrive for years and years — you gotta set your own agenda.

One last example of a deeply sick agenda: Americans who say, "My bond portfolio is so large, I get more income from it now than I could ever spend. Why do I have to fool around with stocks?"

I actually hear that one fairly often, so I'm good and ready for it. I say, "Please hand me a picture of your grandchildren." At first they're startled, but ultimately they produce the photo. As they're doing so, I take out my business card — the new one, with the 1995 32-cent Florida Alligator stamp juxtaposed with the 1975 10-cent Apollo-Soyuz space linkup stamp.

Without a word, I hold up in front of the prospect the stamps (in one hand) and the grandchildren (in the other). The next person who speaks, loses.

What I've done, of course, is re-set the agenda. The prospect set the agenda (selfishly, but humanly) in terms of his own income needs. I re-set it in terms of his grandchildren's need to inherit purchasing power rather than wallpaper. (Indeed, I often tell older, "risk-averse" people that I'm an advocate for their grandchildren. Straightens 'em right out.)

If you genuinely want to succeed in this business — that is if you really want to help people — you have to be the one who sets the agenda. No matter how clear folks are about what they want, very few Americans have any real concept of what they need.

Let me give you my answer, in the hope that one day it will become your answer, as well. My product isn't mutual funds, or equities, nor The Great Companies in America, nor the miracle of dividend growth, which is to inflation what St. George was to the dragon. I talk about those things a lot, and try hard to get people to invest in them. But they're not my product.

I am my product. (Amateurs sell investments; the professional sells himself/herself.) My years, my experience, my sense of the cycle, my personal knowledge of some of the great money managers working today, my faith in the future, my commitment to the client (yes, and to his children and grandchildren); that's my product. In a phrase: my advice is my product. Americans don't need products, they don't need service, they don't even need information. *They need advice.* That's my profession; indeed, it's my calling.

Someone who rejects that advice hasn't hurt me, he's hurt himself and his heirs. That is my belief, and it's what makes me impervious to rejection.

And that brings us full circle, to the first of these four questions — or rather, to my answer to that question. You may not be able to double your income tomorrow (you may, but you may not). You may not be able to open two new accounts tomorrow, try as you may.

But you could resolve — couldn't you — not to leave the office today until you got rejected 15 times. And if you did that for 10 days straight, you could resolve to get rejected 16 times in each of the next 10 days. And so on, and so on... .

Until, by becoming a gold medalist in the Rejection Olympics, you fulfilled all of your dreams for success in this business.

That's my wish for you in the second half of 1995, and forever after.

BELLING THE CAT: HOW TO CONVERT TO A FEE-BASED PRACTICE

Old Aesop, as he so often did, told a fable for our times. Seems the mouse population was being ravaged by a cat, whose approach was so silent that the mice wouldn't know he was there until one of them became catnip.

At the mouse town meeting it was suggested that the problem could be solved by tying a bell around the cat's neck. That way, he'd be heard coming in plenty of time for the mice to take cover.

This idea was greeted with universal enthusiasm, and it was clear that the problem had been solved in concept ... until a wise elder politely inquired how, exactly, the bell was to be tied around the cat's neck, and which mouse would volunteer to do it.

Converting a financial planning practice to a fee basis, i.e. one whose compensation to the planner is a percentage of the assets, rather than commissions on transactions, is a lot like belling the cat. That's because one major argument (some would say *the* major argument) for fees is that they eliminate the huge potential for conflict of interest that's implicit in commissions. Fees, according to this line of reasoning, allow the planner to be completely objective.

This unassailably great concept raises a very significant practical problem, however. How do we enunciate it to our clients without implying that up until now, our interests have been in conflict with theirs, and that we may not always have been completely objective, for selfish reasons?

Pondering all the sinuous and complex aspects of this enigma may be relevant entertainment, capable of filling many hours. But, to me, it is a little like Butch and Sundance, surrounded in that stable down in Bolivia, analyzing the social forces in late 19th century America that caused them to turn to a life of crime. To wit: you may not really have time for it.

My essential thesis is that the momentum behind the fee-based movement is so powerful that, if you don't call this question with your clients pretty soon, some other planner will. At that point, someone who isn't actually your friend will have set your agenda for you, and you'll be on defense — but you can't win on defense.

This is not to say that commissions aren't defensible — they are eminently so: (a) In a long-term, low-turnover investment strategy, commissions may very well be "cheaper" than fees over time. (b) Why should anybody get paid 10%-20% of the investor's total return (i.e. 1%-2% on a total portfolio return of, say 10%) to tell him to do nothing? And (c) no matter what the compensation structure, good advisors will always take good care of their clients, and bad advisors will always find a way to hurt 'em.

And if that's your conscious strategy, more power to you. Besides, you can still use fees as a fallback position. After reciting (a), (b), and (c), above, you can add, "Of course, I can — and cheerfully will — handle your account on a fee basis. The way I'm compensated for my advice is never going to be the critical variable; my advice is what counts. I'll do it any way you want. But if I were you, I'd stay put."

But if you are actively considering converting to a fee-based practice, and are dithering about it, you're going to find yourself in a difficult position when (not if) your competition calls the question. Because at that point your response, no matter how logical and even heartfelt it may be, is going to boil down to "me, too." Maybe "me, too" will save the account, and maybe it won't. But even if you keep the account that day, the seeds of doubt will have been sown. The client will think, "If he didn't tell me about this until I asked, what else isn't he telling me?"

So, if you've been giving any thought at all to kicking open the stable door and making a run for the horses, I'd like to suggest you do it now — before the whole Bolivian army gets here. The best defense is a good offense.

First and foremost, though, you have to remember to set the agenda in terms of the fact that compensation isn't the main concern here. The critical issue is your relationship with your clients, and your (clearly enunciated) desire to serve them and their families in the best possible way.

The folks have to be made to feel that you are raising this issue in a very specific context: The desire to have everyone be aware of his options, so that you can be of the optimum value to the client.

If a dramatic new medical breakthrough occurs which retards the onset of heart disease in people over 55, a family doctor's patients wouldn't want to wait until they were getting angina pains for him to tell 'em about it. They'd hope and expect that their doctor would bring the new therapy to their attention as soon as was practicable.

So let it be with fees, in our business. Your attitude has to be just like the doctor's: hey, look, this is something that might help you, my client/patient. When *you* raise the issue — and especially when you raise it in this context — you gain the moral high ground, and suspicions about ulterior motives tend to evanesce. (If they don't, the client already doesn't trust you, and your relationship is already dead. Fees ain't gonna bring it back to life.)

Make yourself the issue. When clients sense a genuine desire on your part to serve them well, they'll at least consider anything you suggest.

Here's a track to run on, that may turn all these abstractions into a workable plan of action.

(1) Write to the folks. Tell 'em what's on your mind. Do not, among many other things, say, "We're converting to a fee-based practice; here's why; do you want to come along?" That commits two unpardonable sins: (a) it presents people with a *fait accompli*, which just naturally gets everybody's back up; and (b) you're trying to make the letter do your selling for you, rather than you doing the selling for yourself. Amateurs rely on pieces of paper, professionals rely always (and only) on themselves.

Instead, write something like this. (Hell, write exactly this, if you want.)

Dear Client:
As your financial advisor, we at (firm) are delighted by the fierce competition in the financial services industry today.

We believe it's extremely healthy — and potentially very good for our clients — that the industry is striving to provide superior products, services, and pricing.

This year as never before, we feel we offer the greatest flexibility ever in terms of allowing you to chose the way our firm is compensated for our services to you and your family.

We'd like the opportunity to acquaint you with all of these new options. (Write one of the three next sentences depending on your style.) (A) I'll call you next week to determine the time when it would be most convenient for us to meet. (B) We can do this when we meet for your mid-year account review, which I'll call you shortly to schedule. (C) We'll be discussing this topic, as well as our current economic outlook at our next Client Appreciation Night, which is scheduled for (date). Please mark your calendar; a formal invitation follows shortly.

In closing, please be assured that we are continuing to handle your account(s) with us just as we always have. We will make no changes unless, and until, you are convinced that a change will enable us to serve you and your family even better.

Because serving you even better is our constant goal.

Sincerely,

Clearly, all of the options here are face-to-face meetings, because that's the only right way to seek fundamental change in a healthy relationship. The most efficient — though highest-risk — option is the Client Appreciation Night. Efficient because you get to call the question pretty much all at once for your whole book (although you still have to sit down with everybody one-on-one eventually). High-risk, of course, because if you get a bomb-thrower in there who forgot to take his medication today, he could get the whole room worrying about stuff they wouldn't otherwise have worried about.

(2) When you see the folks, lay out all their options for them. Don't stack the deck; read 'em the whole menu, and make sure they understand that it's their option, that nobody's going to dictate anything to 'em.

When they ask you — if they ask you — what you'd prefer they do, then you can make your case for fees. And again, don't knock the way they've been paying you up until now; that's punching the tar baby. Stress, instead, what fees do that other compensation modes don't. I always say,

"Fees are the only way that I can be made to suffer financially when you suffer, and I think that's a wonderful way to keep me/our firm focused on loss limitation.

"You see, in a fee-based arrangement, if your account declines x%, so does our fee income. Presuming that we don't want that to happen — and, believe you me, we don't want that to happen — you can see that our compensation will become absolutely, arithmetically linked to your results in a fee-based arrangement.

"Is this going to make us work any harder for you and your family? I sincerely hope not, because I like to believe that we're already working as hard as we can for you — and for all our clients.

"I guess I just feel better — and hope that you feel better — knowing that our identity of interest, going forward, will be based less on good will and a whole lot more on simple arithmetic: We prosper only to the extent that you prosper. And when you hurt, we hurt — not just emotionally but financially.

"That really holds our feet to the fire. And if I were you, I think that's just where I'd want our feet to be."

41

(3) Tell them to take it out and drive it around for a year, and if they don't like it, they can bring it back. The bigger an issue you make this, the scarier it'll be for the folks. That's just human nature. Make your attitude, Try it on; I think you'll like it. But if, one year from now — or whenever — you feel like it's not working for you — never mind why — then the heck with it. Either we'll go back to doing it the old way, or — who knows, by that time they may have dreamed up a whole new way that neither of us has heard of yet.

"Remember: this just can't be the critical issue, so there's no point in getting all caught up in it. The important thing is that you and I, working together, make sure we achieve your financial goals. Nothing can be allowed to take our focus — yours or mine — off those goals. And I can promise you, from my standpoint: nothing ever will."

As endlessly fascinating as this whole topic may be right now, make sure you keep it in the proper perspective. And the proper perspective is always: where does this issue fit in with my lifetime client relationships, as well as with my financial and emotional obligations to the people I love and who love me?

When you frame the question in those terms, you'll find it quite literally impossible to come up with the wrong answer.

STOP WATCHING MARKETS; WATCH PEOPLE'S LIVES

The other day, I was sitting in first class on a flight from my home in the Caribbean to California. The guy next to me was poring over his *USA Today* with an avidity that drew my attention, so I looked over to see what he was reading so closely. It was the daily mutual fund price listings. And I thought: Here's almost everything that's wrong with American investing today.

When I arrived at my destination, I spoke to a group of wholesalers who sell wrap accounts and mutual funds for a prominent small-cap/aggressive growth, bottom-up stock-picking manager. I spoke to these people for about an hour, on issues having nothing at all to do with the current market.

There was a point, however, when I parenthetically slurred the market for no more than about 30 seconds, after the fashion to which readers of this column became accustomed this summer.

At the end of the session, with only moments before they had to get to their next meeting, one of the wholesalers asked me anxiously whether I didn't think we'd already had our correction in the sector-rotating swan dives of '94. "No," I explained, and thought to myself: This is the rest of everything that's wrong with American investing today.

If you read through these incidents without being even a little horrified (for even I don't ask you to be quite as horrified as I was), you yourself may be part of the problem I'm addressing. At the very least, if these two incidents don't disturb you, then — in the immortal words of Sherlock Holmes — you see but you do not observe.

First, let us examine the curious conundrum of my airborne companion. Here was a person of sufficient business/professional accomplishment to be flying first class. He didn't just roll into town on no turnip truck.

43

You'd assume that such a person would know — if anyone would — that mutual funds are a great device for the long-term accumulation of wealth, and that what they do on a given day is less than meaningless. (If the guy had been looking up individual stock quotes, OK; maybe he's a trader, God help him.) And yet here he was, checking one day's price action. Doesn't have to mean anything, but it can't be a good sign.

Next, observe the case of the worried wholesaler. What's he worried about? He represents a small-cap manager, which means that, even assuming index returns, he's got a long-term 20% advantage over all his big-cap competition, right? Moreover, his manager works purely bottom-up. In other words, the issue is whether the manager is right about his stocks. His style totally ignores the market ... but somehow that's not good enough for the wholesaler!

This is all starting to make me feel like Kevin McCarthy in the original *Invasion of the Body Snatchers*. Everyone around me is being replaced by ... pods from outer space! They're going to sleep as sensible, long-term, planning-oriented professionals, but they're waking up ... market maniacs.

Even I found myself talking a lot about the market in this column over the summer — albeit in a very specific context. I said that a significant, generalized price decline of more than a few days' duration is inevitable at some point. And that we are morally obligated to point this out to a new breed of post-1987 fund investors (rather than hoping that "this time it's different," much less that "it happened last year").

We have to either get people to profit from a correction by buying more, or get people to ignore it. But above all, they mustn't panic. And my whole message is: They *will* panic unless we prepare them.

The best way to prepare everybody for everything, of course, is to take people's focus off the markets altogether. Long term, the market's course is inevitable. (The Dow is going to 20,000, on its eventual way to 50,000. If you doubt this, I recommend that you ponder it further over dinner at the Pizza Hut just off Red Square in Moscow.)

Short-to-intermediate term, the market's course is unknowable and inefficient to the point of randomness. (When they put a $2.2 billion market cap on a company that hasn't turned a profit yet, for instance, you know you're in the Twilight Zone.) Moreover, the market's near-term course has nothing whatever to do with the real lives of real people.

The surest cure for market mania, then, is continuously to focus on — and invest all your energy in — planning out the rest of people's lives. (And your own, as well.) A plan is something you and your clients can control. And when you're in control of things, your anxiety levels always decline. Declining anxiety levels, in turn, reduce the chance that you'll make The Big Mistake.

Watching markets — much less obsessing about markets — always raises your anxiety levels. That's because you've invested your energy in a variable over which you have no control. And, as anxiety levels spiral upward, the chance of making The Big Mistake grows like some evil flower.

Market mania is the belief that the direction of the next 25% move in the market (a) is knowable and (b) matters to your long-term financial plan. Neither of these things is true, of course. Then why do people believe them?

The answer goes back to the fundamental inability on most people's part to distinguish between fluctuation and loss. "If the value of my account were to decline 25%," they reason, "I'd have suffered a 25% loss. I mustn't let that happen; it would be a disaster. I have to watch this market like a hawk every minute."

Up go the anxiety levels; up goes the risk of The Big Mistake. Oddly, this is also the case with people obsessing about whether the market has run its course for a while, or whether it could still go up another 25%.

Suppose I could assure you that it did, indeed, have another 25% pop in it — to, say, 6,000. (A) What would you know that you didn't already know? It's obviously going to 6,000 at some point, anyway. (B) What are you going to do when it gets to 6,000? Sell? And risk missing the move to 20,000?

You see, that's the malignant fiction at the heart of market mania: That if you could figure out what was going to happen next — as opposed to simply knowing what's ultimately going to happen — you'd know when to sell.

Selling is for fools. If you're going to be retired for 25 to 30 years, you have to be in the capital markets — and specifically in the equity market — every day for the rest of your life. Only investing (not saving and not trading) gives you any hope of staying ahead of a quarter century of inflation.

Even if someone's retired now, selling because of near-term market concerns makes no sense. To cut oneself off from the inflation-beating effect of dividend growth is suicide. Retirees don't go to the supermarket with their account statements, they go with the income from their investments.

If prices inside the supermarket are going up, but retirees' incomes aren't because they buried their principal someplace "safe" from fluctuation ... well, that's the tragic enigma of watching markets instead of watching life.

"Happier the man who reads nothing," said Thomas Jefferson, "than he who reads only newspapers." In the same vein, I'd like to suggest that we would all be a lot better off never to know the price of our mutual funds if the only alternative were to look them up every day. Daily price data (not to mention, God forbid, real-time price data) are just that: data. But data aren't information, information isn't knowledge, and knowledge sure as hell isn't wisdom.

This month, the good people of the International Association for Financial Planning will convene, as they do every year around now. And I'm sure that, among the exhibitors, there'll be various and sundry market timing/mutual fund trading services. I'm equally sure that the irony of this will be lost on most people.

Folks, when you get back from the convention (and even if you don't go to the convention), here's what I suggest.

For 30 days, turn the computer screen off. Stop reading *The Wall Street Journal.* Don't let anybody tell you the price of anything. And just see how liberated you feel.

If anybody calls to ask you the price of anything (which may happen a lot less often than you think), offer them one or more of the following responses:

(A) I don't know.

(B) I don't think it matters.

(C) Why?

(D) If you knew that, what would you know?

(E) What will it matter 20 years from now?

Take a deep breath. This isn't MTV, where the rapidity with which the image changes — and not the images themselves — becomes the drug.

This isn't even CNBC, which is itself only MTV in suits.

This is real life. And you can trade the markets for kicks, but you have to plan for real life.

BUILD BUSINESS WITH "LIFEBOAT DRILLS"

Ever since the sinking of the "unsinkable" Titanic, passenger ships have conducted lifeboat drills at the beginning of every voyage. The idea is to get all the passengers in shape for any eventuality by showing them how to get calmly and quickly to their assigned lifeboat.

Late in a bull market, when one feels that a meaningful price decline of more than a few days' duration may be getting closer, you can cement current client relationships and prospect very effectively with a financial "lifeboat drill."

As longtime readers of this column know, my core beliefs about common stocks are threefold:

1. The long-term risk is not owning them. They've made it from 40 to 4,800 on the DJIA during a period marked by a global economic depression, followed by a global hot war, followed by a global cold war that threatened the extinction of mankind. What are they going to do now that we've entered the Golden Age of Capitalism?

2. Americans need to own far more equities than they do now, and they need to own them every day for the rest of their lives. Retirement, in the 21st century, will last 25 to 30 years. On average, over that long a period, consumer prices in the United States will triple. People need, therefore, to own investments whose income also has the potential to triple. That means equities, whose dividend growth has always offset inflation over long periods of time. Over 25 to 30 years, the risk of principal loss in equities is historically zero, so it's excruciatingly dumb to shun, in retirement, the only financial asset that safeguards purchasing power.

3. "Market timing" doesn't work. Stocks go up about 70% of the time, punctuated (though not lately) by horrific but evanescent declines.

The declines are temporary; the advances are permanent. (Put another way, stocks go down all the time; however, since they never *stay* down, it turns out not to matter.) No one has ever been consistently successful at calling market tops and bottoms, which is how I define "market timing." So you'd better plan on staying in, no matter what.

These days, however, I find in the unprecedented public enthusiasm for equity mutual funds a sign that this greatest of all bull markets is cruisin' for a bruisin' — that it's overdue for a major correction.

I am not at all beguiled by the argument that people won't panic because they learned from the '87 and '90 experiences that downdrafts are nonevents: (A) $750 billion of the $1 trillion or so in equity mutual funds came in *since* 1990, so I don't know how it would "learn" from an event in which it didn't take part. (B) What if the next one isn't a nonevent?

Moreover, after viewing the massive panic liquidation of government bond and utility funds last year, I don't know how anyone can believe that people are any less prone to panic than they ever were. So if they'll stampede out of the lowest-risk debt and equity there is, what will investors do when their technology stock funds are all trying to dump the same stocks, and there are no bids — an event which I regard as not impossible?

Finally, if equity mutual funds took in $500 billion in their first 69 years, and $500 billion more in the next 27 months, how can you doubt that something very ugly is on the horizon? As I said in August, markets never bestow great rewards on huge upsurges in public enthusiasm. Never, Never, *Never*. (Am I the only one who remembers real estate limited partnerships at the peak of their popularity in 1985?)

So you see the great conundrum of gathering assets as the leaves turn crimson and the air is once again filled with footballs:

(A) You have a moral as well as a business imperative to keep bringing investors under your protection.
(B) You have to put them into equities.

(C) You have to keep them in equities, because neither you nor they can "time" the market.

(D) The equity market is beginning to become overdue for a potentially savage hit. The issue isn't so much "if" as it is "when."

How do you hold this set of beliefs in your head, all at the same time, and continue to function? Easy. Like I said: You do lifeboat drills.

The last thing in the world you want to be selling today is "performance," i.e. total return as a one-variable equation after a dozen truly great years. Performance selling sets people up to fail, especially when, one of these old days, performance is going to be a fairly big number with a minus sign in front of it. Extrapolating an anomalously wonderful period isn't something that smart investors — or their advisors — do.

Instead, they do lifeboat drills, by asking, "What happened to the investments we're now holding, on the last two occasions — 1987 and 1990 — when this ship hit an iceberg?" (Yes, I know: '87 and '90 were more like ice *cubes,* but they're all we've got.) By squarely facing the reality of the effect of normal market setbacks, we can all learn how to behave the next time the ship stops to take on ice. I believe you can find great opportunity in any "adversity" for which the great mass of your competitors is unprepared.

I specifically recommend the following three-phase lifeboat drill:

(1) Between now and year end, go see each and every one of your clients. Show them a list of their investments, with the peak-to-trough percentage decline (not the full-year results) for each investment in 1987 and 1990. (It'll take some work to unearth those numbers, but I think that, when you're finished reading this column, you'll agree that it's well worth it.)

The reason this is so important is that the '87 and '90 declines were so short-lived (both lasted only about 90 days) that the appreciation during the rest of each year obscures the magnitude of the hit, if you just look at full-year returns. Thus, because investments may not have been down much (if at all) for the full year, people may have forgotten — if indeed they ever knew — the severity of the intra-year decline. The Kaufmann Fund, for instance, advertises the best record of any equity fund since the '87 lows, but doesn't mention that you had to sit through a 44.4% decline peak-to-trough in order to be there the day the advertised record started. Nor that you had to absorb another 30% hit in '90.

People don't know this. (That's just another example of performance statistics simultaneously being factually correct, but, in a larger sense, a lie.) So what I'm asking you to do is drill 'em on the '87 and '90 declines as a peak-to-trough phenomenon. Then say, "Something like this is certainly going to happen again at some point. Maybe next month, maybe five years from now. We can't know when it's going to happen, and my main point is: The decline won't matter; any more then it did in '87 or '90. The declines are always temporary, the advances always permanent. Now look me in the eye and tell me you're OK on this."

This is a fairly dramatic tactic. At first, people may think you're saying more than you're saying:

Client: What is it that you want me to do?

You: Quite literally, nothing. I want you to do ... nothing. If and when a perfectly normal, cyclical, temporary 20% to 30% correction comes along, I want to be sure you do ... nothing, except maybe add some more money before the sale ends.

Client: Do you think that such a setback is coming?

You: To be sure; it's in the nature of the cycle.

Client: When?

You: Don't know. No one does.

Client: I'm confused. What is it you're trying to tell me?

You: Merely that the more or less permanent upward march of equity prices is punctuated, at unpredictable intervals, by temporary declines. And, since the last such decline ended almost exactly five years ago (on October 11, 1990), people may have gotten a little complacent.

So, to celebrate the anniversary, I'm conducting lifeboat drills. Now I ask you again: Please look me in the eye, and tell me you're absolutely 100% OK on this.

Clearly, your mission is: (a) to reinforce the concept of the inevitability of temporary declines, and (b) to elicit a pledge from the investor not to panic. And a part of your account base will respond in kind, thanking you for the reality check and pledging allegiance to the underlying uptrend. These are, quite simply, your clients for life, and I assure you that they will be the base on which you'll build all your future success.

The other part of your account book will, when presented with this '87 and '90 peak-to-trough analysis, turn blue. Which brings us to the second phase of the lifeboat drill.

(2) Anybody who says he could not stand another '87 or '90 decline is in the wrong investments and should be moved to (relative) safety. Nobody, repeat nobody, should get completely out of equities. But you have to realize that, over the last five years, an awful lot of first-time fund investors have bought things whose exact risk parameters they either never understood, or have lost sight of.

The lifeboat drill is the most reliable way of identifying potential square pegs in round holes. There are a lot of people today in high-tech sector funds, for instance, who — in the cold light of day — should be in equity income funds, or convertible funds, or high-dividend-paying value funds. (The reason the Titanic hit the iceberg wasn't that the crew didn't see it; it was because they were going too fast to turn out of its way.) Late in a bull market, the best offense may simply be a good defense.

Everything goes down in a generalized market decline. (Because, as I've said before, when the bear shows up at your church picnic, sooner or later he eats everybody's lunch.) But some things go down a heck of a lot less than do other things. Everybody thinks he wants top performance; the lifeboat drill will clearly show some of your clients that they'd a whole lot rather be tortoises than hares.

Having finished the two phases of current-client lifeboat drills, it's time to offer the same service to prospects:

(3) Prospect "no-help" fund investors, and other lost souls, by offering to analyze their investments for susceptibility to icebergs. Five years into mutual fund mania, with the no-help fund industry (and its bought dog, journalism) continuing to insist that only fools pay loads, I'm guessing that at least half of all no-help equity investors have absolutely no idea what they own.

Amateurs in our business think it's tough to prospect right now, because people are so happy with the performance of their no-help funds. I see it exactly the other way around. I can effortlessly prospect these poor people by showing them the '87 and '90 declines of their funds. They simply have no idea of the volatility inherent in peak performance. You think one in a hundred Kaufmann Fund investors knows his fund went down 44.4% in '87? Not a chance. So when I show 'em, they're shocked. And when I show them further that my help and advice cost 1% per year more than no-help ... it gets to be a little like shooting fish in a barrel.

"The only new thing in the world," said President Truman, "is the history you don't know." By doing lifeboat drills — by showing people the historical downside that they don't know — you can convert a lot of prospects into clients ... and a lot of clients into lifelong friends.

PLACES IN THE HEART VS. PLACES ON SOME CHART

On November 6, along with hundreds of millions of other people around the world, I watched television coverage of the funeral of Israel's prime minister, Yitzhak Rabin.

The services were attended by the mighty of the earth. And, one after another, presidents, a king, and other world leaders made eloquent speeches about the fallen hero.

Then an 18-year-old girl, so small that she barely reached the podium's microphones, rose to speak. She was Rabin's granddaughter, Noa Ben-Artzi Pelossof. And she spoke not about her grandfather, but to him.

She didn't talk about abstractions like the peace process or the fate of nations. She told her grandfather how much she loved him, and what his love had meant to her. And if you could listen to her without weeping, you aren't just tougher than I am, you're tougher than I'll ever be. (Ms. Pelossof spoke in Hebrew, and even the English translator on CNN started to break down. And one of my daughters, who didn't see the speech on TV, cried just from reading the printed text in *The New York Times*.)

No one in America today remembers Edward Everett, the great orator who gave the main speech — all two hours of it — at the dedication of the cemetery at Gettysburg on November 19, 1863. That's because Lincoln's 272 luminous words on the same occasion put everything else that was said and done that day forever in the shade of history.

Similarly, I believe that 100 years from now — when Israeli and Palestinian schoolchildren still memorize Ms. Pelossof's speech from their textbooks — no one will be able to say who else, if anyone, spoke at Yitzhak Rabin's funeral.

Forgive me, but I find in this an uncomfortable paradigm for the direction our industry is taking. Often these days, I'll arrive for a speaking engagement a little early to hear the end of someone else's talk, and the Q & A that follows.

The speaker is always some portfolio manager, economist, or other analytical type, whose orientation is entirely toward markets and not at all toward people. And the questioning is always spirited: What does the guru think of the political turmoil in France(!), interest rates, the dollar vs. the yen, small cap vs. large cap over the next six months ... and dozens of other issues that have nothing whatever to do with how people are going to afford retirement, or provide for their grandchildren's education.

In other words, our industry — whose only reason for being is to manage the hopes and fears of our clients, in a way that no-help funds never can — has instead turned inward. We're slicing and dicing increasingly academic issues of asset allocation and modern portfolio theory rather than doing the real work of helping people become very good lifetime investors. (And remember: The combination of a great bull market and no-help fund "performance" advertising may make people speculators, but only you and I can make them good investors.)

Our efforts, more and more, aren't directed to places in the heart, but to places on some chart. While this may be making us "smarter" (in some cold, distant, intellectual way), I'm convinced it is also making us potentially much less effective at our real work, which is the management of our clients' emotions.

I don't doubt for a minute, for instance, that we gave people intellectually rigorous and complete explanations of the bond and utility stock funds that everyone was buying from us at the very bottom of the interest rate cycle in 1993. And yet our exquisitely nuanced understanding of such issues as duration, standard deviation, etc. does not seem to have been efficacious in stemming the massive panic liquidation of those funds in 1994.

Our work in analyzing and comparing these funds seems to have left us insufficient time and energy to counsel our clients on the (always emotional) difference between fluctuation and loss. "Risk" became, for us, synonymous with something called standard deviation. We somehow lost sight of the fact that, in the real emotions of real people, "risk" means losing your money, so that at 80 you are counting out the coins in your pocket by the light of the one bulb in the house that's on.

I'm sorry, but nothing in our increasingly capacious intellects is sufficient to calm the fears of someone whose primary concern is not the Japanese banking system but the cost of nursing home care. Knowledge isn't the antidote to fear; faith is. And faith begins with the ability to place one's trust in another human being: you, in this case ... if you can ever get your head out of your computer long enough to earn that trust.

Intellectual information is always useless in moments of great emotional stress. If you doubt that, try explaining to an extreme white-knuckle flyer that auto deaths exceed those in commercial airliners by 1,000 to one. Or, alternately, wait 'til the next time the Dow goes down 150 points in one day. Then start showing people the University of Michigan study of what happens to you if you miss the market's 40 best days. I anticipate that you will undergo a genuinely religious experience.

Besides, the intellect is purely a bull market phenomenon, anyway. People want the 30% returns that are so commonplace today. (Uh, oh.) So they're willing to sit through your one-hour, PC-based presentation in order to get you to let them buy Gronsky Incomprehensible Technology Fund, which is managed by a 28-year-old genius who spent the '73-'74 bear market in kindergarten.

I'm convinced that they haven't got the foggiest notion what you're talking about. You're like the doctor who insists on explaining the details of an operation that the patient needs to save his life. All he cares about is not dying; the rest is just being polite to the sawbones.

Let the next 30% number they see have a minus sign in front of it, and their intellects will short out on the spot. Indeed, I'm quite sure that even a couple of years of flat results — down a couple of percent in '96, up a couple in '97, so that net after tax you're under water — and many intellectually converted equity "believers" will emotionally drift back to CDs.

After two years of zip, two years of 7% look like Nirvana to Americans. Thinking is great on the way up, but on the way down — or even sideways — the emotions climb back into the driver's seat. And the rep who has lived by "performance" once again dies by "performance."

It is not your job to outperform markets, nor to specialize in investments that outperform most or all similar investments. It is your job to see that the people who rely on you reach their lifetime financial goals. And it is never, ever necessary to do the former in order to do the latter.

It is not only possible but probable to become wealthy, never in your life owning an equity fund with more than three stars. All you have to do is put the same dollar amount in those funds every month for the rest of your working life. And then withdraw, say, 6% a year from those equity funds throughout your retirement. The result will be truly multigenerational wealth.

It is at least equally possible to become destitute, investing solely in five-star equity funds. Just buy them the day they get their fifth star, and then panic out when they're down 25%, which they will one day surely be. Then, wait 'til everyone around you is raving about their mutual funds again — near the top of the next cycle — and plunge into some more five-star funds. (An even easier, surer path to destitution: Buy nothing but five-star bond funds when you're 50, then live to 90.)

It doesn't matter what investments do, either absolutely or relative to other investments. The only determinant of lifetime investment success is what people do. And people in this country don't make their investment decisions in their intellects; they make those decisions in their emotions.

So the presence or absence of a trusted, empathic advisor — one who understands and speaks to their emotions — becomes the critical issue. Such an advisor goes to places in the heart, and helps his clients deal with the painful turning points in their financial lives. An advisor who holds up 17 graphs and spouts "technobabble" at such times gets run over by his customers (they were never really clients — clients listen to you) as they stampede for the exits.

The empathetic advisor says, always and everywhere, "I understand how you feel. You wouldn't be human if you didn't have these feelings. We will get through this together. I'm here. Don't be afraid." Today's "technobabbler" only knows how to say, "You don't understand." And that isn't going to cut it.

If this is all starting to sound terribly touchy-feely to you, you can render it wonderfully concrete by taking a sheet of paper and a pen and performing this simple, elegant exercise:

(1) Write down, in a column, the names of your 25 most important accounts. This list doesn't have to be in order of the revenue they produce; it doesn't have to be in any order at all — just your 25 most important accounts.

(2) Now, next to the name of each account, write down his or her birthday.

This is an open-book test. You can look the birthdays up anywhere you've got 'em written down, if you've got them written down. If you don't, go stand in the corner for five minutes. Moreover, if you don't know the clients' birthdays, but you *do* know the betas or standard deviations of their top five fund holdings, *go stand in the corner for five days.* Am I getting through to you on this?

It's getting near the holidays. Maybe there isn't a whole lot of major investment decision-making going on. So maybe you have a little bit of time on your hands. I suggest that you fill it with some places-in-the-heart attitude aerobics. Try any or all of these exercises.

(1) Call all your clients. Ask 'em what their birthdays are. Then ask them what their favorite charities are. When they ask why, tell 'em you're going to give a part (1% or 2%?) of your income from

your relationship with them to their favorite charities every year on their birthdays. You needn't specify the percentage, nor the amount. It's the thought that counts.

(2) Call all your clients. Ask the younger ones how their parents are doing. Ask the older ones how their children and grandchildren are doing. Ask for the names of those people, as your clients tell you about them. (Don't let the client say, "My grandson ..." Ask the boy's name.) Ask if there's anything you could do to help those people whom he loves.

(3) Call all your clients. Ask them how they're feeling. Tell them there's no business purpose to the call, just that you wanted to say hello, and see if there was anything you could do for them.

It's nice to know a lot about investments, I guess, but remember that investments are never an end in themselves. They're only a means to an end. The end is people's achievement of the Great Goals of Life — financial independence for themselves and for the people they love.

Let the amateurs go to places on some chart. Let's you and I go to places in the heart — the real places where real people really live. Because that's what this business is really about.

CLOSING: IT'S NOT A TECHNIQUE, IT'S AN ATTITUDE

I recently did a workshop with the wholesalers of an excellent money manager — one with a very special niche, and thus no real competition.

The wholesalers had that most elegant of sales problems: too many great things to tell their audience about the manager. My mission was to facilitate the creation of a new presentation that would concentrate only on the greatest, most important truths about their product. We started the day with this huge undifferentiated block of Carrara marble, and our goal was to cut away, in Michelangelo's wonderful phrase, everything that wasn't David.

It took all morning. But as noontime approached, we were pretty convinced that we knew all the drop-dead critical points we wanted to make and had a fairly clear idea of the order in which we wanted to make them. "Now," someone said, "we just need the close." And in the next moment I heard myself say, "If you're really making this presentation from the heart, you've been closing since you opened your mouth."

This is the kind of epiphany that happens to me every so often, and it's just another reason why I'm glad I get to speak as much as I do. In brief: I don't know what I know until I hear what I say. (The humorist Jackie Mason has said much the same thing: that he doesn't write his new material, he says it. In the middle of a familiar routine, his unconscious suddenly yields up a new thought on a subject.)

Anyway, this got me thinking about the age-old problem of "closing": how we get our clients and prospects to take action on the recommendations we make.

I probably get asked for my "closing techniques" more often than anything else (except, sadly, for my answer to the no-load objection).

And my response is always the same: that I haven't got any closing "techniques." (Nor, for that matter, any prospecting "techniques," or sales "techniques.") I hate the whole idea of technique because I reject any notion that what you do can be separated, in any meaningful way, from what you are.

Technique is probably OK for people new to the business, in that having a track to run on reduces one's anxiety. But as you get a body of experience — which can only come from dealing with the hopes and fears of real people, and not from a computer screen — technique should begin to wither away.

In its place comes a deepening confidence in your own prospecting/selling/counseling style — which in turn becomes indistinguishable from your personal style. Technique, in the end, is what you do while you're waiting for the differences between your selling style and your personal style to disappear.

At that point, your financial plans and your investment portfolios cease to be your product. Your product — the thing you are fundamentally selling — becomes yourself. So you reach inside yourself for the strengths and skills you need, rather than looking outside yourself to empty, mechanical techniques.

Technique (in general, and closing technique in particular) is also terribly manipulative in ways that our industry is striving mightily to get away from. I remember being taught to ask "closing questions" such as, "Do you want the account to be in your name, or do you prefer to hold your investments jointly with your wife?"

Today we know that, if we're doing our job right, we should be advising the client on the optimum way for his family to own its investments, not asking to know his whims in the matter. (Indeed, as long as I've known him, Alan Parisse has preached the indispensable truth that real clients need and want us to tell them what to do.)

One of the hardest things for many of us to accept is that you can't educate your way to a close. We want to believe that there is a quantum of information which, when communicated to a prospective client, will cause him to move in response to its sheer intellectual luminosity. When this doesn't work — which is virtually all the time — we stumble on, in a desperate attempt to provoke a decision by piling on more facts, ratios, statistics, charts, and graphs. We seem not to see that it will not matter how much wood you put in the fireplace if there's no fire.

Though we can't analyze our way to a close, we can — and we must — empathize our way. But again, that isn't a function of what we know. Still less is it a function of what we say. The critical issue is how we feel, and how we make the prospect feel.

Thus, I never ask a prospect what he thinks about what I've told him, but how he feels about it.

There's literally no limit to the number of times I can ask this question during a sales/planning interview. And the slower the prospect is coming along, or the more resistance I feel, the more often I'm likely to ask it. And, lo and behold, each time I ask how my prospects feel, I effect what we used to call, about a hundred years ago, a "trial close."

Me: We've established what you're going to need, in terms of an income-producing pool of capital, in order to achieve a worry-free retirement. Do you still feel that that's the right number?

Prospect: Yes.

Me: Given the amount of money that you need to accumulate, and what you can afford to invest in the interim, we've kind of backed into the conclusion that you're going to have to put at least 70% of your invested dollars into equities from now until retirement. Does the math still look right to you?

Prospect: Yes, the math sure looks OK but ... (begins to make low, moaning noises).

Me: Stop right there. Please tell me how you're feeling about all this.

Prospect: (putting down his calculator, and looking at me sadly) I feel like I might throw up.

Me: Please talk to me some more about feeling like you're gonna throw up.

Prospect: This goes against everything I've ever felt about investing. Why, if my mom and dad could be alive again to see me seriously thinking about putting 70% of my retirement money in stocks, they'd drop dead all over again.

Me: I understand how you feel. What do you say we go 50% equities and 50% bonds. You'll have to retire on less money, but maybe you'll just feel more comfortable.

Prospect: But I don't want to retire on less money. Hell, I *can't* retire on less money.

Me: Then equities feel like the only way to get there. If you need to go down to the corner for a loaf of bread, I recommend you walk. If you need to go over to the next county to visit your son and his wife, I recommend you drive. If you need to go to Australia, I recommend you fly. Do you feel any doubt that, retirement-wise, you need to go to Australia?

Prospect: (Sadly) Guess not.

Me: Then sit back, relax, and enjoy the flight. And I feel I have the right to say that because I'll take the responsibility of flying the plane.

Prospect: But don't you think I need to be worried about ... .

Me: I don't think you need to be worried about anything because I feel that's my job. I insist that my clients plan; I encourage them to hope. But I forbid them to worry, because that's what they pay me to do. Now about this portfolio of funds I've recommended. How do you feel about ... .

The cumulative effect of all this, as I hope you can see, is to arrive at the end of the presentation with nothing left to decide. In other words (I now realize), I've been closing since I opened my mouth.

Let me hasten to add that this will not work if your presentation is based on the merits of the investments themselves, rather than on your portfolio recommendations as funding media for the achievement of your prospects' fondest hopes and dreams. Loving my family as I do, I find I can plug directly into my prospects' love for theirs, and the glow from that empathy can, as President Kennedy said, truly light the world. On the other hand, I find I'm powerless to empathize with — much less cause anyone else to be warmed by — a scattergram. Maybe I'm just old-fashioned.

All "closing" difficulties arise from the failure to make that personal connection. No amount of technique can ever overcome that failure. "What is done for effect," Emerson said, "is seen to be done for effect, and what is done for love is felt to be done for love."

If you can clearly see the beauty of your plan/portfolio for a prospect, if you believe passionately in the ability of that plan/portfolio to fund his dreams, and if you communicate that passionate belief simply and directly, you will have little difficulty in "closing." And when you don't close, you won't see it as a failure on your part, but as a problem that the prospect, God help him, couldn't overcome. For many are called, but few are chosen.

Just realize that you close not on the basis of what you do, but by the force of what you are. And then you'll see that your identity and your "closing technique" must ultimately turn out to be the same thing.

SIX QUESTIONS THAT WILL FIND YOU THREE HUNDRED PROSPECTS

Because prospecting for new clients is the most anxiety-producing thing we have to do, many financial advisors spend an inordinate amount of time thinking about it. Unfortunately, thinking about prospecting and actually prospecting are mutually exclusive pursuits. "How," asked Yogi Berra, "can you think and hit at the same time?"

You can't. So the more we think about prospecting, the less prospecting we do, and the more paralyzed we become. In turn, as paralysis itself breeds even more guilt and anxiety, we retreat into increasingly bizarre behaviors ("I'm loading my prospect files into my computer"). It's a downward spiral.

But suppose there were a way to prospect for new clients without actually having to prospect for new clients. That might really reduce the anxiety involved, and help you function more effectively.

Moreover, suppose this nifty new form of prospecting (or non-prospecting, if you'll pardon my Zen) had the additional benefit of focusing your conversations not on markets or investments, but on the real lives and emotions of real people. In markets that are bound to disappoint, somewhere along in here, that would be a significant benefit. (Or maybe you think we're in for a second straight year of a 37.4% return from the S&P 500.)

So I propose to offer you six prospecting questions. You can ask one or more of these questions of every single person you encounter in any context. And I'll suggest that you start by asking them of everyone in your account book. Then, try 'em on your entire prospect file. And, when your anxiety levels have declined sufficiently (because you're so used to asking these questions and so delighted by the business that flows from the responses), you'll start asking them of everyone you meet.

Beginning this project in your own account book will be so (relatively) easy that it won't feel like prospecting at all. It'll feel like what it is: you asking how you can help other members of your clients' families, thereby deepening your relationship.

The first two questions can be addressed to just about any adult between the ages of 40 and 60, with potentially startling results.

QUESTION #1: *Are your parents still living?*
The dark star that's in a collision orbit with so many baby boomers' retirement plans is the financial status of their increasingly long-lived parents. Few people expected to see a day when the fastest-growing segment of the American population would be folks over 85. Now, that segment is growing five times faster than the population as a whole. The prevailing attitude of their children has, up until now, been one of denial, but I think you can sense that they're awakening to the true scope of this financial planning problem. Question Number One establishes whether your particular client is in this situation.

If the answer is no, that the client's parents are gone, I'll ask if they left legacies to the client or to his children, and if the client is happy with the way those monies are being managed. But if the answer is that one or more of the client's parents (or parents-in-law) is living, I ask ...

QUESTION #2: *Do you expect to become financially responsible for your parents at some point?*
This is, as I hope you'll intuitively see, the mother of all win-win questions. Guy says yes, you get to ask how he's planning to fund that responsibility, particularly in view of his own retirement needs. This can lead to a whole new round of the planning process, in which you get to capture more assets.

But if the client says no, I'll never have to support my parents, he's told you they have sufficient means to be financially independent come hell or high water. Immediately, you know they're substantial prospects. You can quite reasonably ask if the client is happy with the arrangements the parents have made for the transfer of that wealth to him and to his children.

In many cases, the client doesn't know what his folks have planned, and doesn't know how to approach them about it. It's dicey, but you can offer to have that conversation with the parents, either with or for your client. I'm betting that in most cases, the parents will appreciate the help. (Maybe they hadn't fully planned their estates themselves; most folks don't, even today.)

But even if you're rebuffed by the parents, chances are you'll have cemented the relationship with the client just by offering to go the extra mile. And if you discover, in the process, that there probably isn't going to be a whole heck of a lot left when the parents are gone, you can relay that vital intelligence to your client, so that he realizes, and can plan for, the fact that he and he alone will have to provide for himself and his children.

Note that this line of questioning can be applicable to anyone, and has nothing to do with the state of the markets or how many stars your favorite funds have. Places in the heart vs. places on some chart ... remember? Get to the realities of your clients' emotional and financial relationships with their parents. You can't fail to build trust, open accounts, and gather assets, perhaps on a scale currently unimaginable to you.

When you've finished asking every single one of your clients about his parents, and/or are ready to approach those of your clients too old to still have parents, you can start through your book again, like Sherman through Georgia, with either or both of the third and fourth of my six questions.

QUESTION #3: *May I ask you what specific financial plan you have made for the education of your children?*

QUESTION #4: *May I ask you what specific financial plan you have made for the education of your grandchildren?*
This issue is another one where a lot of denial is present. ("College costs aren't going to go up that fast anymore; maybe the kid'll get a soccer scholarship; there's always financial aid.") Yet, particularly with respect to Question Four, it touches some very deep wellsprings of emotion, centered around issues of responsibility for the well-being of the people we (or our children) brought into the world.

Grandparents, particularly, realize that their children may not be in any financial shape to give the grandchildren the education their folks gave them. And there are often some strong intimations of a kind of immortality, here. ("If I endow my granddaughter's medical school tuition, and she's saving people's lives 50 years from now, maybe in a sense I'm still alive.")

If you're the financial advisor who bridges three generations of a family's life in this way, you're going to have this account for the rest of your life. For remember Murray's Law of Multigenerational Marketing, which states:

"The percentage of a family's assets you control, and the length of time you control those assets, are absolute functions of the number of family members you are talking to on a regular basis."

Beyond that, however, look at what a prospecting no-brainer these two questions are. And ask yourself: Other than my own anxiety-based prospecting reluctance, what would prevent me from asking one of these two questions of every adult I meet in the course of a day? Doesn't this issue go right to the heart of everything real people really care about? And don't I present myself in the best possible light by asking them about the people and the issues they care about most?

The last two questions in my six-shooter are a pair:

QUESTION #5: *Do you own any no-load mutual funds?*

And, when the answer is inevitably yes, ask...

QUESTION #6: *Do you fully understand the real risks of those funds?*

If you remember my "lifeboat drills" column from September '95 (and even if you don't), I expressed the devout belief that, when it comes to equity funds, no-load investors have no idea what they own.

On September 30, 1990, 11 days before the bottom of the Saddam bear market, there were $224.9 billion in equity mutual funds. On December 31, 1995, that number was $1.21 trillion. In other words, four out of every five dollars in an equity mutual fund today have never experienced a 10% market decline on a closing basis. People have no idea that they're in funds that can (and do) go down 20% to 40% in a major market correction ... nor that those funds will, one fine day, surely do so again.

What have I got to lose by asking a no-load investor these questions? Nothing. And what have I got to gain? Everything.

PROSPECT: Whaddya mean, the real risks of my funds?

ME: I simply mean, do you know exactly how much your funds can go down — and indeed have gone down, well within the last 10 years — when a perfectly normal bear market occurs?

PROSPECT: Well, uh ... no, I guess not.

ME: Would it be helpful to you if, without any cost or obligation, I found out for you?

PROSPECT: Can you do that?

ME: I can, and I will. Cheerfully.

PROSPECT: Well, I sure wouldn't mind knowing, if you don't mind finding out.

ME: My pleasure.

Since no-help fund investors tend to chase peak performance, with no concept that this almost always entails peak volatility, the percentage hits their funds took in 1987 and 1990 — which is the information I give them — are usually pretty blood-curdling.

ME: And you realize, of course, that — the nature of the cycle being what it is — this is going to happen again.

PROSPECT: You mean ... this could happen again?

ME: No, no, that's not what I said at all. I didn't say it *could* happen again, I said it *will*.

PROSPECT: I couldn't take that.

ME: I didn't think so. Now, since I end up costing about 1% more annually than a no-help fund, do you think it might be worth your time to sit down with me and look at some funds which balance your need for growth with your need to protect your capital?

PROSPECT: Where have you been all my life?

Once again, please see that the only barrier preventing you from trying one or more of these six questions on virtually everybody you meet is your own anxiety.

Start slow, if you like. Ask a question five times a day for 10 days, six times a day for the next 10 days, seven a day for the next 10, and so on. Train, don't strain. Because, even at that rate, you'll have asked one of these questions about 2,400 times by Thanksgiving.

And if you've got fewer than 300 prospects ... well, by that time, the Post Office will probably be hiring for the holiday rush.

Am I getting through to you on this?

THE MYTH OF "PRICING PRESSURES"

If this year is anything like last, I'll probably have about 100 speaking engagements — to brokerage firms, financial planning organizations, life insurance companies, banks, and mutual fund groups.

The fundamental thing one notices, in talking to all these different kinds of groups, is how similar they've all become. When I joined E. F. Hutton & Company 29 years ago this month, there was absolutely no overlap between a stockbroker's products/services and those of a bank or a life insurer.

Today, those products and services are not merely similar, but virtually identical. When you encounter New York Life agents earning most of their income from mutual funds, Citibankers selling life insurance and annuities, and Merrill Lynch betting the (retail) ranch on financial planning, you know you've entered … The Homogenized Zone.

So, not surprisingly, the things these once wildly disparate entities ask me to speak about are taking on a great sameness. And these days, no topic is more widely requested than, and I quote, "pricing pressures."

I have to confess that I find this "issue" mysterious to the point of otherworldliness. That is, I admit, a personal reaction, based — perhaps too much so — on my own experience.

People ask me what I charge, and I tell 'em. Most say OK (having decided, I guess, that I'm worth it); some go away (having decided … who knows what, and who cares?). A very few ask if I'll negotiate. I say, "Sure; always happy to negotiate. Let's start with you. What are you prepared to give up?" This seems to nip the issue in the bud rather nicely. And I think you can infer from it, however anecdotally, Murray's Law of "Pricing Pressures," which states:

YOUR PRICE ONLY BECOMES AN ISSUE TO THE EXTENT THAT YOUR VALUE IS IN QUESTION.

In this view, "pricing pressures" are never really about price, but are always and everywhere a proxy for some other issue. Specifically, I think you can (and should) assume that any "pricing pressures" you may be feeling are not an industry problem but a personal problem.

Although you may be reluctant to accept this seemingly harsh reality, eventually you'll come to like it. You see, you have no capacity to solve an industry problem, and infinite capacity to solve problems that are essentially of your own making. Thus, I love problems that are basically my own fault (which is to say: I love all my problems), because if I made 'em, I can fix 'em.

Before discussing the three major issues for which "pricing pressures" are a proxy, let me acknowledge the very real industry pricing trends with which we all have to live — and in which we can all find opportunities.

Remember, though, that no irreversible industry megatrend (of which pricing is surely one) is a problem *per se*; it's just a reality to be dealt with realistically. Gravity is, I suppose, a "problem" for me in that it prevents me from flying, which I'd really like to do. On the other hand, it prevents me from drifting off into the blackness of space while I'm sleeping. And, in the end, gravity just is; no sense fighting what you can't change.

There can be no question that the pricing of investment products and services is continuing its secular fall — nor that the volume of dollars flowing into our industry is continuing to explode. That's how life works. Look at technology: The price of computing keeps dropping like a stone, and the use of computing keeps growing at exponential rates. Equity mutual funds used to charge an 8.75% front-end load, and took in $25 billion between 1924 and 1964. Today they charge 0% to 5.5% (with the blended rate, I'm guessing, in the 2% to 3% range), and they take in $25 billion in a month.

People always ask me anxiously where I think the financial services industry is going. My answer is always the same: to 1%. I'm operating under the assumption that, before too long, commissions will be a vestigial remain (like the little leg bone in the dolphin's fin), and we'll all be working for an annual percentage of the assets, which I think is most likely to settle out around 1%.

I'll be very happy to be wrong on this, and to have compensation stop falling somewhere north of 1%. But I'm not counting on it, and I don't think you should, either. For the same reason that I draw financial plans that assume index returns — so the long-term surprises are likely to be pleasant — I'm planning to be in a 1% business for the rest of my career.

Let's say I've decided that my price for passing this way is an income of $1 million dollars a year, and that I net about half the gross income from my practice. Therefore, I need to gross two million. (See how fast I figured that out?) In a 1% world, I thus need to get $200 million under management.

Being basically a family guy, I think of clients not in terms of individual accounts, but in terms of family units. My average unit (boomers, their parents, their children, and, increasingly, grandchildren) seems to have about $500,000 in investable net worth. So all I have to do is get 400 of these units on the books, and I'm done.

My choices are essentially twofold: I can start contacting the 260 million people who live in the United States, asking if their family would like to join the 400. Alternatively, I can stand here shoveling, uh, shinola against the tide, and moaning about "pricing pressures."

This scenario is neither good nor bad. It's simply real. One percent. That, as the poet says, is all ye know, and all ye need to know.

Now that we've got that out of the way, let's go back to those three attitudinal/behavioral issues I spoke about — the ones that are hiding behind the red herring of "pricing pressures."

Value Pressures. As we've already seen, price can never be the issue by itself. It is always (albeit unconsciously) related to a perception of the value that's being exchanged — or not exchanged — for the price.

Therefore it's the perception of your value on the prospect's part — not the actual quality of your work — that makes him willing to pay the price. This is why people with backgrounds in engineering, accounting, and the physical sciences have so much trouble making it in this business. They're used to getting paid for finding the right answers. But we only get paid when we cause people to act on the right answers we've found. (This used to be called — before it became so grotesquely unfashionable — "sales.")

Paradoxically enough, a 1% world actually liberates you from many or most value pressures. If a family can't see that your plan for multigenerational wealth is worth 1% a year, they can go to, well, to the tender mercies of the no-help fund industry.

Whatever you charge, just make sure you give more value for it than you ask in return. From that will come the strength to keep prospecting until you've found your 400 families. As I said a few months ago, if you do high quality work and show that work to enough people, all pressures — not just "pricing pressures" — will drift away on the wind. Don't subtract from your price. Add to your value.

Amateur Pressures. One of the many evils of a great bull market — and this is the greatest ever — is that it draws large numbers of unsuitable (nay, virtually unemployable) people into the business. As I travel around the industry, it begins to look to me like the Depression-era WPA: we've somehow become the employer of last resort.

In a roaring bull market, professionals always lose market share to amateurs, since the latter are willing to make wilder claims and give deeper discounts.

Worse, the investors themselves become part of this problem, concluding that they can do it themselves, and don't have to pay a professional.

In moments of weakness you may focus on the symptom ("pricing pressures") rather than on the real disease (which is, of course, that this is The Mother of All Amateur Nights).

Stand by your guns. Do high quality work, and charge a fair price for it. The price of transactions can never be the issue; *the value of advice is always the issue.* It is axiomatic that the amateur's price is lower, and that's only fair: the value of his advice is a lot lower, too.

It's the same with "performance." Amateurs always tout higher "performance," and never talk about the risk you take to get that "performance." (That's an integral part of being an amateur in a wild bull market: He can't explain risk because he himself doesn't understand it.) Amateurs think it matters which investments you buy; professionals know the only thing that matters is what you do — or more importantly, don't do — when those investments go down 20% to 30%.

Don't let amateurs set your agenda; don't compete with them for new clients on their terms. Preserve your own clients against fads, fears, and amateurs. And don't worry, you'll get all the new clients you want on the next turn of the wheel, when the amateurs go to the wall. Just keep prospecting, so you can be the professional that people remember when they fire their amateur advisor.

Self-Image Pressures. Price is always the critical element in the decision about where to buy a commodity, e.g., a barrel of oil, a pound of copper, or 16 tons of No. 9 coal. The less commodity-like the product, however, the less important price (as a governing variable) becomes. And in our little world the three least commodity-like things we offer are caring, experience, and wisdom.

Anybody (and everybody) can buy mutual funds cheaper than I am willing to sell them. So if mutual funds are the commodity for which my prospect is shopping, let him go in peace. I don't want his money; much more importantly, I don't want his blood on my hands.

You and I will never again, as long as we live, be the low-cost providers of investment products and services. (In that sense, I guess, "pricing pressures" are never going to disappear.) And that's fine, because products and services aren't what we sell.

We sell caring, experience, and wisdom. We sell our ability to plan for, and execute the attainment of, multigenerational wealth. This ability is quite literally priceless, but only if we are willing to stand up for it.

"A man," said Emerson, "passes for what he is worth." Ultimately, I think, your price is the value you set on yourself. We all price ourselves (or allow the marketplace to price us) based on our own sense of self-worth.

To bemoan "pricing pressures" is, in that sense, to make a statement of negative self-worth. "This is all the marketplace will let me earn" really means, "This is all I'm worth."

Of this I'm sure: Life happens to losers, and winners happen to life. "Pricing" — like interest rates, GDP growth (or the absence thereof), and the weather — is an external circumstance.

A 19th-century Irish novelist with the delightful name of Samuel Lover wrote, "Circumstances are the rules of the weak; they are the instruments of the wise."

And Napoleon said, "Circumstances! I *make* circumstances!" Go thou, and do likewise.

WHO'S AFRAID OF A MARKET DECLINE?

Two years ago, I was hearing that asset allocation was the long-sought miracle cure for market volatility. Even if the market went down, a new generation of exquisitely nuanced asset allocation models would keep our portfolios from going down nearly as much.

I thought — and think — that this was a transcendently dumb argument. I know I'm terribly old-fashioned, but I can't seem to shake the belief that markets are extremely efficient in the long run. So my conviction is that any portfolio that will prevent my principal from going down nearly as much as the market when the market goes down will, with equal effectiveness, prevent my capital from going up nearly as much as the market when the market goes up. There's no such thing as an out-of-the-park bunt.

As dreadful as I found the asset-allocation-is-an-invisibility-cloak-so-the-bear-can't-see-you argument at the time, I look back on it now almost with nostalgia. At least it admitted of the possibility of a generalized market decline sometime during our lifetimes.

Then, last year, our industry began to slide away even from that admission. Yes, I heard that the law of market cycles has not been repealed, and you still get a 20%-or-so decline in stock prices every five years on average. So we won't be due for another one until about 1999, because — hadn't you noticed? — we had one in 1994. Three quarters of NYSE stocks had the requisite 20% decline, just not at the same time, so the averages never closed off 10%. This is the Stealth Bear Market argument, which I was at pains to excoriate some months ago in this space. Next to this chestnut, the asset-allocation-as-financial-alchemy thesis looks almost rational. (But just almost.)

This year, the awful state of denial our industry is in has taken another turn on its horrific downward spiral. Now, everywhere I go

I find the amazing argument that stock prices are going to be driven relentlessly upward until the year 2004 (or thereabout) by the insatiable demand of the baby boomers.

In this astonishing fairy tale, stock prices are no longer materially affected by such archaic variables as earnings, book value, dividends, the business cycle, interest rates, inflation, or any of those old Stone Age factors. Instead, prices are drawn inexorably and uninterruptedly upward by the boomers' infinite appetite for "growth."

Then, in 2004, the boomers — who have had the brains and guts to acquire equities massively and stoically for the previous third of a century — will not have the plain common sense to hold on to them during their decades-long retirement. They'll begin selling off their stock funds, and the market will finally go down. No sense thinking about it now, though. Hell, it's eight years away. Don't worry, be happy.

This is the single stupidest argument I've heard since the "synergy of conglomerates" theory, circa 1968. And what I want to ask is: Why are we resorting to more and more bizarre arguments that the market "can't" go down? (Because, obviously, we've gone way beyond talking about whether it will or it won't. We're now saying that it can't. Does anybody but me remember Professor Fisher's "stocks appear to have reached a permanently high plateau" speech of 1929?)

My take on this is that the ferocity of our denial is directly related to the depth of our real fear. And all my experience of life is that the thing you fear most always, always happens.

To say that the market won't experience a generalized decline of 20% or 30%, at least within some significant number of years to come, is to bet one's business — as well as one's clients' financial plans — on an outcome about which one can't be certain. This is simply not something responsible professionals do. And all evasions of responsibility come back to haunt us; the longer it takes, the worse the haunting usually is.

If I'm right that the pandemic denial out there is a symptom of fear, permit me to conduct a therapeutic inquiry into the nature and source of that fear. Because you can never arrive at a workable solution to a problem that you don't fully understand in the first place.

What I think we're afraid of is that, at some point, our clients are going to bolt. Otherwise, we wouldn't be concerned about the perfectly normal ebb and flow of stock prices, because we know that the downs are temporary and the ups are permanent, don't we?

Not long ago, I sat through the presentation just before mine at a firm's annual conference. This is just my way of staying in touch with what the industry is talking about, as well as getting a feel for the room and the audience I'm about to work.

The speaker was discussing something called "style boxes": a method of creating mutual fund portfolios so that the return is maximized without big increments in volatility, as measured by beta. But he didn't just allude to volatility control in the abstract; the speaker kept saying that this was so the clients wouldn't bolt. And that's when I had my epiphany. First, I thought: It isn't some academic, complex portfolio alchemy that keeps people from bailing out. It's the word of a trusted advisor. And then it hit me. *The fear that clients will bolt is an unconscious admission that your clients don't trust you.*

In a certain perverse way, this all makes sense to me now. These increasingly bizarre wishful-thinking theories of what the market is going to do — or, more properly, isn't going to do — are the places we're putting our anxiety. We've made the performance of markets and of investments the central focus of our interactions with people. But deep down, we know that that can never work — that only the advice of a trusted professional, particularly in "bad" times, can save people from their worst instincts, chief among which is the tendency to mistake fluctuation for loss.

The plain fact is that, in this greatest of all bull markets, it has become far too easy to put the focus on "performance." In doing so, we've allowed ourselves to ignore two eternal truths. First, the more we let people regard superior returns as something akin to a birthright, the more we desensitize them to the normality and ultimate meaninglessness of declines. This sets them up to fail. It's no wonder we need to believe "this time it's different," because if it's not, even a "cub" market only a little worse than 1994's will paralyze them at best, and quite possibly stampede them.

The second and even more important casualty of "performance" mania is the truth that volatility is, in and of itself, the price of performance. It is precisely the ability of stocks to decline very meaningfully from time to time that causes an efficient market to demand the superior returns that only stocks produce.

We are like the proprietors of an expensive and highly mortgaged beach resort. In our anxiety about losing our franchise, we have taken it into our heads — and are now heavily advertising — that it isn't going to rain again for eight years. Granted, if we're right, no one's vacation at our property is going to get rained out, so — for a little while — we're going to enjoy an excellent income.

Unfortunately, if we're right that it won't rain again for eight years, the earth is going to dry up, and every living thing on it is going to die. No rain, no life. Similarly, if we're right that the U.S. equity market is incapable of meaningful decline for the better part of another decade, an efficient market will bid prices up to a point where the returns fall to a level commensurate with sharply diminished risk. Indeed, it would be the witch of markets' ultimate, cosmic joke if there were no 20% decline until 2004 — and average annual returns were 7% or so in the interim.

You can't, I'm sorry to say, have your cake and eat it, too. Reward is always commensurate with risk, and if you foresee a secular deadening of volatility, surely you realize that you're also calling for returns below historic norms. (A year like '95, with 35% returns and a maximum peak-to-trough decline of 2.4% — the century's lowest — isn't a norm. It's a miracle. You see something like it once every 20 years if you're very, very lucky. The last year like it was 1975, and need I remind you of what had happened in '73-'74?)

Please see the enormity of what I'm trying to communicate here. It's not just that the "market can't/won't go down for donkey's years" argument is wrong. (That goes without saying.) It's that you don't really want that argument to be right!

So let's return to the fear that clients are going to bolt. Let me give it to you straight: You're right. They're gonna bolt. Unless we do something about it. Now, what are you prepared to do about it?

Well, part of the response — at the risk of harping on this — can and should be "lifeboat drills," i.e., reminding clients of how much their core holdings declined peak-to-trough in 1987 and 1990. This is the best way I've found to impress upon people that the price of wealth in equities is the emotional ability to withstand the occasional harrowing — but ultimately temporary — market decline.

My point is that if you want the wealth, you not only accept the declines, but you actively want the declines, because reward and volatility are always and everywhere two sides of the very same coin.

Another response to concerns about inevitable increases in volatility (at least compared to the five least volatile years back-to-back in history, 1991-95) is the countercultural suggestion that what a lot of Americans need to do is to switch into lower-performing mutual funds.

The last five years rewarded investors for taking on the most blood-curdling risks, by giving them all of the pleasure and none of the pain of such an aggressive posture. And I suppose if you really felt that the next five years would be exactly like the last five, you'd want to leave your assets hanging out over the edge.

However, if you thought — as I, for one, find it hard not to think — that the next block of time will be normative (that is, with returns dropping back toward their historic norms, and volatility rising to its), you might just be shopping for managers whose style is more protective of capital.

You might, in other words, think that equity capital should be vectored toward lower-"performance" management styles, for the simple reason that, in an efficient market, such an approach will expose you to lower volatility.

No matter what your strategy for coping with a return to trendline patterns of reward/volatility, please don't think that denial is an option. If you're afraid they're going to bolt, then for all intents and purposes they've already bolted. Your business is under a death sentence, and just because this market keeps giving you stays of execution, (a) you're never going to be free, and (b) one day you're going to have to walk that last mile.

The secret to making money in stocks, as Peter Lynch said, is not to get scared out of them. We're not helping people by making believe that scary things can't or won't happen until the new millennium. We help people only when we assure them (a) that scary things always happen, or the returns wouldn't be there, (b) that it's OK to be scared, it's just not OK to act on the fear, and above all (c) that you'll be there to help them through the scary nights, so they can still be around when the sun comes up again on another bright day in the Global Capitalist Revolution.

Don't make believe that the temporary downs don't exist anymore. (Indeed, for the sake of your and your clients' future wealth, pray that they do.) Instead, remind everybody (and yourself) of the supreme secret of equity investing: The downs are always temporary; the ups are always permanent.

DO YOU
HAVE CLIENTS
OR CUSTOMERS?

Last month I said that if you were afraid your clients would bolt in a perfectly normal every-five-years-or-so-25%-or-so market correction, for career-planning purposes they've already bolted. It doesn't matter how many stays of execution you get from this most glorious of all bull markets; one of these old days you'll have to walk that last mile.

This month, I'd like to expand my inquiry into the nature and meaning of client control. Simply stated: If you're genuinely afraid that your clients are going to bolt, you haven't got clients. You have customers.

This is always a very important distinction. But late in a bull market, as we draw ever closer (statistically, at least) to one of those episodes in which investors' worst instincts have a field day, the issue of customers vs. clients becomes a matter of career life and death.

Merchants have customers, and exercise virtually no direct control over their customers' decisions. Naturally, merchants try to influence customer behavior through such variables as price, selection, and service. But influence ends very far short of control.

If you're a haberdasher, you can stock the highest quality Harris tweed sport jackets in town at the very best prices. And you can be the only store in your market that offers same-day free alterations. But if the customer browsing in your shop this morning decides he doesn't really want a new sport jacket (even if he actually needs one), you're out of luck.

Merchants are more or less at the mercy of their customers' whims. So they've learned not to question people's rationality. If you go into your local Pep Boys store and ask about a certain type of truck tires, they'll show you their selection and sell you a complete set of tires without ever once asking if you own a truck. A merchant, in other words, addresses your wants on the assumption that you know what your needs are.

Professionals don't have customers, they have clients. Professionals are there to tell clients what they need, even (and especially) when the clients themselves do not know what they need. You don't go to an estate attorney and tell her you need a generation-skipping trust or a charitable remainder trust. You go in and say: Here's who I am; here are my assets; here's what I want to happen; what's the optimum strategy for me? Thus, the relationship between a professional and a client is one in which the former exercises a considerable degree of control over the latter — by mutual consent.

Forgive me, but it is no great accomplishment for you to get a family to put 60% to 80% of its investable assets in equities when the Dow's gone from 2450 to 5800 in less than six years without even a 10% correction on a closing basis. This is like trolling into the middle of a feeding frenzy, then going home and telling everyone what a great fisherman you are.

I want to see what happens when the value of those accounts declines 25% amid reports in *USA Today* (the paper for folks who don't have time for the in-depth coverage of TV news) of the end of economic life on the planet as we have known it. Assuming you're counseling people to do nothing (if they don't have any more money) or to buy more before the sale ends (if they do), we'll then know whether you've got customers or clients. Clients will be the ones who heed your wise counsel. Customers will be the ones who bolt. It's just that simple.

This being the case, you have, as I see it, two options. You can wait until the spaghetti hits the fan, as they say, and find out who's a customer and who's a client the hard way. Alternatively, if (like me) you're not from the thrills-chills-and-surprises school of career management, you may want to start assessing your book right away, so that you can predetermine which is which in time for you to act on (rather than reacting to) this critical issue.

Here are some of the more reliable, and easily identifiable, ways in which clients and customers can be distinguished from each other.

1. Customers are buying investments from you; clients are buying your advice. With something like 7,000 mutual funds out there, and virtually any management style anyone could want available at little or no cost, it should be clear to you that investments themselves have long since become a commodity. And, as Warren Buffett used to say before he invested in USAir, in a commodity business it's hard for you to be that much smarter than your dumbest competitor.

You can't tell anyone anything about mutual funds that he can't find out for free in a public library, or for pennies from his computer (America's leading source of technically correct answers to badly framed questions, and thus our dumbest competitor).

You might wonder, then, why you get into protracted discussions with people who want to know about such ephemera as stars, expense ratios, and the letter rating in *The Wall Street Journal.* The problem is that these people are customers, who think that the critical variable in investing is which investments they buy rather than the quality of the advice they get. (Of course, if it's actually you who brought up all that nonsense — beta, standard deviation, Sharpe ratio — then your problem isn't whether you're talking to a client or a customer. Your problem is you.)

Clients make — and then keep — the investments you recommend because you advise them to do so. The investments are seen not as ends in themselves, but as means to the end of The Great Goals of Life: a retirement in which clients won't run out of money, a legacy for their children, the education of their grandchildren. You are seen by clients as the professional responsible for the attainment of those goals. You're a trusted advisor, not a merchant trying to prove that your tires are cheaper and longer-lasting than the other guy's tires.

2. The more often you have to talk to someone on the phone, the more likely it is that that person is a customer. The converse is

also true. No client's lifetime goals change between Monday and Tuesday. And the appropriateness of a given portfolio as the funding medium for those goals can never change from Tuesday to Wednesday. We may infer from these two great truths that if you get calls from (or are expected to call) someone on Monday, Tuesday, and Wednesday ... that's a customer. Someone who you have to talk to most days is, *ipso facto*, isolating on the wrong variable(s). Presuming that your wise counsel focuses on the right variables, we conclude that this person is not listening to you, which automatically disqualifies him from the status of client, and relegates him to that of customer.

If the growth part of an equity portfolio is shooting the lights out while the value portion is lying there bleeding into the carpet, you know that you've got a properly balanced equity portfolio that is doing just exactly what it's supposed to do. A client either (a) understands this, (b) doesn't understand it but accepts it because you say it's copasetic, or (c) doesn't even think about it, which is why he hired you in the first place.

A customer constantly calls up carping about "that blankety-blank underperforming Gronsky Value Fund." You calmly go through your whole approach to portfolio balance, and solemnly promise him that growth and value will eventually do a role reversal, and that Gronsky Growth will then underperform — according to plan. Three days later he calls back to talk about switching from the Value Fund to the Growth Fund.

Do I have to spell it out for you? Anybody you have to talk to a whole lot is (a) talking about the wrong things and (b) a customer. (But I repeat myself.)

3. Customers almost always focus on markets; clients can be trained to focus on their own lives. With the Dow approaching 6,000, I can be quite confident that it is going to 60,000, and ultimately to 600,000. (Go ahead, ask me when, and I'll smack you right in the mouth.) After all, it went up about 140 times in the past 64 years, a period whose highlights (or lowlights) were the Great Depression, WWII, and the Cold War. You think it can't go up another hundred-fold sometime in a century of global capitalist revolution? (If you don't, I submit with respect that you have somehow missed the entire point of the last seven years of world history.)

This being my essential viewpoint (and given the fact that I'm planning for up to three generations of a family, so my time horizon is typically 20 to 100 years), I'm entirely relieved of the obligation to have a short- to intermediate-term market outlook. And in fact I have none: I know as an article of faith that we're going to 60,000, but I've no idea whether we're going to 7,000 or 5,000 next. And couldn't care less.

Even if they're not predisposed to do so (and virtually all Americans aren't), real clients can be trained to match their true investment time horizons to a market outlook of similar duration. This is almost countercultural in the MTV/CNBC/*Money* magazine/Internet era, so only a trusted investment advisor can bring it off — and only with clients.

Customers always identify themselves as such by returning again and again to market-related issues: trends, sectors, "hot funds" (God help us), and countries. They ask you, in other words, to know the unknowable. And then — the classic sign of a customer — they blame you when you're wrong. Were it three times longer, life would still be way too short for that noise.

4. Clients focus on your value, customers focus on your cost. I talked about this issue at length a couple of months ago in this space ("The Myth of Pricing Pressures," May '96), so we needn't belabor it here. I just want you to see that, in addition to all its other ramifications, cost/value is one of the ultimate customer/client dichotomies.

You never seem to have much trouble getting clients to understand (and to appreciate, which isn't the same thing at all) the value of what you do. On the other hand, no matter how much you do for them, customers are always letting you know — in their patented passive/aggressive way — that they think you cost too much.

Please remember what I said in that earlier column: Your price is only an issue to the extent that your value is in question. No one who is constantly questioning your value is your client; I don't care what you're telling yourself.

5. Clients tend to become friends, and friends tend to become clients. Customers just tend to become progressively more hostile. Almost by definition, if you find yourself in the middle of an argument — any argument — you are talking to a customer. Clients may express concern, disappointment, confusion, and other similar emotions; if they didn't, they wouldn't be human. But those issues are always dealt with in a way that doesn't seek to strip you of your dignity. A certain bedrock respect for you and for your professionalism underlies even the most difficult client encounters. And if you haven't oversold or misled the client in some other way, chances are you'll arrive at an understanding ... which in turn can only deepen and solidify the relationship.

I know any number of advisors who were stunned late on October 19 and all through the next day in 1987 to get calls from clients expressing concern about how the advisors were holding up. (At the same time, of course, customers were trying to cut out their advisors' hearts with a butter knife.) It was ever thus: there's a human bond between advisor and client that simply can't be replicated with customers ... not least of all because customers don't want it.

Of course, the advisor has to show the same fundamental respect (and, if possible, affection) for the client. And the advisor has to show those things first. What goes around comes around, but it's our job to set it in motion.

6. Customers victimize you; clients empower you. This is the least specific but most important difference between clients and customers, and indeed it summarizes all of the others.

On some level, all of life is the journey from victimization to empowerment. When you were a child (and especially if you were a first child), perhaps you came home one day with a report card containing four A's and a B. And all of the feedback you got from your parents may have been about the B. That's victimization. (Your folks didn't mean any harm by it, but you don't have to mean harm in order to do harm.)

Today, you may have people in five funds, four of which are doing just great, and one of which is lying there like a beached whale. A client, after having commented appropriately on the four favorable situations, will ask you politely if you're still happy with the laggard. That's empowerment. A customer will go straight to the laggard, and suddenly it's a quarter century ago, and you're clutching that report card, wondering why nobody's talking about the four A's. That's victimization. Don't stand for it.

As the bull market ages, it's time to spend a great deal of thought and effort reinforcing your client relationships. It is also time — and there may not be a moment to lose — quickly, efficiently, and mercilessly to **fire your customers.**

JUST SAY NO TO "PERFORMANCE" SELLING

"*Darn,* we were hoping for forty." This is the headline of an ad that was running in the financial press in late June. The ad was for a "no-help" small-cap fund, and went on to say that the fund had done 37.25% *for the five months* through May 31.

Five-month performance figures! Even when I saw the much, much smaller print, which acknowledged that short-term results are less important than the fund's strategy for long-term success (would that be ... 10 months?), I knew that the game was now over. The malignancy that is "performance" mania is in metastasis, and my guess is a whole bunch of people are going to die from it.

So I hereby declare all "performance" numbers of 15 years duration or less to be statistical truths that are also — and much more importantly — moral lies. And I order you (or beg, or plead, or wheedle, or cajole, or whatever approach you'll go for) to stop selling "performance." (In case there's any doubt in your mind, I'm speaking *ex cathedra* on this, so don't bleep with me, or I'll excommunicate you.)

What is an investor supposed to infer from a five-month "performance" figure? That this is a superior, or even a good, fund? That the fund can do 37.25% in the next five months (or 10, or 15, or ever)? That the fund is even appropriate for him?

A five-month "performance" ad can't even suggest any of these things — and, indeed, this ad doesn't suggest anything. The ad just hangs the number out there, and leaves America to take its own "performance"-maniacal inference.

The problem is that the only inference which can be drawn with any certainty is the last one on earth that investors are likely to draw right now. Namely, that in an efficient market, a fund portfolio that has the capacity to go up 37.25% in five months also has the capacity to go down 37.25% in five months. Peak performance and peak volatility are simply two ways of saying exactly the same thing.

The American mutual fund investor simply does not know this. And the more our industry knuckles under to "performance" mania (and I see lots of one-year 50% to 60% "help" fund ads, even from members of the Mutual Fund Forum who should know better), the less likely investors are to find out the truth any way but the hard way. And if we leave them to find out the hard way, there is, I promise you, going to be a lot of blood on the floor — theirs and ours.

It is, of course, a linchpin of our denial that we believe people do not "panic" anymore. Indeed, at the recent ICI conference, Fidelity Chairman Edward C. Johnson III said, "Mutual fund investors have never panicked — never." Well, never is a long, long time (it even encompasses 1973-74 and 1969-70), and panic is, I suppose, a different phenomenon to different people. But did Mr. Johnson see the huge spike of net redemptions in bond and utility funds in the fourth quarter of '93 and the first quarter of '94? What would he call that: an orderly advance to the rear?

I freely stipulate to the anecdotal evidence that people don't panic as a result of one-to-three-day, 2% to 4% declines, which is all we've had lately. Indeed, the witch of markets' coup this year was the Friday the Dow went down 171 points — and up 100 points on Monday. Of course, people aren't going to panic if and to the extent that they think that's a typical decline — i.e., not merely temporary, but *momentary*.

But suppose this market just gets sandpapered for a couple of quarters in '97 (or whenever). No crash, no cataclysm, just a slow, rolling 15% to 18% correction that lasts for six months or so. If funds go into nice, orderly net liquidation — if people walk to the exits instead of running, and destroy their lifetime financial plans at exactly the wrong time for exactly the wrong reasons — will we feel vindicated in some way because they didn't "panic"?

And is such a scenario impossible, or even improbable? Almost any minute now, the '96 presidential election may degenerate into I'll-cut-your-taxes-much-much-more-than-the-other-guy-will, with no real prospect of meaningful spending cuts. That's what this whole campaign could turn out to be about — just before the *structural* budget deficit in the U.S. starts rising again.

That kind of backhanded fiscal stimulus — or even the perception of stimulus — might very well be a formula for inflation — or even the perception of inflation — which the economy, already revving pretty high, might not be able to handle. And how would a newly confirmed Fed Chairman Greenspan respond to this? I think you know the answer to that already: He will fight even a hint of fiscal fire with all the monetary fire it takes to strangle inflation in its cradle. That's his thing. That's what he does.

Am I predicting this? Not in the least. Can you rule it out? You'd better not. Could the market handle a scenario even remotely like that without flinching? If you're sure it could, don't waste your time reading the rest of this article, because you're beyond its — and my — ability to help.

It is bad enough that we're now six years past the onset of the last 20% decline in the averages. It's bad enough that we haven't had so much as a 10% decline on a closing basis in the interim. It's bad enough that the only two major declines within most investors' — and fund managers' — living memory ('87 and '90) are invisible, because they were so short, so sharp, and happened in the middle of such otherwise great years that you can't see them on a calendar-year basis. These things are bad enough, I say again, because they put whatever adult sense of danger one has under deep, general anesthesia.

But when you add to that witch's brew a gigantic dose of absolutely unrepeatable, anomalous, dope-smoking, short-term "performance" numbers, that's a formula for disaster.

My belief is that the returns of the last 15 years — so far above the trendline — should be presumed to be a glorious anomaly. Just as the hideous returns of the previous 15 years (for which, I'm convinced, we've basically been making up) were a horrific anomaly.

95

(Alternatively, I suppose, you can assume that we're in a "new era," and that the trendline return of stocks is now the 16% of the last 15 years. Again, this excuses you from reading the rest of this column. It'll only make you angry.)

You may think that all I'm saying is that red-hot, short-term "performance" numbers are the last reason on earth for anybody to buy a mutual fund. Wrong. I'm going way, way beyond that. (It was the catalyst for this tirade. It's not the tirade itself.)

I'm saying that we must cease and desist altogether from talking about "performance." We've got to present mutual funds and other managed investments as what they are: the long-term funding media for the realization of people's deepest financial needs — an income they can't outlive in retirement, a legacy for their children, nursing home care for their parents. Those are the things that really matter, not whether Fund Raindrop A gets to the bottom of the window before Fund Raindrop B.

For God's sake, be a trusted professional advisor. The recommendations you make to people are good because YOU *say that they are good.* Not because some magazine says they're good. Certainly not because they went up 37.25% in five months. And not because The Children's Crusade Mutual Fund Rating Service and Storm Door Company gives them nine moons — its highest rating.

Let "performance" numbers be the answer to a question. Never answer a question nobody asked you. And if you are asked, give the "performance" numbers, but then have the guts (and the brains) to say, "I wouldn't assume that the next five months/five years/15 years are going to be exactly like that, though. Returns during this period have been abnormally high. This is a great investment because it fits in perfectly with what you're trying to accomplish, not because it happens to have gone up X% in the last Y years."

Your listener will either accept that (in which case he is, per last month's column, a client), or he won't (in which case there's a high risk that he's a customer).

96

Prospect: Well, what return do you think it will produce?

You: Well, the long-term return of large-company stocks is about 10 1/2% a year. Small-company stocks have averaged about 12 1/4%. A superior manager should do somewhat better over time, but 55% in a year/37.25% in five months? That is, to put it charitably, unsustainable.

Prospect: So you're telling me to look for 10% to 12% over the long haul?

You: And perhaps a tad more from superior managers.

Prospect: And are these Gronskys superior managers?

You: Well, I certainly believe so. They're managing my and my family's money.

Prospect: Reckon that's good enough for me.

OR

Prospect: Nuts to that. If my idiot brother-in-law Bernie is getting 50%, I gotta get 50%.

You: Right you are. Well, it's been oodles of fun talking to you, but I've got to be running along now. I've got an appointment back on Planet Earth.

If people insist that you tell them they're going to continue getting today's far-above-average-trendline returns, insist on exiting stage left — with alacrity and great dispatch. This is not the time to be helping people inject speedballs of "performance" mania into their veins.

This isn't about your month, or even your year. This is about your career, your self-respect, and your life.

So just say no.

REQUIEM FOR A "NEW ERA"

Well, whaddya know? It turns out stock prices *do* respond to concerns about inflation, interest rates, and corporate earnings, after all. And the members of the peacetime army of post-1990 fund investors were not, in fact, quite as stoical about double-digit NAV power dives as it had been popularly supposed that they would be.

(Forgive me for being somewhat amused by all this. There are, as I've said before in this column, only two kinds of people in the world: people with too much class to say, "I told you so," and people like me.)

As the summer draws to a close, many financial advisors seem primarily concerned with what the markets are going to do next. This is very unfortunate for a couple of reasons: (A) It's impossible to know what the markets are going to do next. (B) What the market does next will have no effect on the long-term results of serious investors.

I know as an article of faith that the Dow Jones Industrial Average is going to go to 50,000 (though I don't know — and don't really care — when). I haven't the foggiest notion whether, on its way to 50,000, it will stop at 4,500 or 6,500 next. Don't know, can't know, don't care, doesn't matter, over and out.

I certainly *hope* it gets to 4,500, as must all sane investors who haven't finished buying yet. (Why anyone with 10, 20, and 30 years of investing ahead of him would want the market to go up has always been intensely mysterious to me.) But since the next 1,000 point move is unknowable, and since the next 5,000 point move is inevitable, I invest — and encourage clients to invest — in contemplation of the latter rather than the former.

All time and energy spent in the quest for a market outlook are, as Warren Buffett and Peter Lynch never tire of telling you, time and energy wasted. Moreover, the people in your account book who are importuning you for a market outlook are customers, not clients. I told you to fire them two months ago ("Do You Have Clients or Customers?" July 1996). If you're still running around trying to quench these jerks' thirst for the unknowable, you've got nobody to blame but yourself.

Which brings me, in a roundabout way, to the subject of this column. To wit: I'd like you to stop thinking altogether about what's going to happen in the next three months. If it helps you detach, let me assure you — with a probability above 95% — that three months from now the market averages will be within 20% of where they are today, plus or minus. There, doesn't that make you feel better?

Instead, I invite you to take those prodigious quantities of time and energy and invest them in a serious examination of what happened to you, to your book of accounts, to your portfolios, and to your business plan in the *last* three months.

People in our profession are not, as a general rule, a particularly introspective lot — except when we're "supposed" to be, usually around the turn of the new year. Even then, we're not real good at it. We get bored easily, and start playing with our "optimization" software — a peerless tool with which to position clients for the recent past.

I strongly recommend that you take three to five straight hours of retreat before or during the Labor Day weekend. Get away from the phone and all other distractions and analyze what happened, financially and emotionally, to you and your clients during the recent break.

As difficult as it may be, try to be as brutally candid with yourself as you would be with someone else, or as you would want a gifted, confidential coach to be with you. Because the more searching and honest you can be in this exercise, the better shape you'll be in to handle whatever challenges and opportunities may present themselves in the next block of time.

Here's a partial list of questions you may wish to use as a track to run on during your retreat. By the time you finish answering them,

I'm sure you'll have thought of other, better questions to ask yourself, that are more pertinent and specific to your individual circumstances. These questions are just to get you started. Let me suggest, however, that this exercise will be about five times more valuable to you if you write out your answers to these questions, rather than just sitting there thinking about 'em.

• **Were you surprised by what happened?** If so, why, and in what ways? Particularly if you've been a regular reader of this column for the last 12 months, you probably should have known that a meaningful setback was inevitable at some point. If you didn't, why do you think you didn't? Does your business "need" for the market not to go down? (If it does, you may already be on your way out of the business.) In sum, if you got surprised, try to analyze why you got surprised and how you can use this experience not to get surprised again.

• **Were your clients surprised? How did they react, and what does their reaction say to you?** If your clients were surprised because you were surprised, at least that makes some kind of sense. (It's very sad, but it makes sense.) If they were surprised while you really weren't, then that's probably a cause for concern. Our value to clients is not the investments we offer, which people can easily replicate at no cost on their own. Rather, the real value-added that we provide is implicit in our advice. If clients were surprised by the Summer Swan Dive and we weren't, it must be because we withheld valuable advice from them. And why would we ever do that?

Again, readers of this column were given a tool with which to call this question over the nine months before the spaghetti hit the fan. I suggested "lifeboat drills," the tactic of showing people the '87 and '90 peak-to-trough declines of their top holdings. The point, obviously, was to drill people on the inevitability, the savagery, and the evanescence of major market declines.

No single other thing I've written in this column (with the possible exception of Dr. Murray Murray, The No-Load Cardiologist) has ever drawn as much favorable comment. Even *The Wall Street Journal* printed something nice about it — a first, and probably a last, for me. And that was before the July meltdown. Since that decline, I've had a flood of calls and notes from people who saved their clients (and themselves) with lifeboat drills.

My point is simply that if you agreed that some sort of correction was inevitable, you could easily and non-threateningly have raised the issue. If you didn't, it's time to ask yourself why you didn't. What were you afraid of, and what did your silence cost you?

Were your clients frightened? If so, are you happy with the way you managed their fear? Or were you, in turn, surprised by the depth of that fear? If so, why? Had you fallen victim to the myth of The New Era of Investor Stoicism? Why, since the '93-'94 bond/utility fund capitulation so clearly showed the inability of investors to differentiate between fluctuation and loss?

• **If you had problems with your clients, to what extent might they be attributable to your failure to manage expectations?** Earlier this year, I called the prevailing mental illness of "performance" mania "a crisis of rising expectations." Then, last month, in a column written about three weeks before The Crack-Up, I went completely berserk, and forbade any use of "performance" as a form of persuasion to invest.

I said then (and say again now) that all "performance" numbers of 15 years' duration and less were statistical truths but moral lies because they encourage investors to believe in something that can't happen, i.e. a repetition of the last five, 10, or 15 years.

It should be clear that an investor's surprise at, and fear of, the July meltdown were directly related to the height of his expectations. In other words, the higher the dosage of the drug "performance" you'd prescribed, the more agonizing were the patient's withdrawal symptoms.

If your answer is that you had to show the investor top "performance" or the account would have gone elsewhere, (a) you never really had the account; you were just the investor's drug dealer, and (b) you're admitting that you sold your serenity and your self-esteem for thirty pieces of silver, which the professionals in this business simply don't do. Putting your month ahead of your life is the ultimate one-way ticket to Palookaville.

• **Did you find yourself getting angry at clients? Did you find them getting angry with you?** Few, if any, emotions drain the positive energy you need to deal with stressful situations as thoroughly as anger. And an angry flare-up, no matter how legitimate or real the issue that precipitates it, will often poison a client relationship incurably. (Also, just because you dodged an arbitration bullet this time, don't think the other person is out of bullets. He isn't.)

In general, over the last two years, we've been able to open accounts and gather assets under the most favorable economic and market conditions imaginable. The combination of declining interest rates, negligible inflation, and exploding corporate earnings over these five years fostered such high investment returns and such low volatility that I, for one, never expect to see their like again in my lifetime. (And, no matter how much younger you are than I, I don't think you should, either.)

So it's no wonder that tensions between us and our clients might have been held to a minimum, swept under the rug by each succeeding market upsurge. But an episode like July's that maximizes shock and destabilizes people's equilibriums quickly brings emotional issues to the surface.

During your retreat, identify those situations in which you became angry. Who were the people who provoked the anger? And who were you really angry at? (In the case of a "performance" junkie who bought his drug from you and then turned on you, I think you'll find that you weren't as angry at him as at yourself, which is actually worse.)

Did you see in the anger-provoking situation a dynamic that's likely to recur? If so, what do you propose to do about it? Aren't there, upon mature reflection, accounts with whom you now know it won't be possible to sustain a healthy relationship? If so, why not bite the bullet right now, instead of waiting for the next crisis to arise?

All it takes is an exquisitely polite note: "Events of the past few weeks have made me realize that I probably am not able to offer you what you seem to need in a financial advisor. That being the case, I believe you'd be better served by another advisor. I've asked my manager, (name), to help you find someone in our firm who is better suited to your needs than I. I wish you every investment success."

Yes, I know, you want to write, "I hope you freeze to death in the dark, and your cat dies with you." But that lowers you to the level of your antagonist and suggests that your anger, not his, is the problem. It takes a big person to fire your biggest PITA (pain in the, uh, neck) account, but an even bigger person to do it in a way that doesn't seek to strip the PITA of his dignity.

Finally, here's the ultimate rubber-meets-the-road test of how you fared during the recent unpleasantness:

• **Did you sell?** No matter what else you may now believe you did wrong, if you didn't sell — if you didn't disturb the investments that were (and are) supposed to be the cornerstones of your clients' lifetime programs — you're a success.

And no matter what else you did right, if you sold — or "allowed people to sell," which is, if possible, worse — it's time for an agonizing reappraisal of your entire belief/behavior system, because I assure you that that system is in sorry (and quite possibly moribund) shape.

I say this irrespective of whether you think we've seen the bottom yet. (My own belief is that we've probably seen a bottom, but not The Bottom.) Lifetime investment programs are not trading programs. They are a long-term commitment to accepting temporary declines as the price of permanent advances. If you accepted this intellectually, but weren't able to stick to it emotionally, your belief/behavior system is in need of an immediate, major overhaul. Don't go past Labor Day without it.

On the morning of the day in July when the Dow went down 160 points, only to close up nine, a branch manager for an excellent stock brokerage firm asked me pleadingly, "What do you say to brokers who are selling?"

I thought hard about this for a couple of moments, because I wanted to offer him an answer that was, if possible, pithy, wise, but not smart-alecky (always a stretch for me). Then I thought of a one-word answer, which I believed then and now to be the only right one: "Goodbye."

VOODOO PORTFOLIO THEORY

On the day in August that *The Wall Street Journal* announced that 401(k) money had fled from equity funds during the July mini-meltdown, I re-read an article that appeared in this magazine that month.

This article concerned something called post-modern portfolio theory, and it was, for me, a nearly encyclopedic review of everything that's wrong with this business today.

Before embarking on my rant, let me offer two important caveats. First of all, it's clear that the extremely hard-working people who appeared in the article have their hearts very much in the right place: They want to do the best possible job for their clients.

Second, I don't begin to understand post-modern portfolio theory. I don't know the difference between symmetry and asymmetry, nor between variance and semi-variance. I never had a course in theoretical statistics, and forgot everything I knew about calculus the day I walked out of the exam, more than three decades ago. Finally, I surely do not comprehend the concept of the "lower partial moment." And I feel it only fair to warn you that the first person who tries to teach me this concept is going to die.

I only know two things, but those two things are among the more important (if they aren't actually *the* most important) truths that people in our business need to know in order to be really successful.

Unfortunately, the first of these two truths is, in effect, denied by post-modern portfolio theory. And the other truth is simply ignored by this and all other mind-numbingly complex attempts to get past "performance" to reveal the future.

Transcendent Truth #1: You cannot step into the same river

twice. Past "performance" doesn't actually tell you that much about the future, for the simple but very compelling reason that the future is usually quite different from the past.

Over shorter periods of time, I freely confess, this general randomness does not prevail. Indeed, as I've tried anecdotally to demonstrate in my forthcoming book *The Excellent Investment Advisor*, five-year relative "performance" is often a startlingly effective *perverse* indicator. Whatever happened over the last five years is not merely different from what will happen in the next five, but may often be just the opposite.

To get to a state of belief that future "performance" (much less *relative* "performance," which is a different matter entirely) will be like the past, you have to make assumptions that are of questionable validity. For instance, you'd have to believe that any future economic scenario is predictable.

The article says, "If you make a guess that we will be in a growth — or inflationary, or recessionary, or essentially chaotic — environment, then the program will pull numbers out of periods with a similar economic history ... ."

The astounding premise here is that a future economic scenario (a) is knowable and (b) will look like other such scenarios. As such epic investors as Warren Buffett and Peter Lynch never tire of telling us, the economy, interest rates, and markets are entirely and unequivocally unpredictable.

Moreover, if I pick a "recessionary" scenario, which recession am I thinking of? Is it 1990-91? How do I separate out the Saddam/ Desert Storm effect from the recessionary effect of that period? And how do I react even if I'm right in concept, but the recession I get is more like that of 1981-82?

Forgive me, but this is portfolio selection as video game. When I read it, I'm reminded of nothing so much as the movie *Wargames*, where the computer says to Matthew Broderick, "Shall we play a game?" This isn't post-modern portfolio theory. It's voodoo portfolio theory.

And, by the way, which "chaotic" periods will this video game replay? Will it be 1987 ... which will lead me to view chaos as a One-Day Sale? Or 1981-82, with Paul Volcker putting the economy into cold-turkey withdrawal after 15 years on the drug of inflation? Or will it be 1973-74, The Mother of All Unrepeatable Chaotic Episodes, when most of today's portfolio managers were primarily focused on getting a date for the Junior Prom back there in high school? Puh-leeze! You not only can't step into the same river twice, you can't even be sure which river you're stepping into.

In nearly 30 years in the business, I've learned that emotional maturity, not intellectual brilliance, is the key ingredient in investment success. And a critical test of emotional maturity is one's tolerance for ambiguity. By flying from ambiguity — by insisting that future investment "performance" must somehow be knowable — our industry hinders rather than helps the investor in his quest for a successful frame of reference. Which brings me to:

Transcendent Truth #2: The governing variable in investment success is not the "performance" of investments but the behavior of investors. Of all the execrable "this time it's different" arguments I heard over the past year, the stupidest and most smug (but I repeat myself) was that 401(k) money — whether out of stoicism or just inertia — would not flee equities in a downturn. July's "cub" market proved, as if one needed proof, that this was wrong.

The essential problem of the American investor is not that he doesn't know the difference between variance and semi-variance. It's that — in his Depression-formed, principal-obsessed unconscious — he can't tell the difference between temporary decline and permanent loss. Mistaking the appearance of the former for the onset of the latter, he grows fearful and sells.

The real enemy of investment success isn't ignorance, it's fear. And abstruse mathematical "analysis" is not the antidote to fear (not least of all because fear, in its advanced forms, is entirely insusceptible to reason).

The antidote to fear is trust. And people don't place their trust in increasingly bizarre computer programs. Generally speaking — if they trust at all — people only trust other people.

The primary function of an investment advisor is, therefore, a right-brain rather than a left-brain function. He does not primarily wage a battle of knowledge vs. ignorance, but of faith vs. fear. And the excellent advisor is neither an educator nor a mathematician, but a behavior modifier.

I'm convinced that about 65% of total lifetime portfolio return comes from how much of your money you have in equities as opposed to bonds. Another 30% comes from how you behave in declining markets.

The last 5% — tops — of lifetime return comes from which particular investments you selected. To put 95% of one's time and energy into the last 5% of the equation is completely to miss the point of this business.

Portfolio theory (post-modern, modern, ancient, or voodoo) is to investment success what alchemy was, in the first half of this millennium, to the development of science: not its precursor but its nemesis. By vectoring the efforts of Europe's best minds toward a fool's errand, alchemy — the search for a way to turn base metal into gold — probably delayed the onset of true scientific inquiry a couple of hundred years.

In the end, our industry has to distinguish, and to help the investors who rely on us to distinguish, between knowledge of the future and faith in the future.

The former is ultimately unavailable, and doesn't make much difference. The latter is limitlessly available, and gives the investor an emotional framework for a lifetime of patient equity investing — which is all that matters.

But faith in the future cannot be obtained from some computer program. It can only be obtained from another human being. Places in the heart vs. places on some chart ... remember? Our value to our clients is in our appreciation and understanding of their psychology rather than in our knowledge of higher mathematics.

The key to your success is not in changing the funds, but in changing the folks. Where you stand on this most basic issue may very well be the primary determinant of the outcome of your career.

THE GREAT BOOM BEHIND

I'd originally planned to make this month's essay another excerpt from my new book The Excellent Investment Advisor, *which I self-published in November. But when The Great Nor'easter of 1996 rained out both the first game of the World Series and my trip to the IAFP Conference, I decided to print my talk here. This may not be my most popular column of the year, but I can just about guarantee it'll be the most important.*

October 11, 1996, was a milestone without precedent in the history of the American stock market. For openers, it was the sixth anniversary of the bottom of the last bear market. On October 11, 1990, the DJIA completed its last 20% decline, closing at 2365.

The six intervening years have been, simply stated, the longest and strongest bull market in history. That is, this period now holds the record for both the largest percentage gain (152%) and the longest period (2192 days) without a 10% correction. The previous record, according to Birinyi Associates, was 150.55% in 1127 days, ending on August 25, 1987. *In neither duration nor percentage gain is any other previous advance equal to even half the current one.*

As you begin planning for 1997, I'd suggest that you think long and hard about what you've just read. Because the evil flower growing out of this wildly ahistorical experience is, quite simply, the greatest crisis of rising expectations among American investors that I've ever seen.

As viscerally certain as I might have been about the gravity of this crisis, I've just gotten (and you should get) dramatic statistical proof. In a recent survey of mutual fund investors conducted for Liberty Financial Companies by Louis Harris and Associates, Inc., 29% of those surveyed expected that in the next 10 years the stock market will do *better than* the 14% annual returns achieved (by one measure) in the past decade. Another 56% of those surveyed expect the return to be about the same as the past 10 years' 14%.

Only 14% of those surveyed (I know, this gets a little confusing) thought that the next 10 years' return would be less than 14% annually; 2% said they didn't know.

Am I getting through to you on this? In an asset class whose 70-year return averages 10.5% (up from 10.25% in just one year, the *annus mirabilis* 1995), 84% percent of the fund investors surveyed are looking for another 10 years of 14% or more! And wait, it gets worse.

Less than one-fourth (23%, to be exact) of the fund investors surveyed expect a yearly downturn in stock prices of 20% or more *any time in the next 10 years!* Never mind that we've had a 20% decline on an average of every five years or so since the end of World War II. Never mind that the last decline ended over six years ago. More than three out of four of these people don't think we'll have one for the next 10 years! Aaarrrgghh!!

Nearly three years ago, when the Dow was still well below 4000, I asked that everyone adopt the mantra, "Russian Businessmen." I said that if this phrase (which 10 years earlier had been an oxymoron, and 10 years before that a capital crime) didn't make you long-term bullish, probably nothing would. And I thought that only the most raging, table-pounding, frothing-at-the-mouth, long-term bullishness was adequate to the circumstances.

That was then; this is now. I hereby decree a new mantra which you are to repeat over and over to yourself, chant-like, until I tell you to stop. It is, of course, "Unrealistic Expectations." For, ladies and gentlemen, make no mistake about it. *The dominant theme of our time is unrealistic expectations.* There is simply no historical basis for what's transpired over the last six years and what the huge preponderance of investors apparently believe will continue to happen.

Please note that I didn't say there was no economic justification for the market of the last seven Octobers. There was all you could want, and more: a cyclical (if somewhat muted) economic expansion, secularly declining interest rates, continuing commodity deflation, and explosive earnings growth facilitated in part by radical downsizing and layoffs, which kept a lid on labor costs.

These trends are (a) well-documented, (b) well-discounted by the markets, and (c) largely over. Going forward, the pop is going to have to come from someplace else. It probably isn't going to be exports, at least for a while. Look at the dollar rallying and our European and Japanese trading partners' stumbling economies.

Anyway you slice it, the economic recovery that began in the first quarter of 1991 is getting mighty long in the tooth. So if history is any guide — and it's still the only guide I've got — we're going to get a recession sometime in the next Presidential term. (And, even though I'm writing this a couple of weeks before the election, I'm prepared to predict with 100% probability that the next president will be one of the two white male candidates with zero business experience.)

The market, of course, will start discounting the onset of recession upwards of six months in advance of the fact. This means, among other things, that your equity portfolios may take an arrow through the neck while you're still scanning the horizon for your first sight of the hostiles.

If and to the the extent that this line of reasoning makes any sense to you, you probably want to put a lot of energy into vectoring new money away from peak "performance." This is because, of course, when you buy peak "performance," you're also buying peak volatility — an eternal truth that may evidence itself sooner than later. (Following this thought process to its supremely logical conclusion, the last fund on earth you'd buy today is the one that advertises "best return of all equity funds since the 1987 lows.")

Next, you probably want to take all your clients back to the last recession (of 1990-91) and show them how their core holdings behaved during the last perfectly normal, cyclical, and above all temporary market decline. While you're back in that neighborhood, show 'em '87 as well — not on a calendar-year basis, but peak-to-trough.

This exercise, which I call "Lifeboat Drills," is a quick, efficient way to create some overlap between expectation and reality.

Alternatively, I suppose, you can simply go into denial and decide that you don't need to intervene in your clients' expectations, because they're not unrealistic! Because "this time it's different!"

The nearly universal "this time it's different" argument *du jour* is, of course, the heartstoppingly stupid notion that demographics is the primary determinant of stock prices over most of the next decade. In this malignant fairy tale, the baby boomers (and their surging retirement-savings propensity) sweep all petty economic/earnings cavils away. Only one thing matters: the mindless, limitless appetite for equities on the part of a generation that can relate to "Blowin' in the Wind" as the soundtrack for a bank commercial.

Once again, this is an idea that I viscerally knew was a total crock in the complete absence of any corroborating data. But a stunning research paper just published in the *Brookings Papers on Economic Activity* provides irrefutable proof that the demographics argument is an utter fiction.

(Now, before you go thinking I routinely read — or even *can* read — such weighty material, let me assure you that I was tipped off to this study by Morgan Stanley's Stephen Roach, who not only read it, but understood what it meant to our industry.)

The paper is titled, "Understanding the Postwar Decline in U.S. Savings: A Cohort Analysis." Its three authors are Jagadeesh Gokhale, of the Cleveland Federal Reserve Bank; Laurence Kotlikoff, of Boston University; and John Sabelhaus, of the Congressional Budget Office.

They look at the spending and savings behavior of several generations of Americans since 1960. Their finding: Far from generating a savings boom, there has been "a dramatic rise in the consumption propensities of older Americans."

People just don't go immediately from college to marriage and child-bearing the way they did years ago. They marry later, have

114

children later — and then often marry again, and start new families later than any past generation ever has. Moreover, they remain active (and are active consumers) much longer then past generations, so past spending/saving shifts are misleading.

Specifically, the study finds that in the early 1960s, 60-year-olds consumed only 71% of the amount consumed by 30-year-olds, which is consistent with the conventional wisdom. But by the late 1980s, 60-year-olds were actually consuming 18% *more* than 30-year-olds! Far from sparking a largely mythical mid-1990s savings boom, the authors argue that the skewing of the population will actually lead (and is already leading) to a *declining* national savings rate well past the turn of the century. (The study found the U.S. savings rate to be 9.1% per year in the 1950s and '60s, 8.5% in the '70s, 4.7% in the '80s, and just 2.7% in the first five years of the 1990s.)

This would, if you'll forgive an appalling play on words, tend to put a "dent" in the prevailing denial. If you were waiting for a demographic *deus ex machina* to come and pluck you from the cruel necessity of dealing with the reality of the economic/market cycle, you'd better start formulating Plan B.

At the Battle of New Orleans, when his artillery's first cannon volleys went completely over the advancing British lines, Andrew Jackson is reported to have said, "I reckon you better elevate them guns a little lower." We desperately need to adapt this as our industry's 1997 rallying cry: "Reckon we'd better elevate them expectations a little lower." The deathless disclaimer, "Past performance is no guarantee of future results," may just be turning into the understatement of the millennium.

The equity market has simply never done what it did in the last six years. And while I'm never prepared to say it can never do that again, I'm as sure as I can be of anything that it can't do that again in the next six years.

So we all have a pretty basic and very simple choice to make. We can talk about the wonderful historical returns of equities: nearly 7 1/2 % a year above inflation (in relative terms), or 10 1/2% to 12 1/2%

(big-cap and small-cap respectively, in absolute terms). Add something to that for emerging markets, something else again for superior management (if such is your belief, as it is mine), and something yet again for dollar-cost-averaging.

Or we can degenerate into financial drug dealers, peddling the investor another hit of recent past "performance." Forgive me, but this is a moral as well as a business decision, and my advice is: You'd better make it, and right quick, before the market makes it for you.

If there's one thing I've learned in nearly 30 years in the business, it's that markets never deceive us. Rather, we deceive ourselves. Or — worse — we allow our clients to deceive themselves.

Reckon we'd better elevate them expectations a little lower.

WHO ARE YOU, AND WHAT DO YOU WANT?

Take my word for it, fellows and gals (and do take my word for it, 'cause you don't want to prove this to yourself): There's nothing like four days in the intensive care unit to restore your perspective. (Well, maybe *five* days would work even better, but I didn't get to find out.)

Now, not being from the everybody's-health-stories-are-boring-except-mine school of raconteurism, I won't subject you to the details. Suffice it to say that my illness was pretty sudden, pretty serious, and of absolutely no lasting consequence — other than the consequences I have chosen to attach to it.

Nor do I propose to bore you with yet another take-time-to-smell-the-roses essay of the type that is always cropping up in professional magazines, usually written by guys who just got out of the hospital, having seen the light.

But when you're lying there, and you're not going anywhere for a while, and you can't talk because they've got you breathing through a tube, you get to do a lot of thinking. (You also get to cancel eight speaking engagements because even when they let you up, you ain't moving too fast.)

What I decided to think about most are the two questions that, above all others, I've been asking my audiences to ask themselves. They are (1) who are you, and (2) what do you want?

Modern, urban, industrialized society is full of people who have no idea what the answers to these questions are. (By contrast, I've lately been reading Ellis Peters' delightful Brother Cadfael mysteries, which take place in England in the 1140s — nearly at the apex of the Medieval Synthesis in Europe, when everyone knew *exactly* where he stood in society — nay, in the universe.)

Our business has a disproportionately high percentage of people who don't know the answers to those questions. I suspect that's because our profession is a haven for the "other-directed": people who get their basic sense of self from the way other people react to them.

The sales psychologist Aaron Hemsley has always said that we think we enter this business looking for money, but that, in fact, we're looking for the approval we didn't get earlier in our lives. This, he feels, is particularly helpful in explaining why the sales side of the business is so rife with first children, who never seemed to be able to do enough to meet their parents' expectations.

Thirty years ago, in his howlingly funny book *The Money Game*, "Adam Smith" (George J. W. Goodman) repeatedly said that if you don't know who you are, the stock market is a terribly expensive place to find out. (Incidentally, everybody better hurry up and read *The Money Game* again, before it's too late. There may not be a moment to lose.)

I'd just like to expand this dictum to read: If you don't know who you are and what you want, this business is an absolutely killing place to find out. For of this I'm sure: There's no such thing as an other-directed Excellent Investment Advisor. The direction simply has to come from within, and it has to proceed from the Two Great Questions that form the title of this essay.

Part of what we love about our business is the almost infinite capacity for choice that we have every minute of every day. Will I call a prospect or a client in the next five minutes? If a client, will I ask for a referral? If so, how? If not, why not? If I call a prospect, what will I say? How will I feel if he says no? How, for that matter, will I feel if he says yes?

Sometimes our choices are conscious; more often than we suspect, they're unconscious. But in either event, we choose as we do because of our witting or unwitting answers to the questions: Who am I, and what do I want?

You had to know that Bob Dole was going to lose the minute you heard he'd said to his Republican colleagues in 1995, "I'll be Ronald Reagan, if that's what you want." Not that you have to be inner-directed to get elected president (the incumbent is living proof that you don't); it's that you can't let the audience define you and still hope to be truly successful. Life happens to losers; winners happen to life. The Excellent Investment Advisor acts, always acts; the journeyman permits himself always to be acted upon — by people, markets, and "circumstances," whatever the hell those are.

So what I'd like to do now is to ask you a series of questions, not dissimilar to the ones I asked myself during those four days in ICU. None of these questions, taken by itself, will give you the Big Answers you're looking for. But, taken as a whole, they may serve to put you on the track toward those answers.

1. If you went under a bus tomorrow, would the people who depend on you be all right financially? If the answer is anything less than an unqualified yes, then in some sense you're a fraud, aren't you? How can you purport to sell what you don't own: financial security, reasonably assured by a formal plan? I promise you that that fraudulence is corroding your soul; prospects are getting bad vibes from you, and they don't know why. And the harder you struggle to sell intellectual proof of what you yourself haven't emotionally embraced, the more mixed a message you send out, and the more you turn people off.

I recently did a workshop for a wirehouse region that is having trouble getting its brokers to sell a very basic, lots-of-value-for-not-many-bucks financial planning profile. So I simply asked how many people in the audience had this profile done on themselves. Fewer than 10% of the audience raised their hands. I then asked if there was anything else anybody wanted to talk about for the rest of the session, since the basic problem was, on its face, insoluble: You can't sell anybody else's family what you can't be bothered owning yourself.

If you need to go out and buy a big box of term insurance, go do it. (Maybe you'll find you like talking to people about having an extra million bucks of protection for very little money.) How's your disability insurance situation? Sure you've got the right kind?

119

Is your own retirement plan clicking along OK? Kids' college funds in shape? You don't have to be putting away the gross national product of Portugal to be able to hold your head up on these issues — you just have to have a plan that's reasonable and be funding that plan reasonably. For purposes of your own self-esteem, *the discipline is to the dollars as nine is to one.*

Managers and principals of financial planning practices take note: The effectiveness of your employees will rise no less than 300% when they can empathize with all your clients through the prism of their own financial plan. Conversely, an employee who wants no part of a plan is telling you he's (a) short-term, (b) never going to be a real asset to your practice, and quite possibly (c) both of the above.

2. Does your family know what the plan is? It doesn't really matter how good your plan is (or even how lame it is) if your family and/or a trusted associate can't access the plan. I know from my own experiences that the more my family has understood that there's a plan and how it works, the more comfortable they've all been — or should I say we've all been. It also makes them somewhat more philosophical than they might otherwise be regarding my travel schedule. They see themselves as partners in, rather than competitors of, my business. And I'll bet that a clearly delineated plan would have a similar effect on your family. Hey, it can't hurt.

3. If you were in a hospital bed for a couple of weeks, are you happy with who'd be running your business? If so, great; I was, and, if possible, I was even pleasantly surprised. But if the answer here is no, then it's time to be thinking about making some changes. (Actually, it's probably time to start implementing changes you already subconsciously know you need to make.)

Who's your go-to guy (or gal)? And are you in shape to play the same role if it's that other person who gets sick? Here again, what's the plan? We tend to like to play lone hands, most of us, but ask yourself: Might that be disserving the clients, as well as the value of your practice?

4. What are you putting off? Procrastination, that most elegant entertainment for people who basically have too many choices, is a hydra-headed enemy. I can tell you for a fact that you don't want to be thinking, "Why didn't I get that done?" just before they wheel you into surgery. For me, the knowledge that I'd just finished the single hardest thing I've ever done — writing and self publishing *The Excellent Investment Advisor* — was a phenomenally comforting thing. I wasn't planning on it being my testament, but if that's how it shook out, it felt very OK to me.

Your agenda doesn't have to include anything as ambitious as a book, though. Whether it's saying "I love you" to somebody, writing a long-postponed letter, or revising your will, beware what you're putting off. It may be chipping away at your sense of who you are in ways that aren't immediately obvious.

5. What do you stand for? How are your ethical standards? How's your professionalism? What were your clients able to do with your help that they couldn't have done without you? (Not without somebody like you — without *you*.)

In whose life are you making a difference, and why would you subject yourself to customers who won't *allow* you to make a difference? Who's the most corrosive account you've got? Why do you keep it? If you let someone with a low opinion of you stay close to you, are you not in some way accepting the validity of that opinion? Why would you do that? *Do you have the business you'd like to be remembered for, or do you just have the business you've got?*

The answers to these questions, like the questions themselves, aren't to be found outside yourself. (Hint: No one reading this column will, at the end of his life, be remembered as having stood for asset allocation.) And all the answers are ultimately subordinate to the ones you find inside when you ask the Two Great Questions:

Who am I? What do I want?

THE CEILING THAT ISN'T THERE

Not long ago, I got a call from a veteran wirehouse broker who asked if he could hire me to coach him. I thanked him, but said I didn't do that. "But if you tell me what the problem is, I'll try to refer you to someone who could help," I said.

"Well," he began, "I'm grossing about $400,000 a year." I allowed that so far I didn't see what the problem was. He continued, "I've been grossing $400,000 a year since 1982."

More recently, a prominent financial planner contacted me about reviewing his business plan, the goal of which is to quadruple his assets under management by the year 2000. When the "plan" arrived, it turned out to be pages and pages of the most minute, process-oriented activity (down to issues like which kinds of clients get gifts of cookies). It did not have a single real prospecting initiative anywhere in it.

Please note that these were accomplished, intelligent members of our profession. They were certainly not failing. Having shown themselves capable of working consistently and well over protracted periods of time, they'd arrived at well-above-average levels of income.

And then, for reasons they could not begin to understand, they'd closed themselves off to significant further progress. Both people had constructed exquisitely elaborate (and supremely effective) ceilings through which their businesses could not pass.

And both men were trying to hire me to help them break through barriers that were quite literally imaginary. They had invented the barriers in their own imaginations; therefore, the barriers did not (and do not) really exist.

In the years just after World War II, a tremendous effort was aimed at "breaking the sound barrier" — flying a piloted aircraft faster than the speed of sound, and having the pilot live to tell about it.

And for the better part of two years, everybody who tried it got killed, which only gave the sound barrier a more and more mythic aura of impenetrability. It seemed to be, in Tom Wolfe's wonderful phrase, "a farm that you buy in the sky."

Then Chuck Yeager spoke up and said he'd be willing to give it a try. And 50 years ago this October 14, Yeager blew right on through Mach 1 — and then accelerated. You see, not being an engineer, Chuck didn't believe that any such thing as a "sound barrier" existed — and, of course, he was right.

We're in a business that has absolutely no externally imposed income limits, which is one of the two big reasons we chose it. (The other is, of course, no real boss.) You may infer from this that any limits that are set *on* us are set *by* us. This realization will, in turn, lead you inevitably to the conclusion that if you put the limit on yourself, you — but only you — have the power to remove it.

Please note that it is not strictly necessary to understand how or why you built the imaginary ceiling in order to break it. You can go lie on the couch every night for five years, and replay for the nice doctor all your childhood traumas. At that point, you'll either know exactly where your success-reluctance comes from ... or you won't. And you'll either see exactly what you have to do in order to bust through the ceiling ... or you won't. Hmmm.

Alternatively, you could — and I would — view the problem as behavioral, and decide that if you were capable of behaving your way into the problem, you're capable of behaving your way out of it. "All chronic production issues," as the sales psychologist Aaron Hemsley has always said, "are behavior issues."

There are probably as many behaviorally sound approaches to dismantling the imaginary ceiling as there are people bumping against that ceiling. (That in itself should encourage you: Your way can be the right way simply because it is your way.) But as someone who has spent a whole career first running into and then (as recently as this year) breaking through self-imposed limitations, I'd like to outline the process that has worked for me.

(1) Accept that you have a problem. In talking to the guy who'd been grossing $400,000 a year for 15 years while the market septupled and CD rates went from 14% to 4%, I found that he bristled when I used the word "problem." (His position was simply that he was doing well, but knew he could do better.) Such is the siren song of "comfort zones."

Until you fully accept and acknowledge that you have a problem — that something is significantly and seriously wrong — you can't solve the problem. It will always come back, as anyone who deals professionally with substance abuse will tell you. And it'll probably come back worse.

In the case of our business, this issue is particularly pressing because if you're not accomplishing just about everything you want to accomplish now — in the longest, strongest, most positive investment environment there ever was — what are you going to do when the markets head south for a year ... or two? (Or what if they just go into a prolonged trading range, so that every month CDs look a little better?)

If you begin by accepting your imaginary problems now, you'll be in infinitely better shape to deal with real ones later on. And you'll be ready to take the next step.

(2) Take complete responsibility for the problem. Please do not confuse this with beating yourself up. "Oh what a rogue and peasant slave am I" self-flagellation doesn't get you anywhere. More to the point, neither does blaming anybody or anything else. ("My manager's a transaction-oriented troglodyte; our research stinks; my sales assistant is from Mars.")

The great thing about accepting total responsibility (as distinctly opposed to blame) for the problem is that you become the owner of the problem. That is, if no one but you is responsible for the problem, you need not rely on anyone else to change in order for the problem to go away.

Which is really good, when you come to think about it. You see, I've found that I have virtually no capacity to change anyone else and almost limitless capacity to change myself. So if my problem is totally my responsibility, I have total power to overcome the problem through healthy change.

Blame, no matter whom (including you) it's directed at, only compounds your feeling of victimization. Accepting responsibility empowers you to change your own behavior and thereby to vanquish the (always behavioral) problem. Own the problem, and you own the solution.

(3) Identify one behavior you'd change if you were already where you want to go. Change it immediately. At a certain point in my career, I wanted to make a major step up and could not see how to do it. So I said, "Suppose you were already there. What one thing in your life would you change?"

The answer was immediately obvious. I'd commuted to high school, to college, and to work on the subway for 25 years, and I hated it more every day. And I knew that when and if I ever got where I wanted to be professionally, I'd start being chauffeur-driven to and from work. So I made that change immediately and very quickly achieved my goal — a goal that seems absurdly modest to me now, but was a very big deal to me then. (Remember that we're dealing here not with reality, but with the way you currently perceive reality.)

"I'd never fly coach again." Start flying first class on your next trip, and never go back. "I'd have my suits custom-made." Make the appointment to have your measurements taken before nightfall today. "Act as if ..." "Fake it 'til you make it." Call it what you will, it is an instant energizer, and I've never known it to fail.

(4) Fire your biggest PITA account. I have to confess, this is my answer to everything: When vexed, becalmed, distracted, or unnerved, look around to see if one large client hasn't become such a huge Pain in the Ankle that dealing with him or her is a terrible energy drain. Ask yourself if this relationship can ever be put on a healthy, productive basis characterized by mutual respect.

When (not if) you conclude that it can't, fire the account. But do it with class. Fax and overnight a letter that says, "I'm making some fairly big changes in my practice and my life; in thinking about our relationship over the last couple of years, I've concluded that I can never serve you the way you seem to want to be served. It's not fair for me to keep the account on that basis. I've asked my manager to help you find an advisor better suited to your needs than I. I wish you every success."

Then you just have to do one more thing: Do not under any circumstances take this passive/aggressive scorpion's call when (not if) he/she tries to seduce you again.

"I'm capable of doing much better/I need this scorpion to do even the level of business I'm now doing" is obviously the worst mixed message you can send yourself. It always leads to paralysis, and thus to even more self-recrimination. Firing the scorpion puts one huge, consistent message up in lights: "I deserve better, and I can find better outlets for my talents than this."

(5) Lose the bottom third of your account book. They're doing much less than a third of your business, and probably causing you more than a third of your really troublesome administrative problems, particularly around tax time. Why, then, do you keep 'em?

Easy. You're waiting to win the lottery. In your fantasy, one of their Aunt Sylvias is going to die and leave them five million bucks, and they'll come running to you.

It ain't gonna happen. You don't win the lottery, but poor people keep playing it because they don't know what else to do. But you and I *do* know what to do: Take responsibility; stop waiting for lightning to strike; prune the dead branches; and renew our climb to the top of the tree.

(6) Enlist in a holy crusade. Invest all the time, energy, and self-esteem you've freed up (via these last two steps) in a major prospecting effort aimed at the top third of your book. In the next 90 days, see all these high-potential folks, and ask them the five questions in The Great Goals of Life interview (Chapter eight of my book *The Excellent Investment Advisor*).

Or do Lifeboat Drills with the top third of your book. Or *do both*, Great Goals *and* Lifeboat Drills.

Fall in love with something: small-cap (totally trashed in the mob's rush to Nifty Fifty names); or biotech (hell, even Jim Grant loves biotech, and he's been bearish since Eisenhower's first term). Find something in which you believe passionately, and preach that belief with all your might to your best clients and prospects.

If they go for it, immediately ask for a referral. If they don't go for it … immediately ask for a referral. You *deserve* referrals — now more than ever, as you forge singlemindedly toward even higher levels of professional achievement.

Give yourself permission to go to the top. Start acting like someone who's really on the way to the top, and you'll go through that imaginary ceiling like it isn't even there.

Because, of course, it isn't.

A CONSPIRACY OF SILENCE

The outpouring of patriotism and martial ardor that greeted the Declaration of Independence can hardly be overstated. Men of every colony rushed to take up arms, vowing to fight to the last drop of blood in order to drive the tyrant from our shores.

Just 70 days later, George Washington wrote to Congress, describing a "battle" in Manhattan. "To my great surprise and mortification I found the troops that had been posted in the lines retreating with the utmost precipitation and those ordered to support them ... flying in every direction and in the greatest confusion, notwithstanding the exertions of their generals to form them.

"I used every means in my power to rally and to get them into some order, but my attempts were fruitless and ineffectual; and on the appearance of a small party of the enemy, not more than 60 or 70 in number, their disorder increased, and they ran away in the greatest confusion, *without firing a single shot.*" (Italics, I freely and even gleefully admit, mine.)

Now, I'd be willing to bet you just about anything that if those troops had been surveyed anytime between July 4 and September 15 (the day this ignoble rout took place), they would have sworn *to a man* (a) that they were in this war for the long run, (b) that they would not panic, and (c) that they would stand by their guns and do their duty, knowing they must win in the end.

This is precisely what came to mind as I was perusing a report by the ICI, issued in July 1995 (guess I'm not getting to my "To Read" file as fast as I used to). It is called "Mutual Fund Shareholder Response to Market Disruptions." Surveying several unrelated and evanescent unpleasantnesses of 1994 — the big interest rate spike, derivative hits in/bailout of money funds, the tanking of Orange County, and the meltdown of Mexico — the ICI drew some really remarkable conclusions.

To wit: (a) none of these disturbances "produced a bank-like run on mutual funds"; (b) shareholder response was "rational"; (c) that's because the fund boom has been fueled not by novices, but by institutions and "seasoned investors"; (d) these very cool customers have a "long-term investment horizon"; (e) they "may not be prone to react to short-term market volatility"; and (f) most investors say they'll stay in through a 15% decline ("*I'll* never run from those redcoats").

This smugness would probably be laughable if it weren't so downright horrifying. Because it is symptomatic of the growing conspiracy of self-deluded silence that is, I believe, spreading across our entire industry. The twisted logic of the conspiracy seems to be: (1) Investors have not panicked during recent short, meaningless declines. (2) All declines are essentially short and meaningless. *Ergo*, (3) investors will not panic, and thus we are excused from talking to them about the reality of meaningful setbacks.

All my years in the business and all my experience of human nature tell me that this conclusion is false, not least of all because the premises are false. (Was it "rational" that domestic bond funds were in net redemptions in all but one month between February 1994 and March 1995, turning positive only *after* the bond market had made new highs?)

But let me be as fair as I can about this: I can't *prove* my thesis, any more than the ICI and its equally sanguine co-conspirators can prove theirs. I would simply like us all to agree that our positions can't be proven, in other words, *that no one knows what mutual fund investors will do in the face of a serious, prolonged market decline.*

If we really embraced this conclusion — that 90% of all mutual fund assets got here since the bottom of the last bear market in 1990, so *nobody* knows how they'll react — we would, individually and collectively, embark on a massive bear market training program.

That is, after a 2,400-day, 330% run in the DJIA without a 10% correction on a closing basis, we'd be making it our business to vaccinate (and thereby immunize) everybody with a crash course in the price of performance. We'd be showing them the 1987 and 1990 peak-to-trough declines of their holdings (my "Lifeboat Drills"). We'd be reminding them that the Dow has declined more than 20% 10 times since the end of World War II, for an average hit of 28.4% ... punctuating an advance from 200 to 7800. We'd be cautioning them that equity returns over the past 15 years have been close to double the historical level.

This is what courageous, ethical, and rationally self-interested career advisors would do late in the biggest bull market of all time. They'd do everything in their power to prevent their audience from getting carried away. To put it charitably, we're doing just the opposite.

The conspiracy of silence basically takes two forms. In the more virulent strain, it denies that a major market decline can take place; therefore, we need not bother our clients' heads about it. This is the "paradigm shift" (a/k/a "this time it's different") school of denial. (Again, in fairness: Is it possible that there has indeed been a paradigm shift? Yes, surely. Are we justified in betting our clients' portfolios and our businesses on that thesis? Of course not.)

This is the school that pays a certain individual a couple of million bucks a year to go around telling it an interesting but highly speculative demographic hypothesis to the effect that there can't be a bear market until 2008, or some such year.

And today, for the first time since the summer of 1987, this is the school that is frantically reviving the Japan argument. At just about this time in '87, when America was in its last great speculative frenzy and all value in the market had been extinguished, the following argument gained instant and total currency: It's OK that we're at 22 times earnings, even though that's marked every top since Hector was a pup, because Japan's at 40 times earnings.

That line of "reasoning" told me we were close to the top in '87 (although I had no idea a crash was coming). And suddenly this summer, I'm hearing the Japan argument again. It's OK that we're at 7800, I'm told. The DJIA and the Nikkei were both 200 in 1949, and the Nikkei's been to 39,000. Even today, it's at 20,000. Don't worry, be happy. (This is a reason that it's starting to feel a lot like 1987 again, but it's not the only reason.) Even in an age of massive denial, the Japan argument, as Samuel Johnson said about patriotism, is the last refuge of a scoundrel.

Please note that this is not me suggesting that there's about to be a bear market. It is me decrying the meretricious arguments of the we-don't-have-to-warn-people-about-bear-markets-because-there-isn't-going-to-be-one school of conspirators.

The second major rationale in the conspiracy of silence is one that takes no position on future market events; it simply says that, no matter what happens, people won't panic. But it draws the same evil conclusion: We're excused from talking to people about bear markets because they're all mature, seasoned, long-term investors who won't bolt. Possible? Again, yes. But do we have the right to bet our clients' retirements on this notion, *without even consulting them*? I assure you we do not.

And meanwhile, our industry keeps caving in further and further to the short-term agendas of a new generation of market maniacs. A very fine regional brokerage firm is now putting out buy, sell, and hold recommendations on mutual funds — as if they were stocks (which they're not) and as if you could improve your performance with a lot of portfolio changes (which you can't). A highly regarded, veteran fund executive recently told attendees at an ICI meeting that she is downloading her funds' portfolios to her big producers *every night* — as if they could or should try to make intelligent short-term judgments about whether the fund managers are right or not. Do we really not see how this is just pandering to investors' (and advisors') very worst instincts?

Please: We've got to initiate an industrywide crusade to lower people's expectations, here. Not so much because the economy or the market is at risk — but because the investors are at risk. Their goals are noble, and their instincts are fine, but they just don't know what it's like to get shot at. You and I have the power — and, I believe, the obligation — to train them to behave appropriately under fire. And we may not have a moment to lose. Because I don't know about you, but a lot of my informal sentiment indicators are at

DEFCON Two (DEFCON Five being world peace, and DEFCON One being global thermonuclear war).

The Conference Board's index of consumer confidence has reached astronomical levels not seen since August of 1969. Does anybody remember what the market did in the next five years, through 1974? It *halved,* is what it did. Forgive me, but consumer confidence is the mother of all perverse indicators; when it is making new highs, you can be sure that value in the stock market is flickering out.

Meanwhile, the CBOE put/call ratio, a marvelous contrary indicator near market turning points, reached the mid-0.50 level on a 10-day basis in late May (i.e., investors bought about half as many puts as calls). This is a level not seen since May 1990 — a couple of months before the onset of the last real bear market.

Also this May, Consensus Inc.'s survey of futures traders found an astounding 91% of its respondents bullish on Treasury bills. Can unanimity — that rates won't rise, or about anything else — ever be right? One more time: Maybe. But that isn't the way to bet.

Still, as revolting as I may personally find current market conditions, I am not making a market call; I'm making a people call. (I don't know which way the next 1500-point move in the Dow will be, but I know exactly the direction of the next 7800-point move. The only issue is: How can we ensure that our investors stay that course? How can we help them absorb the temporary downs, so they can be enriched by the permanent ups?)

And what I know about people is this: They are fundamentally much more fearful of loss than they are hopeful of gain. And when losses mount — especially when they mount quickly — people tend to panic.

Smith Barney's Consulting Group recently published a very useful paper called, "How Behavioral Idiosyncrasies Impact Investor Decisions and the Stock Market." The paper reviews a study of 900 institutional and individual investors that was done by Robert Shiller of Yale shortly after the 1987 crash.

Shiller concluded, "The suggestion we get of the causes of the crash is one of people reacting to each other with heightened attention and emotion." Smith Barney adds, "In effect, the piece of information most relevant to investors was declining stock prices, not a fundamental change in the expected future value of corporate earnings. As stock prices fell, investors adopted a herd mentality, causing the cascade in stock prices."

Smith Barney sees this as entirely consistent with an SEC study that was done after the market dropped 6.1% on September 3, 1946 — 40 years earlier. The SEC found that 46% of the interviewed investors cited "declining stock prices on September 3" as their reason for selling. New eras may come and go, but nothing much changes in the human psyche.

I'm not suggesting that there's anything fundamentally wrong with the economy, nor even with the market. I'm suggesting that the bullish camp is about as crowded as I've seen it in the past 10 years and that whenever everybody goes to one side of the boat, the smallest wave can capsize it.

It is, as Bear Stearns' chief market strategist Elizabeth Mackay recently observed, when the outlook is brightest that people become careless. At the end of the day, people are paying us — whether they realize it or not — to save them from themselves. So I think it's time we asked ourselves: Are we part of the solution or — by our silence — part of the problem?

For, make no mistake about it, one of two things is going to teach people the reality of major market downturns. Either we will do it before the fact, and thereby really immunize people to panic. Or the market will do it. But then, like Washington and his generals, we will be powerless to stem the panic and the flight. And then a whole generation of investors (and their advisors) may be lost. If not us, who? If not now ... when?

IF IT AIN'T BROKE, FIX IT ANYWAY

In last month's column, I suggested that if you aren't currently earning just about all the money you could possibly want — with stock prices eight times higher and CD rates two-thirds lower than they were 15 years ago — you've got some major behavioral issues that need to be addressed.

This month, I'd like to ask a corollary question. Simply stated, if your client relationships are not blissfully harmonious — when everything that can possibly go right is going right — what's going to happen when the market backs up?

The former issue is obviously played out essentially between your ears; you alone are the problem and the solution. But the latter concerns your relationships with other people, who are under no obligation to see any situation exactly the same way you do.

So it's one thing for you to be sitting there saying, "Well, dammit, they certainly *ought* to be happy." And it's quite another thing to ask yourself, "But are they really happy; if not, why not; and what am I prepared to do about it pretty much right away?"

All this is the critical issue in the next major phase of your career. Because at this point, the question is not how much longer this bull market is going to last. Rather, the critical concern is how are you going to preserve your book until the next bull market is well under way.

Make no mistake about it, someday this market is going to peak. (Where and when it peaks is not as important as acknowledging — emotionally as well as intellectually — that it will.) At some subsequent point, another bull market will start (or this greatest of all bull markets will restart), and the markets will soar to much higher peaks. So the only issue is: How are you going to keep your wagon train intact as it works its way down through the valley between the peaks?

(If your view is that a demographic *deus ex machina* has constructed a "permanently high plateau" between peaks, or that asset allocation will somehow cause your wagons to levitate across the valley, you are excused from reading the rest of this essay. It will only make you angry.)

Note that neither the height of the next peak nor the depth of the subsequent valley are important to this analysis. (And that's good, since neither can be foreseen.) The only thing that matters is making the descent through the valley as stress-free as humanly possible, so that the settlers (your clients) are able to complete the journey in one piece and maintain their faith in (you) the wagonmaster.

And the time to strategize for that descent is before you get to the peak, not when the wagons start careening down the valley, seemingly out of control.

I suggest that your primary initiative in the fourth quarter of 1997 should be to conduct a Total Client Satisfaction drive. By New Year's Eve, you should have only three classes of clients: (1) those who are, by their own statement, completely satisfied with the relationship; (2) those with whom you are working on a specified program, agreed upon by both of you, which will bring them to a state of complete satisfaction; and (3) those with whom you've agreed (or about whom you've decided on your own) that it ain't gonna work, and whom you've instructed to get another advisor.

Clear the air completely. Let nothing fester. Even the smallest residuum of toxicity, no matter how inert and harmless it seems in a raging bull market, may blow a big hole in your business when ignited by the hot breath of the bear. And I am reliably informed that it is almost impossible to serve good clients (much less to prospect) when you are giving depositions.

Here is a suggested program.
(1) Make a list of the 10 clients with whom your relationship is most strained. Rank them in descending order from your single, most-troubled relationship down to the least difficult (of these 10, anyway). Develop your skills by working *up* the list.

See each person in turn and candidly acknowledge that things seem less than ideal between you. Ask for an equally candid statement from the client of what the problem is; if you can *and* if you care to, suggest a solution; ask if that would completely satisfy the client; fix it if he says your solution works, and fire him — on the spot — if he says it wouldn't.

If the thought of performing this exercise produces a lot of anxiety, consider working over the list for an hour or two with a psychologist who deals with people in our business (Ted Kurtz and Aaron Hemsley come most readily to mind). You may find that there are other issues you need to address before approaching the clients, and/or you may get just the corroboration and encouragement you need.

(2) Based on what you learn from the exercise above, send your remaining clients a survey form. Be as open and direct as you can. "We want to enter the new year in a state of total client satisfaction. That's what you deserve, and that's what we can deliver — so long as we completely understand each other. Please help us help you by filling out the enclosed survey. If you'd like to discuss any of this with us directly, either instead of the survey or as a result of it, please call us and we'll schedule an appointment to meet with you right away."

What questions will you ask in the survey? My guess is that you will be able to answer that yourself after you have had your pow-wow with the Ten Most Troubled, above. But if you want a track to run on, consider:

(A) What do you like best about dealing with us? What do you like least?
(B) What service that we don't currently provide would you like to see us begin?
(C) Do you completely understand the statements you receive from us? Would you like an appointment to go over them?
(D) Have we adequately explained why we've recommended all the investments you now own? Would you like further information on any of your investments?
(E) Is there anything material to your financial situation that we've failed to ask you about? Please tell us what it is.

(F) How is our telephone etiquette? Do we respond to you in the way you want us to or could we improve in this area? How?

(G) What one thing could we do that would make us easier for you to deal with?

(H) How is our outgoing communication? Do you hear from us too often, too infrequently, or just about right?

(I) Do you have a "pet peeve" about any aspect of our dealings with you? Please tell us about it, and be as candid as you like.

If you would have any reluctance to ask these questions, one would have to conclude that you probably already know — and don't want — the answers. But if you can find the courage to do this, the answers — good and bad — may really surprise you. Moreover, your responses to constructive criticism will delight your good clients — and tell you once and for all who the incurable carpers are.

(3) When you call the people to respond to the concerns or comments voiced in the survey, first thank them for responding, and ask them what their favorite charity is — if you don't already know. Make a small donation in their honor, and consider doing so again at holiday time, rather than giving a small gift that may quickly be forgotten.

(4) Try to see everyone who indicates a need or desire for an appointment by year-end. Demonstrate a willingness to respond directly to their concerns, clear the air, and to deepen the relationship. Focus on client goals, and on the long-term plan for achieving those goals, rather than on your economic and market outlook. At the end of these interviews, when good feelings should have been restored to their best level, *immediately ask for a referral*. There may never be a better time to do this.

(5) Write the client a brief summary memo of the conclusions and agreements reached in the post-questionnaire interview. That will reinforce your commitment and allow you to show that you believed, in good faith, that these issues were resolved.

(If issues you thought were behind you recur, it's usually a sign that the client didn't really accept what he said he was agreeing to. This is always a bad, if very human, sign. It suggests that maybe the client never really wanted the relationship repaired. Better to find out soon, rather than after the Dow goes down 1500 points.)

(6) Continue to be sensitive — and to let the client clearly see that you remain sensitive — to the issues he's raised. If you find yourself starting to do things again (or fail to do things again) that have irked the client in the past, maybe your unconscious is trying to tell you that *you* never wanted the relationship repaired. In that case, have the guts to go back to the client and suggest that it just isn't going to work. Then try to find him someone else who may serve him in ways that are more likely to make him comfortable.

This is not, at the end of the day, a business about investments. It is a business about people, and the fuels that it runs on are trust and mutual respect. As in every other aspect of life, the more of those qualities you give, the more you will receive.

The converse is also true: The more you let suspicion, distrust, or frustration enter into the way you deal with a client, the more of those negative emotions you'll get back, explosively, just at the wrong time.

You can act today to accrete the positive emotions in your client interactions, or you can wait and react to the negative emotions when the market starts to maul people. The choice is entirely up to you. Consciously or unconsciously, you make the choice every single day.

EVERYTHING
OLD IS
NEW AGAIN

Once upon a time, monied America had one financial advisor, with whom the whole family dealt, and who was the custodian of the family's entire financial life.

The advisor may have farmed some of the work out to other professionals — legal, accounting, or investment specialists — but he coordinated everything, and the family spoke only with him.

Then, in the great slamming of the barn door after the horse had been stolen in 1929, the society decided to trifurcate (a wonderful verb that I just this minute made up) financial services. That is, it created a set of laws and regulations the net effect of which was to force a family to go to at least three financial services providers in order to get its needs met.

Did the family want to get a home mortgage, create a checking account, or save some money in a government-insured account? It had to go to a bank. But then the family would certainly want to insure life and health, protect against loss of income because of disability, and perhaps buy an annuity for its old age. Fine, said the society, but you have to go to a second financial services entity called a life insurance company.

Finally, with its most basic financial needs covered, the family might decide to invest its surplus income in stocks, bonds, and/or mutual funds. Bully for you, the society cheered, but of course for those assets you'll have to see yet a third financial services provider called a securities dealer.

The result of all this was a situation in which America could have all the financial *products* it wanted — savings, insurance, and investments — *but it couldn't have a plan.* For all too many families, their financial life was like an orchestra with no conductor.

You and I grew up, personally and professionally, under this trifurcated synthesis. And because it's all we've ever known, we may not have noticed how deeply unnatural it is. Indeed, only government could have thought of it. It certainly isn't something that real people would ever have dreamed up.

To reality-check this thesis, consider your family doctor. Most of us still have one primary health care provider to whom we go, and to whom we take both our parents and our children. We certainly seek the advice of a specialist if our family GP counsels us to do so, but only if and when he advises this. And we almost invariably go to the specialist the GP recommends.

I don't know very many people who have two family GPs. And I've never met anybody who had three. In that sense, health — like money — represents a complex of needs to which our intuitive response is *convergent*. Regardless of the specific complaint or issue of the moment, we naturally seek the counsel of one trusted professional, rather than several.

And make no mistake about it: Trust is the overwhelming factor in our choice of a primary health care provider. We don't require the doctor to be board certified in every ache, pain, and flu strain we come down with. Rather, we gravitate toward a humane healer who knows our health history and who genuinely cares for us.

And in the end, people's approach to issues of both health and money is quite similar. (1) Our responses tend to be emotional rather than intellectual. (We don't say, "I wonder if my throat is closing due to epiglottitis or a particularly virulent staph infection." We say, "Please don't let me die.") (2) Our response to problems is primarily one of fear, which is largely insusceptible to reason. (So we do not say, "My primary concern in life is optimizing my position on the efficient frontier." We say, "Even more than death, I dread running out of money in my old age and becoming a burden to my children.") And therefore, (3) we do not seek to be educated; *we seek to be cared for.*

But while our society was more than happy to see us have one primary health care advisor, it all but forbade us to have a similar primary financial advisor. Until now.

142

Today, the dominant impulse of the financial services industry is convergence. Consolidation (and a general raising of the ante with respect to the capital required to be a major player) may appear to be the megatheme, but the Excellent Investment Advisor will be far more directly affected by the resulting *convergence.*

For when the smoke clears, what you'll find is that virtually all the remaining financial services providers will be able to provide virtually all financial services. And I believe passionately that when America can once again have one primary financial advisor, it will surely and instinctively choose one. The winner will be: the person whom the family trusts the most (as distinct from — just for example — the person with the most subtly nuanced understanding of the difference between variance and semivariance).

Now, the most important thing for you to realize about the race for the position of primary financial advisor to a monied American household is that it is a zero-sum game. For every winner there is going to be at least one — and quite often more than one — loser.

Moreover, this is a battle to the death, and you can't declare conscientious-objector status. You can't say, "Listen, I'm a really good investment advisor and I really have no interest in these other areas, so I'd really like to be left alone." You'll just be a casualty waiting to happen.

American households are inexorably becoming two things: older and richer. And I'm convinced that there's a phone call coming from every one of those monied households. The only question is whether that call is coming to you, or to another advisor (or advisors) because of you.

That call will go something like this. "Listen, you know we've always been friends, and I hope we'll always be friends. You're the only person I buy stocks/bonds/mutual funds from. We've done a lot of business, we've made a lot of money, and I appreciate all your help.

"But the thing is, I'm getting older, and my family's been after me to get a comprehensive financial and estate plan. It turns out my daughter went to law school with a woman who's now a senior trust officer at NationsBank, or my son's fraternity brother is an estate planning specialist at Mass Mutual or … (fill in the name of any other entity that would dearly love to hang your scalp from its lodge pole).

"And they've created this total plan that, of course, involves their taking over the management of all my assets. So they told me to tell you — they said you'd know what this means — that the document coming out of your fax machine even as we speak is called transfer papers. So goodbye, and have a nice life out there on the efficient frontier."

You see, America doesn't really need more or different mutual funds/wrap accounts/life insurance policies. What America needs — and what it is beginning consciously and even desperately to want — is a plan, with a primary financial advisor to keep the family on that plan.

Note that it is not necessary (and may even be inadvisable) for the primary financial advisor to be either the author of or the technical expert on the plan. The technical staffs of the surviving/converging firms will only grow bigger and better. Let them write the plan; there are far better uses for your time and energy. (I recently spoke at an insurance department meeting of a major investment brokerage firm. By actual count, there were more staff support people from the firm's life insurance vendors in the room than there were brokers. This was the best argument I ever saw that the brokers need learn absolutely nothing about insurance. They need only put the clients and the experts together.)

Convergence only narrows (i.e., worsens) the distribution bottleneck, which only makes the vendors and your staff work harder to serve you. This trend will progressively free the primary financial advisor to do what she does best: manage her clients' emotions while others manage her clients' money.

As you broaden the scope of what you propose to do for a family — as you graduate from whichever of the three trifurcated camps you grew up in and become a primary financial advisor — you have to see that your essential product is going to change as well.

For instance, the primary product of an investment broker is surely investments. And investments are a left-brain, intellectual business that runs on the fuel of knowledge. But the product of the primary financial advisor is sound advice. (The investment portfolio, then, can never be an end in itself. It's the servant of the plan, or it's random.) And advice, as we've seen, is a right-brain, emotional business that runs on the fuel of trust.

This will be a very big leap for a lot of veteran trifurcated campers to make — and many indeed will not be able to make it. If you have spent your whole life saying things like, "Trust my optimization software," or "Trust the dividend projections in my split-dollar illustrations," you may have more than a little difficulty learning to say simply, "Trust me." Still, that's going to be the key to everything.

This, in turn, tells you why the primary financial advisor will be compensated by fees. In the end, the strongest foundation upon which to build trust is perfect identity of financial interest between advisor and advisee. And that's what fees (including "C" shares) do for me. When the client/prospect asks me why his family might want to hire me as their primary financial advisor on a fee basis rather than any other arrangement, I get to say the 10 words I've been waiting to say for my whole career: "I prosper as you prosper; I suffer if you suffer."

What the fee-based primary financial advisor will say, in effect, is: "I will give you the very best plan that my firm and I are capable of creating for you. We ask of you and your family only three things. (1) Give the plan enough money. (2) Give the plan enough time. (3) And above all, never lose faith in the plan nor in us. If you will do these things and if history is any guide, you will ultimately be able to fund all of your family's deepest financial hopes and dreams, and you will cause your deepest financial fears to fly away and be gone.

"For our part, we will tie our compensation directly to the success of the plan — in other words, to the correctness of our advice. Our relationship with your family will be profitable to us only to the extent that our advice proves to be right.

"Indeed, even when we're sure our advice is sound, but your

investments go down simply because the markets go down, we'll willingly absorb the same proportionate decline in our compensation. We'll be stoical about that, in the hope that this will encourage you to be stoical as well. Because sometimes all you have to do — and all you can do — is keep faith with the plan."

Personally, I would never want to be anybody's first financial advisor, but I expect to (and believe I'll deserve to) be the *last* financial advisor that they'll need during my lifetime.

Because my focus is not primarily on outperforming either markets or other advisors, but rather on helping the family achieve all of its most important financial goals.

The primary financial advisor is not selling knowledge of the future, since that is unavailable to man. He is selling, above all, his own limitless faith in the future, and in what he and his clients can accomplish through the three golden attributes of planning, patience, and discipline.

How to go out to one's existing clients, and start running for the position of Primary Financial Advisor? Well, I'm prejudiced, of course, but I can think of no better way than to go see 'em, ASAP, and have the Great Goals of Life Conversation. (This is Chapter eight of my book *The Excellent Investment Advisor.*)

This is a 15-minute, five-question interview, the purpose of which is to illumine the state of a family's planning (or the lack thereof) for the interconnecting financial needs of up to four living generations of the family, as well as to examine its financial relationship with its favorite charity.

The Great Goals of Life Conversation does not, in any rigorous way, offer any answers (although it leaves your listeners in no doubt that you and your firm have access to those answers). Rather, it seeks to help the family get the really important questions framed right. And the most critical of all those questions is, of course:

What's the plan?

A NEW YEAR'S RESOLUTION — OR TWO

Not long ago, I heard a presentation by the president of a broker/ dealer whose firm has an excellent mutual fund wrap fee program. He was enthusiastically describing the program's very attractive features, when suddenly he said something that absolutely froze my blood.

I can't remember his exact words, but he spoke about how easy it is to switch the funds in clients' portfolios. That was important, he said, because you'd want to change funds every so often *in order to convince your clients that you were earning your fee.*

I sat bolt upright in the back of the room, waiting for the audience (inevitably, I thought) to start throwing things at the guy. Nobody moved. If possible, this horrified me even more. Heaven help us, I thought, these people don't see anything wrong with having the integrity of their client relationships impugned.

Never reluctant to conclude that everybody's out of step but me, I have to admit that I started to think I might be reading this wrong. So I sat there quietly, doing the arithmetic in my head:

Okay, I met with the clients. I spent all the time and energy necessary to completely understand their financial (and emotional) situation. I comprehend and empathize with their hopes, dreams, and fears. We've made a written plan together. I've funded that plan with a beautifully diversified portfolio of professionally managed investments that are superbly appropriate to the clients' long-term goals. *And soon I'll have to change those investments, just so my clients will "know" I'm earning my fee?* Yecchhh!

I've always felt — and continue to feel, more strongly than ever — that one of the great glories of fees vs. commissions is that I can get paid to tell my clients to do nothing, when nothing is the right thing for them to do. Which, if I've done my job right in the first place (i.e., made a coherent, all-weather, long-term plan and hired disciplined money managers to execute the plan), it almost always is.

I don't get paid to change investments; I certainly don't get paid to pander to clients' misperceptions of how I earn my fee. I get paid to tell my clients what I most sincerely believe is best for them, as I'm given light to see what's best for them, and to do so with sufficient professionalism and moral weight that they believe me — even (nay, especially) when they don't understand me. And what's best for most people most of the time can easily be summed up in four words: steady as you go.

Portfolio turnover correlates negatively with wealth. The more often you change investments, the less money you make. (That is, the more you try to be short- to intermediate-term right, the more long-term wrong you become.) Past a certain level of turnover — as any chastened trader of commodities, futures, CBOE options, or margined stocks can tell you — you actually start losing money. Turn your portfolio over often enough, and you lose it all.

I think this is why Warren Buffett says we should all be issued 20 chits at birth, and have to surrender a chit every time we invest in a different stock. When your 20 chits are gone, you can't buy any new stocks for the rest of your life — although, of course, you can continue to buy all you want of the stocks you already own.

His thesis is that this would make us all very choosy long-term investors in only those few companies that seemed to us to have the most superb prospects for decades to come. Why should it be any different with money managers?

The answer is that it shouldn't. And if we would only quit micromanaging our managers, it wouldn't. What we need to do is to stop working so much on variables we can never really control (e.g., markets and investments) and put all that energy into variables we can almost limitlessly control (e.g., patience and discipline).

Because, as always, the relative performance of similar invest-ments can never be the critical issue in anyone's investing lifetime. No client of mine will or will not run out of money in retirement because of which small-cap value manager he owned for 20 years. He'll prevent himself from running out of money by owning virtu-ally *any* small-cap value manager (and *any* managers from the other major equity styles) instead of bonds and CDs. In that sense, the most important portfolio decisions are the easiest, and you only have to make them once.

The more you shorten your perspective and chase immediate past performance (which are (a) two ways of saying the same thing and (b) why most manager-switching takes place), the more apt you are to lose sight of what really matters.

So I would like you to consider making a resolution for 1998: *Don't change any of your portfolios all year.* Other than if your man-ager goes under a bus or to another firm, why would you even con-sider it? Are your managers seasoned, disciplined professionals? Do their styles complement each other, so that the client is likely to achieve his long-term goals while being diversified out of some of the bumps and the humps? *Then why change,* other than to generate a commission, or to "prove" something ("I'm earning my fee") that cannot — and should not have to — be proven?

Would anything the economy and/or the market could do in the next 12 months invalidate one of your current holdings? If so, it was an inappropriate long-term investment to begin with.

And if your long-term investments are fundamentally short-term event-proof (other than that you might get to buy some more at sale prices), why would you need to switch them in 1998? Answer: You wouldn't. So just decide right here and now that you're not gonna. And look at all the time and energy that resolution will free up.

No need to waste time reading fund research, going to analysts' meetings, perusing charts and scattergrams, playing with your opti-mization software, watching the markets, or massaging asset alloca-tion models. Nothing at all to do every day, in fact, but the real work

149

of this profession, which is finding and nurturing relationships in the mirroring eyes of other human beings — people who need, and who know they need, your wisdom and experience.

If you discipline yourself not to change managers for a whole year, you'll also find out (or rediscover) pretty quickly who are your clients and who are your customers. Real clients may swallow hard, but they'll ultimately accept your re-affirmation of faith in the overall strategy, or in a "lagging" manager. Customers will argue with you, and may even insist on grabbing the steering wheel away from you. My experience is that relationships rarely recover from major episodes of second-guessing. Let 'em go.

The real trouble with a lot of manager-switching, of course, is that you usually end up firing somebody who's been cyclically cold for a while, just before he gets hot. At least one of Mario Gabelli's funds lost half its assets when his value/M&A themes went into cardiac arrest in 1989-90 — whereupon he proceeded to shoot out every light in the joint.

And I can only imagine how many people bailed out on a small-cap value manager like Chuck Royce between 1994 and 1996, when his type of stocks did essentially nothing — just before soaring 50% to 70% in the past three quarters or so. I need hardly add that money that leaves a manager due to impatience almost always goes into a manager who's lately been hot — and is about due to go cold.

You don't have to live like that anymore — at least for a year. In 1998, don't manage your accounts. *Lead* them ... to new high levels of patience, discipline, and a truly long-term focus.

And while you're at it, make a second (and closely related) New Year's resolution. For one whole year, never discuss "performance" unless you're specifically asked.

If you couldn't sell "performance," what would you sell? Particularly in a deeply ahistorical period like this — stocks up 3.5x in seven years with only one 10% correction on a closing basis — one-, three-, and five-year performance numbers are very misleading.

They cause the investor to get a wildly inflated sense of what normal returns are, and they blind him to the historical savagery of typical bear markets. So trumpeting immediate past performance isn't helping the investor, and it may actually be hurting him, because it's setting him up to fail when reality bites.

If you wanted to talk to people about managed investments, but for a whole year you couldn't discuss performance, what could you talk about? Well, character, for one thing. Don't you find that there's a certain integrity to the work of very good managers? I do.

I'm not saying I like them all, or find them all attractive as human beings. But I think we take away from any conversation with a quality manager a clear sense of mission — a sense of "I've tried, or seen other people try, everything else; this is the one way I believe I can achieve superior returns over time. I may look wrong sometimes, and I may even *be* wrong, but I can't turn traitor to my most passionate beliefs." That's not just the kind of person we want running our money; that's the kind of person we want in our lives. (It's also the kind of person most of us want to be.)

But, like all the other human qualities that really count, character isn't something for which a computer can screen. Nor is integrity reducible to some number of stars, moons, or asteroids.

Why, then, are these not the primary (if not the only) attributes of our favorite managers that we discuss with our clients? I believe it's because we've allowed the no-help fund industry (and its bought dog, financial journalism) to set our agenda for us.

A no-help fund ad can't conceptualize. It can't interact with an investor, nor discuss in any meaningful way such "soft" attributes as character, patience, and discipline. An ad has to say, "Buy me now, and don't buy all the other ads." So it's going to go for the simplest, lowest-common-denominator hook it can. And today that's a blockbuster "performance" number, the shorter-term the better.

Financial journalism's agenda is even more insidious. It's not the purpose of journalism to make its audience wealthy; it's to get 'em to buy more financial journalism. Were journalism to tell you the truth ("The thing for you to do is to get a top-notch advisor, make a long-term plan with that advisor, stick to the plan, get on with your life, and stop looking for the answer in magazines"), you'd stop buying the journalism. So they can't tell you the truth.

They tell you, "The most important thing is picking the best funds." (This is a lie; the most important thing is having a comprehensive, written financial and estate plan.) "You can pick the best funds by reading performance figures, expense ratios, etc. in this magazine." (That's also a lie. Past performance may not give you any reliable clue to future performance. And peak performance, in an efficient market, also exposes you to peak volatility.)

"You don't need an advisor to help you read performance figures; just keep buying this magazine." (Narrowly true, and in the larger sense a lie; you need an advisor to help you plan, to balance return with your tolerance for volatility, and to talk you down off the occasional ledge of greed or fear — all issues that don't fit into a six-inch-square ad for a no-help fund.)

This journalistic "logic" leads to the Big Lie: "Six Hot Funds To Buy Now." Or to the endlessly interchangeable "Here's how Stash and Susan Gronsky Are Planning To Retire With $1 Million At Age 40!" cover stories — wherein it is revealed that Stash and Susan (a) read this magazine cover to cover every single month and (b) own nothing but the six hot no-load funds featured on page 268 — all of which are, of course, advertisers in that issue.

We have to have the courage to stand up and say, "It isn't as simple as that. Nothing is. You don't get wealthy running your finger down a performance table in a magazine, nor counting stars on the fingers of one hand. Sound advice from a caring professional who knows you and your family is the issue. Character, courage, patience, discipline, and perspective are the issues."

But that involves us resetting the agenda. If you couldn't sell performance, you'd almost be forced to set the agenda in some other terms, wouldn't you? And in the long run, a different (and healthier) agenda would be best for the clients *and* us, don't you agree? Okay, then: For all of 1998, just say no to "performance."

I think you can see that these two simple but very profound resolutions would affect not just your '98, but your way of relating to people, your career, and quite possibly your life. (1) No changing portfolios unless (a) the manager changes, which they don't that often, or (b) the client's goals actually change — which they virtually never do. (2) No "performance" selling.

You'll have a lot more time. You'll have a lot more self-esteem, because you have the guts to do the right thing (or at least not allow the client to talk you into letting him do the wrong thing for the wrong reasons). You'll have a lot more energy, because you're acting on your own healthy agenda, rather than reacting to someone else's diseased agenda — and acting always accretes your energy, just as reacting always depletes it.

You can do this. The question is, will you?

THE OCTOBER SURPRISE: DID YOU GET YOUR WAKEUP CALL?

There's an old story about a farmer who had a mule that he just loved, but couldn't get to do any work at all. Finally he took the recalcitrant beast to the best mule trainer in the territory. "I want him trained," said the farmer, "but you mustn't hurt him."

The trainer said he understood perfectly. Then, picking up a two-by-four, he proceeded to smash the mule in the face with all his might. The farmer screamed, "You promised me you wouldn't hurt him." "And I won't," said the trainer, "but I had to get his attention."

In this little fable, the mule is our industry, and the market is the trainer. It didn't want to hurt you — in October's global meltdown — but it had to get your attention. The question of the hour is: Did it succeed, and are you paying attention now? Or have you just gone back into denial?

Of all the toxic fictions produced by this greatest of bull markets, I've ranted most in these columns about two. They are that (a) we are in a new era in which significant market declines are no longer possible so we don't have to train our clients to withstand them, and (b) the new breed of sophisticated long-term investor is panic-proof and will never sell into big declines.

(A third lunacy — which is really a variation on (b), above — said that asset allocation/international diversification would stabilize a portfolio so wonderfully that no one would ever again panic out of individual components of the portfolio that might happen to be hemorrhaging.)

I thought — and think — that these notions bespeak a tremendous moral cowardice on our industry's part, as well as a basic misperception of how advisors add value. Letting people live in a dream world — much less encouraging them to do so — doesn't help them.

155

Moreover, long-term investment success is almost totally a function of how one emotionally handles declines in the equity market, *as opposed to how one's portfolio handles them.* Thus, it has always seemed to me that the highest and best function of a professional advisor is to help his clients understand, accept, and even embrace chaotic markets.

And yet here we are, confronted once again with the spectacle of massive liquidation of emerging market mutual funds, *after* declines of up to 75% in countries like Thailand (including the currency effect). Where are the noble goals of asset allocation and international diversification now? Where is long-term perspective? Did people somehow not know that, in an efficient market, the much higher returns of emerging-country investing are purchased with much higher volatility and risk?

And once again we have to conclude that, although markets and the global economy are capable of great fundamental change, human nature is not. It is the most basic human instinct to regard soaring stock prices (i.e., the progressive extinction of value) as good, and crashing stock prices (i.e., gigantic rallies in value, yield, and opportunity) as bad. Unaided, people don't merely get it wrong, they get it backwards. Price and value are always inversely related.

At the end of the day, all value is born out of chaos, and the great values — the real potential lifestyle-changers — are born out of massive panic liquidation. A few years ago, Sir John Templeton said, "People are always asking me where the outlook is most favorable, but that's the wrong question. They should be asking where the outlook is most miserable."

It is precisely because good investing is so utterly counterintuitive — you have to learn to distrust prosperity and calm, and to fly toward chaos — that the Excellent Investment Advisor was sent into the world. The EIA earns treasure on earth (and, I believe, in heaven) by helping people do with their capital exactly the opposite of what they want to do with it, pretty much all the time. Thus, the EIA is not so much an educator nor a portfolio manager. She's a behavior modifier.

156

And behavior modification primarily involves altering people's emotional responses to external stimuli in general, and to market chaos in particular. An EIA has no ability to affect economic or market events, but virtually limitless ability to change clients' emotional responses to those events. Thus, being ever the ultimate realist, the EIA puts all his energy into variables he can control, and manages not money, but people.

Herewith, the Excellent Investment Advisor's 10-point short course in belief-and-behavior modification regarding equity volatility:

1. In the long run, real wealth comes to the owner, not the loaner. The Ibbotson chart of which we are all so fond shows 71-year average annual returns of 10.7% and 12.6% for the stocks of large and small companies, respectively. Long-term corporate bonds in the same period paid an average of 5.6%; long-term government bonds returned 5.1%.

Either these numbers are random, or it looks like you get paid about twice as much to be an owner as to be a loaner. But wait: These are merely the nominal returns. Adjusted for 3% average inflation over that period, the equity investor earns more like four or five times what a debt investor does in real terms.

Now, you know there's gotta be another variable in here somewhere. An efficient market doesn't pay equity investors four to five times the real return of bonds because owners are better human beings. (Even though we are.)

Why do equities return so much more than bonds? The academic answer is: more risk. But I say it's not risk, it's volatility. And I say they're not the same thing. More about this distinction in a moment. For now, just focus on the apparently incontrovertible fact that, in the race for real wealth, bonds are a non-starter.

2. The great risk of the 20th century was losing your money. The great risk of the 21st century will be outliving your money. Our clients may be retired nearly as long as they worked; in retirement, they'll still have to deal with as many as three decades of rising living costs. Twenty years ago, a first-class postage stamp cost 13 cents;

today it (and everything else) costs two-and-a-half times as much. In the same 20 years, the cash dividend of the S&P 500 quadrupled (while the index itself octupled), and bond yields actually went *down.*

My point is that whether you believe in the Ibbotson return relationships or not, you still need to be an owner. If you've got any kind of life expectancy and/or heirs you really care about, bonds are irrational. Don't look at yield; look at total return. And above all, don't mistake certainty ("I'm guaranteed to get my $100,000 back in 20 years") for safety ("Twenty years from now my increased dividends will let me buy everything I do today, even though everything will cost two or three times what it does now").

3. All you have to do to be a great equity investor is watch huge percentages of your capital disappear every so often, and have faith that the disappearance is temporary. Here's everything you need to know about equity price movements, in eight words: The advance is permanent; the declines are temporary. Believing that, you can never fail. The Dow was about 170 at the end of WWII; last August it hit 8300. That's about a 50-bagger — ignoring dividends, which you must never do.

During that time, the Dow took 10 hits of 20% or more; the average was 28.4%, and the market went down for a year or so. (In 1973-74 the Dow fell 45% over two years. And the things people really owned, like the Nifty Fifty growth stocks, went down 60%-80%.)

Here's the key: You couldn't know intellectually how, when, or why any of those declines would end. You could, however, maintain perfect faith *that* they would end. And that turned out to be all you needed to do: just hold on. (By the way, every single thing the bears were saying about the U.S. in '73-'74, they're saying about Japan now. Except, of course, Nixon.)

Long-term equity investment success is, therefore, as I've said so many times in these columns, not the triumph of knowledge over ignorance, but the victory of faith over fear.

4. No panic, no sell. No sell, no lose. If markets are only capable of creating temporary declines, permanent loss can only be created by people — losing faith, succumbing to fear, and selling.

That's a remarkable realization, and it enables people to see that volatility isn't, in and of itself, risk. Warren Buffett's net worth went down $342,000,000 on October 19, 1987 — and yet he didn't *lose* anything. Why? He didn't sell, of course. Markets don't kill people. People kill themselves.

The same people (well, the same *kind* of people, anyhow) who sold the Mexican bolsa during the peso crisis after it went from 3,000 to 1,500, and then watched it go to 4,500 in three years, are now selling Thailand and Brazil. Mark my words, they'll someday sell the U.S. at exactly the same point in our euphoria/panic cycle. Unless they have an EIA, *whose faith is so strong that it vanquishes their fear.*

5. You can't time markets. The only way you can be absolutely sure of participating in every day of the permanent advance is to be willing (nay, eager) to participate in every day of the temporary declines. *That's the deal.*

6. If the volatility weren't there, the returns wouldn't be there either. There's no such thing as good markets and bad markets. There's just one supremely efficient market, in which return and volatility are two sides of the same coin. If the volatility of stocks died down, over time, to match the volatility of bonds, the premium return of equities would disappear, God forbid. The size, scope, and frequency of the temporary declines are responsible for the shape of the permanent advance. *That's also the deal.*

7. A portfolio matched to the great goals of life is an investment. A portfolio driven by a market outlook is a speculation. If your goals haven't changed (which is a way of saying: if your life and the lives of the people you love haven't changed) and if your portfolio is appropriate to your goals, why change it?

Changing your portfolio because of market conditions is virtually synonymous with abandoning your goals. ("Yes, I'm still 54 and my bride's still 53, and our kids/heirs are still in their 20s, so over the two generations, our investment time horizon is about two-thirds of a century ... but I *gotta* sell Thailand and Brazil ... which in my heirs' lifetimes will probably be as fully developed as Europe is today ... because those markets are getting killed *this month!*")

Don't speculate. In other words, don't let your portfolios be driven by a market outlook. Keep your head out of today. Keep asking yourself, "Where will these markets be in 20 years?" Look *back* 20 years, and see how far we've come. Maintain a life-driven, goal-oriented, long-term (indeed, if appropriate, multi-generational) perspective.

8. Focus on the big picture. The central reality of our time is not the downward revaluation of currencies and markets of some emerging countries that got ahead of themselves. It is the global capitalist revolution in these and indeed all the countries of the world. It is the conversion of the world's energies to free-market capitalism. It is the explosive growth of property rights and the concomitant eclipse of big government.

Whatever battles have yet to be fought, the war's over. The good guys won. This is the great gettin'-up morning of universal economic freedom and development. And you ain't seen nothin' yet.

9. Focus on the *other* big picture: technological progress, at a speed and on a scale hitherto unimaginable. And all of it coming from the private sector — which means we and our clients can own it.

Think of the great technological breakthroughs of 50 years ago: jet propulsion, radar, atomic energy, lasers — virtually all products of government research and development. Things aren't like that anymore. So much of today's innovation comes from small, entrepreneurial, capital-hungry companies that we (or, more properly, our portfolio managers) can invest in. And I say again: We ain't seen nothin' yet.

10. Try to remember how relatively elegant today's problems are. Sixty-five years ago, we didn't know if capitalism had a future. Fifty-five years ago, we didn't know if democracy could survive.

Fifty years ago, the Cold War froze the world over; 35 years ago, in the Cuban missile crisis, we probably got as close to the suicide of the species as we'll ever get. The next year, an American president was assassinated.

Thirty years ago, a presidential candidate and our greatest civil rights leader were shot to death within weeks of each other. Twenty-five years ago, OPEC and Watergate. Twenty years ago, stagflation, the Ayatollah, and Oil Shock II. Ten years ago, the crash. Even five years ago, a galloping budget deficit that seemed out of control.

Does anything we have to deal with today (hell, does all of it put together) measure up to these crises? I think you have to feel that today's issues are wonderfully elegant compared to those of yesteryear. And that the investment opportunities created by today's problems are truly historic.

So here's my toast to us and ours in 1998: I wish us a year of elegant problems. Have I gotten your attention?

YOU CAN *BUY* THE RECORD, OR YOU CAN *BE* THE RECORD

The Great No-Help Lie is that you can pick superior performing funds by yourself, without having to pay an advisor.

This conclusion is so clear, simple, and attractive that most folks don't notice — until way too late — the false, toxic, and fundamentally evil premise upon which it is based. Namely, that investing in funds with superior records is, in and of itself, the key to successful investing.

But it isn't. It's not even *a* key. Real people do not get *investment* returns, they get *investor* returns. The latter are always substantially lower — and sometimes grotesquely lower — than the former.

The reasons for this are twofold, and quite simple. (1) Investors contribute the huge preponderance of any investment's net inflows *after* it has built a superb record. (That is, they buy the record.) (2) Then, investors sharply reduce their net investments when, as it inevitably does, "performance" subsequently lags for a while. (This pattern assures that they buy most heavily at above-average prices, which mathematically guarantees below-average returns. Thus, most investors significantly underperform their own investments.)

Carried to its logical conclusion (which sooner or later it always is), this second behavioral pattern produces not merely a decline in net purchases but the onset of net liquidation. (One wishes, here, to write the phrase "*panic* net liquidation," but refrains from doing so on the grounds that it is a redundancy.)

This happens when some extraordinary confluence of favorable circumstances (e.g., low interest rates, stable currencies, competitive costs, etc.), which had previously contributed to a great rise in values, comes suddenly and spectacularly a cropper.

At that point, the investor — having bought a great record only *after* it had been amassed — panics out at or near historic lows. Having bought high, he sells low.

Thus, we see that investment success is not primarily determined (and may not be determined at all) by investment performance, but by investor behavior. And we know that, human nature being what it is, investor behavior will always be instinctively inappropriate. (At critical junctures, it will be wildly, suicidally inappropriate.)

Enter the Excellent Investment Advisor, whose mantra is, "I am not an investment analyst, *I am a behavior modifier.*" The EIA knows that, if she can get people to trust her, she may be able — through the combined effects of her empathy and her wisdom — to persuade them to desist from inappropriate behavior and thereby begin to enjoy lasting investment success.

The difference between lifetime investment success or failure for at least 90% of American households is the presence or absence of an Excellent Investment Advisor. We are not the thing that matters most. *We are, ultimately, the only thing that matters.*

Believing that, you can look forward to a professional life of psychic and financial income whose only limits are those you impose on yourself. Failing to believe it, you will think that Ameritrade and Schwab OneSource are your competitors; that way lies failure, madness, death, and bad skin.

If you doubt any of this, (a) I'm really worried about you, but, more to the point, (b) two wonderful statistical studies reached my desk in late December. And, being your friend, I want to share them with you.

The first is an article from the December issue of *Morningstar Investor.* It's called "The Plight of the Fickle Investor," and it looks at the returns of the average dollar invested in some select funds vs. the returns of the funds themselves. And for us EIAs, it is truly heartwarming, if not at all surprising.

The article begins by comparing investment vs. investor returns in PBHG Growth Fund over the previous five years. It concludes that "the average dollar in that fund made just 13% annually during the past five years, not the 22% investors would have made by systematically investing throughout the period, nor the 31% listed in the fund ads, newspapers, or the data pages of *Morningstar Investor* (all of which assume a single lump-sum investment at the beginning of the period)."

You really need to look at Morningstar's chart of inflows and outflows plotted against cumulative return to see this pattern in all its gothic horror. But for now let the words paint you a picture:

"From 1992 through 1995, the fund quietly built a superb record, though its cash inflows were moderate. In early 1996, when the fund's average three-year gain of more than 30% placed it on many a leader's list, the money started rolling in. Nearly $2.5 billion poured in during the first six months of 1996, *just in time for the fund's 10% slide in July.*" (Forgive me; the italics are mine.)

"Inflows dropped sharply. Then in early 1997, after the fund had suffered several down months, shareholders started bailing out, missing a strong second-quarter rebound." This is a polite way of saying that the fund went into big-time net liquidation just as its cumulative return was roaring back nearly to peak levels.

(As a very vocal critic of Morningstar's star system, and the deification of immediate past "performance" of which that system has become the unwilling symbol, let me not fail to note that Morningstar did a very classy thing in publishing this study. Don't miss it. Now back to the regularly scheduled essay, already in progress.)

The second study comes from the Leuthold Group. It focuses initially on the $2.5 billion outflow from foreign-focused equity funds last November. "This," Leuthold says dryly, "is the first outflow month in our records since December 1990" — just before the great worldwide Desert Storm rally in January 1991.

Another chart in this study plots the weekly inflows/outflows of foreign-focused funds against Morgan Stanley's EAFE index throughout 1997, and, of course, you watch these funds go into massive net liquidation only *after* the index's slide gets into third gear.

Leuthold then cites the recent survey, done for American Century Funds, which asked investors (*after* the October 27 meltdown) what they would do in the event of a one-day 23% drop in the market, à la October 19, 1987. A staggering 66% of respondents said they would do nothing. Leuthold comments with asperity, "Those equity investors who bailed out of foreign funds in November must not have been participants in the survey." Either that or denial ain't just a river in Egypt, because I still hear lots of people saying that today's new breed of long-term investors simply does not panic.

I confidently predict that the next version of this latter fiction, which you should be hearing any day now, will say, "Sure, people panic out of third world countries like Korea, Thailand, and uh, Japan ... but not the good old U.S. of A." And let me say to you, from the bottom of my heart, that if you'll believe that, you will quite literally believe anything.

But I digress. I'm not trying to prove the herd mentality response, or even the panic response, *per se.* I'm suggesting, as I always do, only three things:

(1) Basic human nature has not changed, because it does not change.
(2) Basic human nature, untreated, guarantees investment failure.
(3) In this context, the only known antidote to basic human nature is the Excellent Investment Advisor.

The critical variable in lifetime investment success is, therefore, never the investments people own, but always the quality of the behavioral advice they are getting — or not getting. (Speaking of mantras, take mine ... please. "It's not load and no-load. It's help and no-help.")

So what this issue comes down to — indeed, what our whole business comes down to — is your willingness to stand up for the primacy of your advice. The problem is not what's going on in the investors' heads, but in yours.

If you understand the business and your role in it, you will always be resetting the agenda in your client/prospect interactions. You'll be steering the discussion away from issues of the "right" portfolio mix and toward the issue of the right behavior. Otherwise, you're just another tinpot investment commentator, claiming to able to say what the market will do next, or whether mutual fund raindrop A will get to the bottom of the window, over the next five years, before mutual fund raindrop B.

If this is starting to sound as if your client's biggest problem just might be your own self-esteem, you've got it. A quick, self-administered test of your self-image levels: Have you worried at all in the last 90 days about whether technology is making you irrelevant? If you have, you're in trouble.

If your livelihood could be affected by a machine that can only manipulate data, transmit "information," and give the investor faster, cheaper ways of behaving inappropriately — you're in the wrong business. Specifically, you're in a commodity business, but you're not the low-cost producer of the commodity.

But if you have taken rank with the EIAs of the world — if your product is that rare, elusive, and invaluable thing called sound advice, you've basically got it knocked. From this point on, the business is just a numbers game — being willing to look in the eyes of enough people and to say that your wisdom, experience, and empathy are what their family needs in order to reach their financial goals.

Again, please note that this is always a matter of resetting the agenda — which has already been set in the wrong terms throughout America: "Six Hot Funds To Buy Now," which is the apotheosis of buying the record.

Now is the time for truth. Now is the time to help people climb down off the gerbil wheel of investment "performance." The choice is simple and stark: You can enable people to follow their own diseased agenda, or you can genuinely help them and their families. But you can never do both.

And remember that replacing the fiction of investment "performance" with the truth of investor behavior is one of the most liberating and empowering things you can do for people. I like to tell investors that, in the long run, no mutual fund manager controls their family's investment fate. *They* control it.

Patience, discipline, and faith in the future — all virtues that, with a good advisor by your side, you can practice limitlessly — will determine at least 90% of your lifetime return. Don't you find that exhilarating? I certainly do.

You can buy the record, or you can be the record. Almost by definition, you can't do both. So the question becomes, how do you want to spend the rest of your investing lifetime? Do you want to keep serially buying whatever went up the most in the three years before you bought it, only to be disappointed (if not massacred) on the next turn of the wheel?

Or do you want to chart a course that has always led to long-term investment success, and then — with the aid of a great professional navigator — follow that course all the way home?

When we have the courage to put the choice to investors just this way, everybody wins ... in the long run.

WHAT ARE YOU TRYING TO PROVE?

A couple of months ago ("A New Year's Resolution or Two," January 1998), I suggested that we take a year off from changing — or allowing clients to change — their portfolios.

In a particularly Blinding Glimpse of the Obvious, I said that portfolio turnover correlates negatively with return. That is, the more you act on the illusion that you can outthink the market zig for zag, or capture small inefficiencies in the relative pricing of different securities, the wronger you'll get to be in the end. And, worn down by wrongness and transaction costs, the more you'll sandpaper away your return (and ultimately your capital).

No sooner had this column appeared than my office got an urgent call from an advisor, asking for the "statistics" to back up this contention. Seems the advisor had a client who'd been bitten real hard by the trading bug, and she wanted to "prove" to her client that he should cease and desist.

I confess I found this unutterably sad. The advisor's heart was in the right place, but she wasn't using her head. (This, in my experience, is a formula for banging your head against a wall *and* getting your heart broken.) First of all, she was trying to prove the obvious. Second, she was trying to reason with somebody who wasn't listening to her advice. Each of these is something you should never do, and this advisor was doing both simultaneously.

I believe that in our genuine desire to do good for people (even — and sometimes especially — when they so signally do not want good done to them) we all find ourselves sparring with this tar baby from time to time. It's what I would characterize as a good/bad instinct.

Not to feel this instinct would, I'm quite sure, be a sign that we'd surrendered to cynicism. (And never is that temptation greater than when the world around us has turned into frothing, gibbering "performance" maniacs — as it has now.)

So it's okay — and it may be very important — to feel that feeling. It's just not okay to act on the feeling. And that's what we do every single time we try to "prove" something, especially when it's something a client or prospect so assiduously does not want to hear. I recommend you save your strength.

Inappropriate behavior — even in a good cause — arises from inappropriate beliefs. So let's look at some of the harmful beliefs that may be informing your good/bad instinct to "prove" stuff.

1. The client is rational and genuinely wants investment success. He will therefore respond to intellectual "proof" of the better course of action. This has never been my experience, least of all now. In the unconsciously revealing commercials for National Discount Brokers — in which the passion for trading is unsubtly analogized to sex — we are reminded yet again that portfolio "action" is often used to meet all manner of dark psychic needs. And addiction is quite insusceptible to reason.

2. My prospect/client has a right to expect me to support my recommendations with objective evidence. Yes, but only up to a point, and that point is very finite. Reasonable evidence is one thing, and it's usually based on past experience; "proof" is quite another, because you're trying to prove a future outcome, which, of course, can't be done.

I can easily demonstrate that the long-term nominal return of stocks has been twice that of bonds, and that in real terms (net of inflation) it's closer to four times. At best, this is evidence.

But I certainly can't "prove" (nor would I ever try) that these relationships will continue to prevail. Hell, I can't "prove" that the sun's coming up tomorrow. You want me to "prove" that small-cap will keep providing a 20% premium return over big-cap between now and the time your kid starts college? Much less "prove" that mutual fund raindrop A will get to the bottom of the window before

170

mutual fund raindrop B between now and your retirement date? I'll pass, thanks.

Only the amateur in this business accepts the burden of "proof." The Excellent Investment Advisor accepts — at most — the burden of reasonable probability, based on common sense and the evidence (if any) at hand. *In that order.*

3. After I "prove" my contentions to my prospect/client, he will begin to trust me. Never happens, in my experience. The more strenuously you try to "prove" the future — which everyone knows is unprovable — the less people are inclined to trust you.

The converse is, quite wonderfully, also true. The *less* I try to prove ("This is the way the cycle has played out in the past, and the logic is that it will continue to do so in the long run, but in the end you've got to kind of trust my judgment"), the more people seem inclined to trust me, *not least of all because I don't give them any other choice.*

You can never educate your way to trust. It's a gift that has to be given out of faith, not out of knowledge. "Proof" and trust are oil and water. And all successful client relationships are based on trust. Remember that the next time you're tempted to whip out your optimization software.

Is it possible that, with all your intellectually powerful, data-driven arguments, you may be actively discouraging people from trusting you? I think it's more than possible. It's bloody likely. Because when someone says, "Prove it," in however many words, you have my permission to hear, "I don't trust you."

You can't blame people for this, but you mustn't enable them, either. And wrangling is simply a way of enabling people to continue to distrust you. As soon as you integrate that perception into your deepest beliefs, you will more or less instantly stop behaving inappropriately. And you'll start sounding something like this:

Prospect: Prove it.
EIA: Can't. Probably wouldn't if I could. (Silence.)

Prospect: Then I can't work with you.

EIA: Nor with any other advisor who tells the truth.

Prospect: Huh?

EIA: (Gently) What you seem to want — and it's only human, so don't worry about it — is high returns with a high degree of certainty. Now, it isn't just that I can't give you that combination. It's that no one can. It does not exist in nature, much as we both might wish it did.

Prospect: But ... what about ... I read somewhere ...

EIA: Let's do certainty first. I'm about to offer you as much certainty as has ever been offered to any investor on earth. Ready?

Prospect: Sure.

EIA: It's called a 30-year U.S. government bond. It is, without question, the most certain security ever crafted by the hand of man. It pays about 5.9%. After inflation and taxes, this is a return of about one-half of one percent. Now, that's not certain, but it's highly probable. So you'll get virtually no return, but you'll be certain to get your investment back. Of course, over 30 years, your capital will probably have lost about two-thirds of its purchasing power. That's the price of certainty. How many do you want?

Prospect: Ugh. None. What a disaster.

EIA: Correctamundo. Certainty will kill you every time. This is perhaps the single greatest truth of long-term investing.

Prospect: So ... what do you recommend?

EIA: Same thing I've been recommending all along: *prudent, controlled exposure to higher levels of uncertainty.* I recommend ambiguity.

Prospect: Is that on NASDAQ?

EIA: It's not a security; it's a concept. The more ambiguity you can tolerate, the greater the returns in the long run — which is what you and your family are investing for. Anyone who comes to you and says, "I can get you high returns and certainty" is lying. So your choice is my uncertainty or some other advisor's uncertainty.

Prospect: And of course you think I should hire you.

EIA: The absolute truth is that I want you to hire the advisor you trust the most. I don't want a client who doesn't trust me implicitly, and I don't want you to have an advisor you can't totally believe in. I want the right thing to happen for you and your family.

Prospect: Well, okay, I suppose we ought to give each other a try.

I think you see that you engender trust precisely by selling against "proof" and against certainty. That is, "The proof that my approach has the potential for very attractive long-term returns is implicit in the fact that *I can't prove it.*"

If you want certainty on the front end of your investing program, you will get terrible insecurity on the back end. Conversely, the more uncertainty you can accept on the front end, the greater the long-term opportunities for financial independence for you and wealth for your heirs.

Prospect: But how can you be sure this is the right time to invest?
EIA: There you go again.
Prospect: Now what?
EIA: I can't be certain. This is a great long-term portfolio, and *therefore* it offers no near-term certainty. And, of course, in the long run it's always the right time to invest. It's kind of like life: As you get older, you don't regret what you did; you regret the things you didn't do — because you weren't sure the time was right.
Prospect: So for you, the fact that you can't be sure is a good thing?
EIA: Exactly.
Prospect: This is probably a bad sign, but I'm starting to think you must be right.

Now, I'll be the first to admit that today's problem is less a reluctance to invest than a reckless eagerness to do so. People are currently inclined to unconsciously accept far more uncertainty than they realize; such is the nature of the epic investor complacency ("buy the dips") *du jour.*

Thus, the problem today's advisor faces is a demand for a different kind of certainty, but one that is equally unavailable.

Prospect: Prove to me that your mutual fund portfolio will "outperform."
EIA: Can't. Nobody can. Doesn't matter.
Prospect: But I read in *Money* magazine ...
EIA: Yes?
Prospect: They picked the "ultimate" six great funds ...

EIA: Based on what they've done in the past?
Prospect: Sure.
EIA: What period of time?
Prospect: I dunno ... three years, I think.
EIA: How old are you again?
Prospect: Fifty-one.
EIA: So your investing time horizon is maybe 30 years, and your heirs' is, say, 30 years beyond that. Let me ask *you* a question: What do you think "performance" over the past three years — the three best years in the history of American stocks, by the way — proves?
Prospect: Uh ... nothing?
EIA: Bingo.
Prospect: Then how do you pick funds?
EIA: As a professional advisor, I (and my firm) use two criteria. The first is appropriateness: Are these funds truly a fit with your long-term financial goals? (As opposed to: Are they "hot" in today's market?) Second is relationship: Do my firm and I have a personal relationship with the fund managers, and do we personally believe them worthy to be stewards of our clients' most serious money? The first criterion lets out the huge preponderance of funds; the second lets out nearly everybody else. We build long-term wealth for our clients on the few who pass both tests. And we say you're going to reach your goals, which very few Americans ever do ... as opposed to saying what nobody can prove: that you'll "outperform" everyone on your block.
Prospect: Well, it's reaching my goals that I'm really concerned about... .
EIA: Right again.

The Excellent Investment Advisor knows (and never stops preaching) that real investment success comes only to those courageous enough to embrace high levels of uncertainty. "Proof" is the opposite of courage, and the EIA will have no truck with it.

Because, hey: We can't "prove" the sun's coming up tomorrow.

THE FIVE-MINUTE "RISK" SEMINAR

"Risk" is one of those words ("safety" is the other) that mean a thousand different things to as many people. When it shows up in a conversation between an advisor and his prospect/client, therefore, it maximizes the probability of a communications breakdown.

Some time ago, I consulted for a bank investment program that was struggling with this very issue. Its Depression-scarred, principal-obsessed, current-yield-driven client base was all too willing to foray into equities when they were soaring. But when the stock market backed up, the bank's investment reps came under tremendous pressure from clients about the "risky" nature of equities.

The reps waved their obligatory Ibbotson charts, and chanted their mantra ("long term, long term ..."), but to little or no avail. How, they asked, would I illustrate the curative power of time on the "risk" of equities?

I replied, as politely as I could, that they were framing the debate in the wrong terms. It isn't just that "risk" declines over time, I said. It's that *the very nature of "risk" changes with the passing of the years* — that the obvious "risk" goes away and is replaced with a different and even more implacable "risk."

I illustrated this phenomenon on a sheet of paper, as follows. (When I finished, the bank sales executives grabbed the paper and ran straight to their compliance cops to see how they could get it approved for distribution. I have not heard from them since, and can only assume that, in the ensuing firefight, they were all killed.)

First, I said, draw a simple graph; make the perpendicular axis *RISK* and the parallel axis *TIME*, thus:

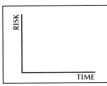

Then start by graphing the progress of the obvious "risk," which is principal loss. I think we would all agree that over very short periods of time the principal risk of equities is astronomical. Why, one day not so long ago the American stock market lost 23% of its value between sunup and sunset. And that was an *average.* So we're talking huge short-term risk.

As I say this, I make a big dot on the chart, as follows. You see that, because it's very low on the *TIME* axis, the dot is very high on the *RISK* axis.

But almost immediately a funny thing happens. With the passage of time, the risk of holding equities declines, quite literally to zero. Indeed, there is no 15-year period in history in which stocks (with dividends reinvested) have produced a negative return.

Now, there's nothing sacred about 15 years (any more than your potential short-term loss is limited to 23% — or any other number). So the graph is illustrating a concept (indeed, as you'll see, two concepts); it's not predicting or calibrating the future.

The concept is simply that, over some period of time, the risk of holding equities falls all the way to zero ... and stops there, because it can't go any lower. (This last point may seem so obvious that it needn't be mentioned, but it's about to become very important. Just watch.)

I illustrate the decline of principal risk to zero as follows, and then label the resulting bar:

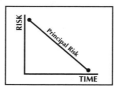

Now, I say, let's look at the *other* risk of your economic life — the risk that does *not* decline but only keeps rising, without limit, for as long as you live (and then goes on rising throughout the lives of your heirs). That is the risk of the loss of your purchasing power — the risk that your cost of living will outrun your income.

In the short run, purchasing power risk is exactly the opposite of principal risk, in this sense: While short-term principal risk is astronomical, short-term risk of purchasing power is virtually nonexistent.

What is the chance that you'll walk into the supermarket tomorrow and find that a diversified basket of your household needs is markedly more expensive than it was today? I would say that risk is close to zero. So let's start graphing this risk literally at zero, by putting our starting dot right where the axes meet:

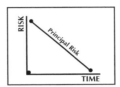

Here, though, we find that with each passing day the risk of losing our purchasing power — through the slow, steady increase in the prices of nearly all the goods and services we consume — *rises* over time. But unlike principal loss risk, *it has no finite limit*, other than the days allotted to us and to the loved ones who will survive us.

(Let me just stop here and acknowledge with the appropriate disdain the currently fashionable, essentially journalistic notion of deflation. The time to start talking about this was 17 years ago, when disinflation though not deflation started. Now that it's virtually run its course — anybody watching labor costs? — it's all the rage. Give me a break. When the U.S. Postal Service lowers the price of a first-class stamp, then I'll allow you to say the "D" word to me. Until then, you do so at your own risk.)

So when we graph the progress of purchasing power risk — which is the last step in this visual presentation — our chart ends up looking like this:

Forgive me; I just couldn't resist putting the infinity sign up there. (Maybe *that's* what got all the bank guys killed.)

The concept, then, is not simply one of the declining level of principal risk over time — an intellectual fact that rarely vanquishes the emotional experience of watching one's NAV going into a power dive.

Rather, this back-of-an-envelope seminar is intended to show the *mutation* of risk — from something that starts out very scary and then weakens and dies, into something that starts at zero and then can't be stopped, growing limitlessly more malignant with the years.

High "risk" today, security and serenity in the long run. Low "risk" today, devastation and destitution in the long run. That's the choice ... as opposed to the illusion that you can choose "safety" over "risk."

Friends and colleagues, I wish there were someone else here to tell you this, but since there isn't, I've got to go ahead and say it. If you walk in to see a risk-averse prospect with every chart, graph, and scattergram known to man, and then I go in carrying only a piece of scrap paper and a No. 2 pencil with which to draw this diagram — I'm going home with the bacon. (No brag, just fact.)

There are some things, as I suggested in last month's column ("What Are You Trying To Prove?", March 1998), that are so self-evident that you actually hurt yourself when you try to "prove" them. What does my little conceptual risk graph "prove"? Why, nothing, of course. It just says what reasonable people already know in their hearts, but of which they sometimes need a gentle reminder from someone who really cares about 'em: **There's no such thing as no risk.**

There's only the risk you accept today (because you can control it), so that you're not devoured by the risk that nobody can control tomorrow, and tomorrow, and tomorrow ... .

Clip the completed graph out, and keep it in your wallet. You may not have a lot of use for it while the market keeps making new highs. But when stocks head south for a while, you may find that it's a lifesaver.

And the life it saves just may be your own.

NEVER
FLY
COACH

The thing about flying to New York from Minneapolis on a week-day evening is simply this: If you want to go non-stop, you fly at 6:05 p.m. or not until 9:50. During the intervening four prime business travel hours, there's nothing.

This is because Minneapolis is a hub of, and in a stranglehold by, Northwest Airlines (currently forming a strategic alliance with Continental, to create an entity that may finally wrest from Russia's Aeroflot the title of World's Worst Major Airline).

So, on a recent day trip to Minneapolis, I was given the choice of flying coach at 6:05 or first class at 9:50. Now, for reasons that will shortly become clear, I never fly coach. I'll go business class where it's available, and first when it's not. I do this on my own nickel because I still don't have the face to ask my (non-West Coast) clients to pay the bump. I'm just funny that way.

But to stand on ceremony for three hours and 45 minutes in the Minneapolis airport seemed a bit much. After all, I reasoned, if I take the 6:05, I'll be back in New York before the later flight even takes off. Just this once, I'll go coach.

Big mistake. Never mind all the gory details; suffice it to say that coach was even more an assault on the sensibilities than I remembered it. The guy about my age in the middle seat next to me, victimizing the twentysomething woman pinned to the window with the details of his twentysomething daughters' checkered romantic lives ... the dinner service (a choice between "meat loaf" and "meat loaf") ... the flight attendant telling me to bring my broken seat forward every 20 minutes ... God, it was awful.

But at least this experience gave me an opportunity to renew my vow: *Never fly coach.* It also gave me ample time to reflect on how

I had come to make that vow. Herewith, I pass those reflections on to other seekers of excellence — which is what these columns (and, I hope, all my work) are about.

Aristotle tells us that excellence is not a state of being but a habit — a constant way of behaving, as distinctly opposed to a way of thinking. This distinction is critical in that I believe many of us *think* like potentially Excellent Investment Advisors, but then compromise in our behavior. We put up with any number of petty indignities in our daily lives, thinking that when we get to our goals we will be able to afford to root out these indignities.

In my experience, this never works. The unconscious mind will, I believe, release limitless reserves of energy to us *if we present it with a clear, non-conflicted demand.* However, if we think about excellence but compromise like mediocrities, the unconscious receives a mixed message — and responds with similarly conflicted results.

You will never get to be an EIA "someday" by behaving like a mediocrity today. And today is the only thing you've got. Yesterday is long gone, and tomorrow never gets here. Put another way, today is the tomorrow that you swore was going to be different ... yesterday.

I don't really have any capacity meaningfully to augment the amount of assets I'm gathering, or new business I'm doing, today. (Those things were determined by the level of prospecting I did — or didn't do — six months to a year ago.) But I can instantly change the quality of my behavior, not just in terms of the actions I take, but also in the compromises I elect no longer to accept.

"Start where you stand." "Act as if ... ." "Fake it 'til you make it." All these slogans are expressive of one fundamental concept: *It changes when you change.* And you can only change (therefore you must change) now. Mediocre behavior is a predictor of nothing more or less than continued mediocre behavior. Excellence predicts — and begets — excellence. What would you change if you were suddenly an EIA? *Change it now,* and you will become one.

180

At a point in my career when I was still working for a large investment banking/brokerage house, I craved a certain corporate title. (Such was the poverty of my ambition at the time ... but I digress.) If I were suddenly to attain that exalted rank, I asked myself, what would I change in my life?

The answer was immediately obvious. Having commuted to high school, to college, and then to Wall Street by subway for over 30 years, I'd never take the subway to or from work again. Okay, I said, it's time to "act as if ... ." I grabbed the phone, called the car service my firm used, and arranged to be chauffeur-driven from then on. (Yes, I got the title, and yes, it was meaningless. But there was only one way for me to find that out.)

When I began to do a lot of speaking around the country, I started flying coach. It quickly became obvious to me that coach is the IRT Lexington Avenue subway of the air — and it's always rush hour. I just couldn't reconcile *(for me)* excellence and sitting in the back of the bus. Hence: Never fly coach.

Next, I'd often find that the places I was speaking were remote from the airports. Then I'd rent a car — and get lost and/or exhausted driving (usually at night) on unfamiliar roads to destinations I didn't know. So I 86'd Hertz; if the client won't send a car for me, I'm not going. (It's never been a problem.) Same with driving myself the 100 miles between my home and the New York airports. I get a ton of work done in the back seat of those cars, and also stack a lot of well-deserved Zs on the way home.

What small (and maybe not-so-small) indignities do you put up with in the name of economy, and is it possible that they are actually false economies? That is, might the energy and self-esteem you give up be worth more than the money these indignities allegedly save you? What is your time worth? What is your dignity worth? *Who are you, and what do you want?*

Let me ask you a few questions that may help you begin focusing on things that drain your energy and might be (relatively) easily replaced with energy-accreting behaviors.

1. What's the most annoying piece of machinery in your life?
Upgrade or replace it *at once.* If you're Mr./Ms. Handyperson, this
question may seem strange to you. But for the rest of us humans,
there's often a clunker car/loud refrigerator/fuzzy TV/quitter
lawnmower that drives us nuts. Get it fixed or replace it ere Apollo's
chariot transits the heavens one more time (English translation: by
tomorrow night). Then ask: What's my next most annoying inani-
mate object? Fix it/replace it next month. Do this 12 times, and see
how much better you feel about yourself.

2. What's the garment you wear to work that you like least?
Replace it today. Then do the same thing 11 more times, at 30-day
intervals.

**3. What's the one aspect of our business you feel you most
need to know more about?** Buy (do not go to the library and borrow)
a book about it. Get up an hour earlier every day, and read this book
till you're done. Then do it again. And again ...

Asset allocation? Why don't you read — I mean *really* read —
Jeremy Siegel's *Stocks for the Long Run?* (You may be surprised at
how little you actually need to know about asset allocation.) Bear
markets? Try Charles Kindleberger's *Manias, Panics and Crashes.*
NAFTA, GATT, free trade, protectionism, stuff like that? *How Nations Grow Rich: The Case for Free Trade* by Melvyn Krauss. Everything you could possibly want to know about the economic realities
(as opposed to the myths) of trade in 120 pages of text. Are you a
manager of people, particularly salespeople? *Organizing Genius,* by
Warren Bennis, will give you priceless ideas on making teams out of
very bright, very independent, not-too-stable individuals. (Read this
even if you're not a manager; you'll find useful insights into your
own psychology.)

Unless you are a turnip, you'll mine a minimum of one heart-
stopping, mind-blowing insight out of each of these books. Reading
them (magnified by the discipline of getting up early to read them)
will be a huge jolt to your self-esteem, and to the way you see yourself as a professional.

4. Do you have a comprehensive, written financial and estate plan? If not, you're like the shoemaker whose children go barefoot. How can you preach a discipline you yourself won't practice? How can you sell what you don't own? Get going on a plan today, and get your whole family involved. You will be amazed at the reserves of energy and self-esteem that this will release.

5. Do you have one account whose very essence curdles your blood and corrodes your soul? Fire him or her. (The bigger the account, the more vital to your self-regard this tactic is. You will never achieve excellence selling your dignity for 30 pieces of silver.)

By 10 a.m. tomorrow, fax and overnight this letter: "I'm considering some major changes in my business and my life. In reviewing our relationship over the past couple of years, I've concluded that I will never be able to serve you in the way you seem to need. It doesn't seem fair for me to keep your account on that basis, and so I am resigning it. I've asked my manager to help you find an advisor whose talents are better suited to your needs than mine are. I thank you for all your past business, and wish you every future success."

Then you only have to do (or actually not do) one more thing: Don't take this passive/aggressive scorpion's call — a call which (a) I promise you is coming, and in which (b) he/she will try to win you back with extravagant pledges of a clean slate. This is the scorpion trying to buy time to figure out how to sue you.

Every six months, do this again.

6. Want to lose at least half of your smallest but most vexing administrative problems, particularly around tax time? Lose the bottom third of your account book, which (a) produces way less than a third of your income, (b) produces way more than a third of your mosquito-bite-type paper problems, (c) doesn't have any money, (d) doesn't particularly like you, and (e) all of the above.

Why do you keep the bottom third of your book? Easy: You're trying to win the lottery. Stop it. You don't win the lottery. But poor people keep playing it because (I assume) they don't know how to prospect.

Do you know how to prospect? I thought so. Do it. And stop behaving like a poor people. Remember Murray's Third Law of Metamorphosis, which states that a caterpillar can become a butterfly, but a poor people can never become an EIA.

7. Do you know what each of your kids is most interested in? If not, why not? If so, do you have a minimum of one hour per week per kid to devote to that thing each cares so much about? (Hint: There's only one right answer to this question.)

Or: Take each kid to a museum for just one hour. They have fifteen minutes to pick out the painting/sculpture/dinosaur they dig the most. Then you spend the other 45 minutes finding out all you can about that work of art/artist/critter. Then: Mickey D's. If this doesn't oxygenate your soul, you ain't got one. Sorry. The point here, of course, is that you're never going to become an EIA by compromising your family. So look for creative ways to gin up some high-quality time in relatively short bursts.

8. Did you wake up this morning (a) not dead and (b) able to do for Americans what they can't do for themselves, i.e., to secure for them true, lasting financial independence? That's a miracle. In point of actual fact, it's a couple of miracles. And as Einstein said, "There are only two ways to live your life. One is as if everything is a miracle, and the other is as if nothing is."

Remember, before you get swamped by all today's busy business, to be grateful for (at the very least) these two miracles. Who or what you're grateful to is entirely up to you.

But let me assure you, pretty much as an article of faith: The first requirement to becoming an EIA is being grateful for the opportunity to become an EIA. Trust me on this. And never fly coach.

WHY I'M PRAYING FOR A BEAR MARKET

"Every second counts." That sentence about sums up our society's passage from late bull-market investment mania to full-blown overtrading psychosis.

And no, it's not the come-on of some fly-by-night market timing service or commodities infomercial.

It's the headline of an ad for the Chicago Board of Trade's new futures/options contracts on the Dow Jones Industrial Average. Using these tools, the ad says, "You can react to market-moving events the minute they occur." (Knee-jerk reaction as investment philosophy: sure sounds like a winner to me.) And to reinforce this point, if you call for the CBOT's new trading kit, they'll send you a free "limited edition" stopwatch. Yes, a *stopwatch.* So you can, in the words of the ad, "trade what you know ... the Dow." And we all know how good most folks are at calling short-term zigs and zags in the Dow, now don't we?

"Big news can mean big opportunity," says another ad for an online trading service; "points can be made *in a heartbeat*" (italics admittedly mine). And *anything* online is, of course, the tulip *du jour.* America Online sells for 200 times trailing earnings, making it a big blue chip compared to Amazon.com, a company with a market cap around $6 billion with no earnings in a business with no barriers to entry.

K-tel International merely announces that it's going to start selling compilations of yesteryear's hit tunes online, and the stock sextuples.

(The business logic here is really a hoot: People who loved 1950s rock 'n' roll when they were in their teens, and who now — in their 50s — make up a disproportionately large population of the computer-illiterate, are going to flock to buy Dion and the Belmonts off the Web.)

Is anyone but me old enough to remember 1968, when stocks would double just because they announced that they were going into the computer-leasing business? Doesn't anybody read *The Money Game* anymore?

Margin debt is at a record 1.7% of gross domestic product, four times what it was in 1991. And Gail Dudack of UBS Securities calculates that *all* personal savings for the six months through April went into stock mutual funds.

And in May, I listened in horror as a portfolio manager from a major fund company told an audience of brokers (a) "Who am I to say that Coca-Cola can't sell for 100 times earnings?" and (b) "No corporate MIS manager can get fired for buying Cisco Systems equipment." (In 1972, when this guy was probably still in sixth grade, that's exactly what people said about IBM ... at 60 times earnings.)

This has all got to end. At this point, it almost certainly has to end badly. And we'd all be better off, believe it or not, if it ended sooner rather than later. That's why I'm praying for a bear market.

I don't think it's going to be enough for the market to settle down into a trendless trading range, or some other gently corrective scenario that — under more normal circumstances — might let all the bad air out slowly. Trendlessness would just provoke a panic in needle park: All the action junkies would get even more desperate for a fix, and nobody would really get cured.

No, we professionals need an old-fashioned bear: a decline of at least 20% that takes the better part of a year to go from peak to trough, and that long again to recover — so that "performance" numbers have minus signs in front of them for a good long time.

Are we going to be lucky enough to get such a market anytime soon? Probably not, but there's always hope. So while we wait in hopeful anticipation, let me share with you the reasons why I love the bear:

(1) Who the hell needs me in a bull market? How do I add value when investors can throw darts and make 30% a year, year after year after year? If a guy can pick a mutual fund that's done 60% in the past 12 months, do I win his trust by recommending something that did 70%? ("You should buy drugs from me rather than another drug dealer because mine will make you higher.") Professionals love to be leaders, and indeed are most useful and effective leading (as opposed to managing) their clients. How do you lead people when they don't even see why they need you?

But in a bear market, people really feel the need for help and good counsel, and we get to exhibit the leadership characteristics — chief among which are courage and faith in the future — that distinguish the real professionals in this business.

I hate being a wet blanket, which is what you almost have to be at a time like this. I like rallying the troops and leading the charge, and you only get to do that when the going is hard.

(2) I'm not finished buying yet, and neither is anyone else I know. In the Berkshire Hathaway annual report, Warren Buffett says, "Even though they are going to be net buyers of stocks for many years to come, (many investors) are elated when stock prices rise and depressed when they fall ... This reaction makes no sense. Only those who will be sellers in the near future should be happy at seeing stocks rise. Prospective purchasers should much prefer sinking prices."

They should, and I do. And since I'm dollar-cost-averaging, my enthusiasm for declining prices goes double, because my same dollar investment buys me that many more shares.

(3) I love big sales. I don't generally go to the manager of a supermarket and ask for a list of the priciest, most-marked-up stuff he's got. I pick up the sale circular and look for the big markdowns.

I like to buy higher investment values and higher yields, which means I like to pay lower prices. When tuna fish goes from a dollar a can to three for a buck, I buy more. I do not, among other things, try to sell the tuna I bought last week for a dollar back to the supermarket.

Let traders look for momentum. I'm an investor, and I look for value. Momentum comes from a perception of perfection. ("Maybe Coca-Cola *should* sell for 100 times earnings, it's so great.") Value is born out of problems. The greatest values are born out of chaos. Bring on the chaos. Bear markets are periods during which stocks are returned to their rightful owners. Like me.

(4) Bear markets expose the no-help lie for what it is. Bull markets induce people to think they can do it themselves; that's a mistake, because they can't (especially since they don't really know what "it" is). No-help funds, aided and abetted by most financial journalism, confirm to people that they can do it themselves: This is a lie, and lying is evil.

A bear market reminds investors (or, in this case, will teach a whole new generation of investors) that the critical variable isn't what you pay or don't pay, but rather the advice that you get or don't get. It is irrational for investment professionals not to want investors to realize this. So if a bear market is the only thing that can convince people of the primacy of advice, we professionals say: Bring it on.

(5) Only a bear market is going to restore realistic investor expectations. Today's neophyte equity fund investors don't think 10% is an average, they think it's a floor. The balance and caution that mark the perspective of an investment professional are everywhere trivialized by the power of this greatest of all bull markets.

That's just not healthy. The returns of equities are the reward for one's willingness and ability to withstand equity volatility. This point is utterly lost in America, and only a major dose of negative returns can bring it back. When investment advisors are getting fired for holding 5% cash, the system is so sick that it will only respond to shock therapy.

(6) It's time to bring down the curtain on amateur night. Sad but true: The quality of the retail financial services profession varies inversely with the level and trend of the market. So eight years (or 16 years, depending on how you're counting) into history's greatest bull market, the business has become The Mother of All Amateur Nights. Like the WPA or the 1962 Mets, we've turned into the employer of last resort.

188

A bear market will solve this problem nicely. Four years ago ("Hallelujah! A Lousy Market!", May 1994), when amateurs who'd never seen a bear market thought we were having a bear market, I wrote: "In markets like this, the amateur obsesses about how upset his clients are, and freezes up. The professional focuses on how up-set *everybody else's clients are,* and goes after them like there's no tomorrow."

It isn't just stocks that return to their rightful owners in a bear market; it's accounts, as well. When the amateur does his deer-in-the-headlights routine, the professional riding to the rescue seems like even more of a godsend. And she is.

(7) Accounts you gain in bear markets, like friendships formed in combat, often last a lifetime. When you carry a wounded client off the battlefield, after his "new era" advisor went back to working at Starbuck's, you'll very probably be his hero. And you'll get to reposition his account at or near panic lows. Of such experiences are great relationships (and major referral mills) made.

(8) Finally, bear markets enable you to put the focus back where it belongs: not on markets, but on life. Investing for the Great Goals of Life — as distinctly opposed to trading for points that "can be made in a heartbeat" — is what our calling is about. After years of ingesting larger and larger hits of the white powder of "per-formance," many investors have lost sight of this. So, if you'll pardon a mixed animal metaphor, the bear becomes their cold turkey.

"Performance" isn't a goal. It's just a way of keeping score when you've forgotten — or never knew — what game you're supposed to be playing: the game of life. The game of a long, worry-free retire-ment followed by meaningful legacies to the people you love.

If your retirement date is your 65th birthday, it'll be here on the same day whether the next 20% move in the market is up or down. If your granddaughter is two years old, she'll start college in 2014 whether growth outperforms value over the next 12 months or vice versa, and whether or not Coca-Cola ever sells for 100 times earnings, God forbid.

Investing (a) is very different from trading and (b) is a means to an end, not an end in itself. At this point, it's going to take a bear market to restore that perspective. And then we'll once again be faced with the task of keeping people fully invested through that temporary decline, so they can be fully invested when the permanent advance resumes.

That'll present us with a different set of challenges. But anything's better than this.

YOUR DEEDS ARE YOUR DESTINY

In our profession, we tend to see ourselves as being acted upon by any number of very powerful external circumstances, which are neither of our making nor within our control.

It is one thing to hope that these circumstances will, on balance, continue to be favorable — as they have so signally been since the stock market blasted off in August 1982, when it first decisively surmounted Dow 1000.

But it's something else entirely to *rely* upon a favorable confluence of circumstances, much less to hope that we can achieve lasting excellence because of the economic/market environment as opposed to our own exertion. *Hoping* for a continuation of good times is, as I've said before in this space, only human; *needing* it is among the greatest mistakes we could be making right now.

Moreover, the stuff of which lasting excellence is made is not usually a product of good times, easy money, or huge upsurges in investor enthusiasm. Rather, the qualities that give rise to excellence are most often formed and tested in periods of great adversity. But even if we aren't treated to such a period anytime soon, there's nothing to stop us from currying the iron self-reliance (the inner — as opposed to other — directedness) that is a pre-condition of true and lasting excellence.

Over three decades in this business, I hope I've progressed from a callow stock jockey hoping for "the breaks" (which, when you most need them, you can't even buy) to someone who truly feels that if I don't make my own breaks, I don't deserve to get any. Today, my belief/behavior system rests on four unshakable pillars, which support it — and me — regardless of "circumstances."

191

1. "You play basketball against yourself. Your opponent is your own potential." The legendary basketball coach Bob Knight of Indiana said this to the sportswriter John Feinstein in the best-selling book *A Season on the Brink*. I remember being astonished at it when I read it, because it seemed at first blush to be so deeply counterintuitive.

Yes, I'm playing my heart out, I thought. But look at all the other people who affect the outcome of the game. There are my four teammates on the floor with me; there are the five players on the other team. Our bench, their bench; our coach, their coach. And the refs — who knows what controlled substance they ingested before the game, making them not see fouls they don't, and hallucinate the fouls they think they see?

That seemed to me very analogous to our professional situation: yes, I'm doing everything I can, but there's my broker/dealer, my in-house fund managers, my branch manager, my compliance cops, The Market (whatever that is), my clients and prospects... . Look how much the outcome of the game is affected by them.

But then I began to realize what Coach Knight must have meant. Regardless of the other factors affecting the game, the only thing I can control — and the thing that will ultimately help my team the most — is for me to play up to my potential.

Closing the (often enormous) gap between our performance to date and our potential is (a) within our control and (b) something no circumstances can prevent us from doing. I have no capacity to change outcomes, but almost limitless capacity to change myself. So let me work on changing myself — specifically, by striving to reach my potential. If I *can* do better, I *must* do better. *That's my responsibility.*

2. All my professional limitations are self-imposed. One of the things we initially find so attractive about this business is that there's no income limit. Indeed, everything and everyone around us conspire to help us prosper, because we're the producers, and everyone else feeds off us.

No one is better served if our income tops out — if we hit a plateau, or get stuck in a rut, or simply run out of time or energy. So no one is trying to make any of those things happen to us — except possibly us.

If we're honest with ourselves, then, we have to admit that any professional limitations which have been imposed *on* us have been imposed *by* us. And if we've built an imaginary ceiling over our heads, as I suggested some months ago ("The Ceiling That Isn't There," July 1997), only we can dismantle it.

This is certainly not to suggest that everyone's working environment is perfectly supportive, nor that excellence can be achieved easily. It is simply saying that there are no systemic, externally imposed limits. Satchel Paige asked, "How old would you be if you didn't know how old you was?" Similarly, I ask, "How much would you earn if you didn't know how much the top person in your office — or even your firm — earns?"

What hinders me, other than myself? If the answer is "nothing," as it surely is, then the removal of all hindrances is *entirely my responsibility.*

Which brings me to the third pillar of my belief/behavior system. It's changed a lot over the years, but here's how it started:

3. If I can own the problem, I can own the solution. Although the honesty required for me to accept the first two pillars did not (and still does not) come easily, when it comes it's very liberating.

If I've signed up to play the game of my performance vs. my potential, and if I accept that the limitations I'm encountering are self-imposed, I can take title to my problems ... which means I can also take title to the possible solutions. (If my problems are caused by something or someone else, they are only soluble by ... something or someone else. That ain't good.)

So I begin by formulating the principle, "If I can own the problem, I can own the solution." That works OK for a while, until I get a

THE CRAFT OF ADVICE

little more honest with myself, whereupon I see that it's still a cop-out. (Maybe not as egregious a cop-out as "It's somebody else's fault," but a cop-out nonetheless.)

And then, kicking and screaming and fighting it every inch of the way, I have to get even more honest with myself. I have to admit that "owning" the problem isn't enough. Because, you see, my problem isn't really my problem. Invariably, it's *my reaction* to the perceived problem that's the real problem.

Do I not have enough prospects? Well, I can "own" that problem 'til the cows come home but it's not going to get solved ... because it's not really the problem. The problem is that, having gotten hypersensitive to hearing "no," and having become depressed about how poorly my prospecting efforts have been paying off, I've let my prospecting activity tail off. Thus, the problem isn't "no," it's my totally optional (albeit unconscious, at the moment) *reaction* to "no." I don't own this problem; *I am this problem.*

Is my manager a passive-aggressive, transaction-oriented troglodyte, always beating up on me to do more syndicate business? Not my problem. My bottled-up anger, and the way it's poisoning my client/prospect interactions, is my problem. *I am my problem.*

Do I have a very large but cold and critical client, and does my frustration at his callousness drain my energy? He's not my problem, I'm my problem. Why do I keep this client? Why do I tolerate, accept — and thereby invite more — abuse? He is not the problem; this is not the problem; *I am the problem.*

And so, finally, you see what the last iteration of this third pillar must be ... and is: *I am the problem. I am the solution.* And the fourth and final pillar:

4. "All chronic production issues are behavior issues." I spent a long life-changing day in 1983 with the sales psychologist Aaron Hemsley. Of all the great things he said that day, this was, for me, the key to everything.

Why do I plateau? Why do I permit jerks in my professional life, then build up anger and frustration at the jerks, and then take out those negative emotions on everybody but the jerks? Why do I fear "no," when I know that risking it is the only way in the world I'll ever get to hear "yes"? Why ask why?

In pillar #4, Hemsley gave me (and I hereby bequeath to you) permission to stop worrying about "Why?" He said, in effect, "You behaved your way into whatever box you're in. You can behave your way back out again."

The great Zen mystic Lawrence Peter Berra said, "How can you think and hit at the same time?" I'm not sure I know what that means, but I know that I can't worry about "Why?" and do anything productive at the same time. And I certainly don't have a guarantee (or any particular reason to believe) that if I suddenly figured out "Why?" anything would change.

My professional life is the sum of my behaviors. If I'm not totally satisfied with my professional life, (1) I've identified a gap between my performance and my potential; (2) the gap is self-imposed; (3) I am the problem and I am the solution; and last but not least (4) when (but only when) I modify my behavior, the gap will go away.

I behaved my way into this mess. Let me now (a) stop asking "Why?" (b) stop beating myself up (responsibility is productive, but blame is destructive), (c) observe the inappropriate behavior, and (d) slowly, systematically, with a lot of self-administered "attaboys," habituate myself to healthier, more appropriate behaviors. This is not about what I think. Still less is it about what I know. It's all about what I *do.*

"Decide to construct your character through excellent actions," Epictetus tells us, "and determine to pay the price of a worthy goal."

I'm determined to pay that price. Not that I have a choice, because this business is the most just employer on earth — you get out of it exactly what you put into it — so I know that an excellent outcome is wholly dependent on habitually excellent inputs.

And by basing my habitual behavior on the four pillars — on, as I hope you've seen, a code of total personal responsibility — I insure that I'll get the outcome I want, *eventually.* "It does not matter how slowly you go," Confucius assures us, "so long as you do not stop."

Don't stop. Don't waste time and energy *thinking* about excellence; it doesn't get you anywhere. Accept total responsibility. Habituate yourself to excellence, however long it takes. Your deeds are your destiny. *You are what you do.*

THE TOXIC ILLUSION OF TECHNOLOGY

"Computers are useless," scoffed Pablo Picasso many years ago in the mainframe era. "They only give you answers."

How far we've come since those early days. Today, each of us has on his or her desk more computing power than existed in the world in 1950. And all those computers apparently think that the day after December 31, 1999 is January 1, 1900. How I wish Picasso had lived to learn this. He'd have died laughing.

But this is to trivialize Picasso's point, which is an excellent one. To wit, that computing answers is infinitely less important than asking the right — indeed the essential — questions. A machine can (and should) do the former, but the latter can only be done by thinking human beings.

Moreover, since in our industry we counsel individuals and families who don't think about money so much as *feel* about it, even the process of critical thought becomes secondary to our ability to empathize with very non-linear emotions. And if thought is beyond computers, how much further above their capacity must feeling be?

Thus we must ask, with Picasso: What are you trying to get technology to do for you and your clients? And is there any reason on earth to believe it can do those things? And if there isn't, might you be using the computer to hide from the cruel necessity of dealing with the murky financial emotions of real people? *What are you trying to prove?*

I freely grant that the following observations are those of a computer-illiterate technophobe. (Not a Luddite, mind you. The Unabomber is a Luddite. I don't want to blow technology up; I just don't want it encroaching on my profession, which is — I sincerely hope — wisdom.) That doesn't make me wrong. Indeed, as some one literally unable to hear technology's siren song, I may be able to help those of you who have sailed too close to that fatal shore.

1. There is no system. If there were any usefully predictive pattern to investing, given all the computing power that's been brought to bear on markets over the past 50 years, someone — or, more properly, someone's computer — would have spotted it long since. And that person would not have packaged the system into a software program you can buy for $69.95. He or she would have gone into a little room with the computer and a phone, and proceeded to clean out everyone else in the game. That this has not happened demonstrates to me that it can't happen. The system is: There is no system. *Successful investing quite literally does not compute.*

2. Successful investing is a function of temperament rather than of intellect. This is actually true of the whole of life, not just investing. Oliver Wendell Holmes famously observed of Franklin Roosevelt that he had a second-rate intellect but a first-class temperament. Surely it was that temperament and not his intellect that made FDR the greatest president of this century.

This is not a game, as Warren Buffett has said, where the guy with the 160 IQ beats the guy with 130. Patience and discipline, based on an unshakable faith in the future, are the hallmarks of the successful investor, but these are all temperamental rather than intellectual attributes.

Data may support the conclusion that faith in the future has always been warranted. But data alone cannot infuse someone with faith in the future. Put the other way, nothing that comes out of a computer can vanquish fear of the future. Only human leadership can do that. Computers may inform, but only you and I can (and therefore must) lead.

3. Data help you win arguments. Unfortunately, arguments are inherently unwinnable. Any time that I refer in these columns to some third-party study that supports my (and many readers') beliefs, I get besieged for copies.

THE TOXIC ILLUSION OF TECHNOLOGY

But when people in our industry rely on data to try to "prove" some point, it's invariably because they've already made that point conceptually to a prospect or a customer, and had it rejected.

(This experience, by definition, only takes place when your interlocutor is a prospect or a customer, never a client. A client accepts what you say because you said it — which is, of course, the whole point.)

Rejection of your word or your worldview is not a signal to go get more data. It's a signal to disqualify the prospect or customer you're talking to. Arguments about investing, like arguments about religion and politics, are unwinnable.

If the whole investment advisory profession woke up one day saying, mantra-like, "The decisive reason to buy the mutual funds I recommend to you is simply that I recommend them to you," (a) what a wonderful world this would be, and (b) Morningstar would have to lay off half its staff by nightfall. The demand for the illusion of third-party "proof" would simply evaporate.

There's only one mutual fund (or any managed money) presentation that makes any sense to me, and it is the only one I use. In essence, it says: "(1) I know my money managers — know 'em personally as well as professionally; (2) I know you and your family; (3) the styles, character, and disciplines of the managers I've selected fit just about perfectly with your goals and temperament; (4) I hope to have you and your managers meet at some point, because I think you'd really enjoy each other; (5) any questions?"

It isn't just that I can't do much more than this; it's that I refuse to try. Pouring data on doubt is like pouring gasoline on fire.

4. No matter how sophisticated your data are, the future remains resolutely unknowable. All data are past data, and all manipulation of that data can only help you understand that past. This is highly suggestive, and may even be very useful, in forming a view of the future. But it can never be conclusive. Indeed, I don't think it's rushing to judgment to state my fervent belief that the understatement of the millennium will turn out to be: "Past performance is no guarantee of future results."

You can manipulate all the data on earth, and do so until the last syllable of time, but you will never be able to tell me what any mutual fund is going to do, either absolutely or relative to its peers, over the next five years. The essential aspect of the future is its unknowability. As H. L. Mencken said (even *before* the mainframe!), "Penetrating so many secrets, we cease to believe in the unknowable. But there it sits nevertheless, calmly licking its chops."

I've always felt that the truest test of emotional maturity is one's tolerance for ambiguity — one's acceptance of the unknowable. In that sense, technogeeks endlessly torturing the data for The Answer (variance? semi-variance?) strike me as not merely wrong, but unutterably sad. They're not just missing the point of investing. They're missing the point of life.

And, when all is said and done, adult investors aren't asking us to help them understand the future in any rigorously intellectual way. *They're asking us to help them believe in the future.*

5. The computer was supposed to be a time-saving, effort-saving tool. When did the means become the end? Let us say, just to pick a number off a bus, that computers can manipulate data 10 times faster than they could 10 years ago. (Or manipulate 10 times as much data in the same time. Or whatever. Hey, cut me some slack, here. I'm a technophobe.)

This would mean either that you're able to spend one-tenth as much time at the computer as you did 10 years ago — or that you can do 10 times the business in the same time.

So if you're spending the same or even more time at the computer than you did then, but aren't doing 10 times the business, something has gone very, very wrong. I'm pretty sure I know what it is. And it ain't pretty.

200

Somehow, you've let the means become the end. Instead of freeing you to spend more time and energy doing the real work of this profession — seeing people, as opposed to manipulating data — the computer has ensnared you further. And, deep down in your heart, you secretly love this.

Why? Because when you're sitting there updating your optimization software, massaging your asset allocation models, and reading the ream of research/market commentary that's hit your screen in the last hour, *you can pretend you're doing your work when you know you're really not.* The computer has become the greatest avoidance behavior this industry's invented since charting stocks with a pencil and a ruler. ("How about doing some prospecting?" "No, no; too busy now: I'm loading my prospecting database into my computer!")

This is a human tragedy, not a technological one. It isn't the computer's fault that it keeps giving you answers to the meaningless questions you keep asking it in order to avoid your real work. (Know when I'll get a computer? When they teach 'em to say, "Hey, wait a minute. The stuff you're asking me is either unknowable or not that important, and you'd be better off talking to a prospect." Then, and only then.)

A couple of months ago, this magazine profiled a very interesting practitioner. He's obviously dedicated and hard-working, and has had to overcome a lot of adversity that he suffered growing up in another country. But in the course of that interview, he said something that absolutely made my blood run cold.

It seems that he's been in the business since 1988. His total gross revenues are running at the rate of about $150,000 a year. And he has spent over 3,000 hours doing research on his own trading/investing system. *Three thousand hours!*

I certainly mean no disrespect to this gentleman when I say that I was (and am) appalled by this datum. At seven hours a day, that's 430 days. At eight hours, it's 350 days. Split the difference, and call it 390 days.

Now, assume there are 22 working days in a month. Unless I'm doing the math all wrong, that's 17 months of "research." Seventeen of the 120 to 130 months he's been in the business! And what has it all added to his clients' well-being? Or to his, for that matter?

How much further along could he be — how many more clients could he be helping today, how much more money could he be prudently managing — if he'd invested even half that time and energy in doing rather than knowing?

For heaven's sake, get on with it. There isn't one person in a hundred reading this column who doesn't already know a hundred times what his clients need him to know. And besides, as Thomas Huxley said, "The great end of life is not knowledge but action."

(A) Turn that damned computer off. (B) Get the hell out of the office and go see somebody who might need your help. (C) Do not mistake either (A) or (B) for a request.

CREATIVE DESTRUCTION

In a starburst of alliteration worthy of the speeches William Safire once crafted for Spiro Agnew, Warren Buffett's 1995 shareholder letter said, "Fear is the foe of the faddist, but the friend of the fundamentalist." Wiser words were rarely written.

Presumably because I've been leading a good life, when I prayed for a bear market in this space in July, my prayer was instantly and quite spectacularly answered. I didn't just get a bear market, I got a real old-fashioned crash. And boy, am I happy. How could a professional not be?

First of all, I've gotten to watch a couple of our industry's most pernicious pseudoeconomic fads come a cropper, to my delight and that of everyone with an adult memory that extends further back than 1995.

One of these base canards held that American's demographics, regardless of any and all other economic/market variables, would render a bear market impossible before 2008, or whenever. The corollary craziness claimed that a "new breed" of long-term investors wouldn't sell into a bear market that couldn't happen anyway. Both of these "ideas" were casualties of the market's great summertime Jonestown Kool-Aid party.

(One need not and probably should not gloat over this, and yet I can't help myself. There are, after all, only two kinds of people in the world: People with too much class to say "I told you so," and people like me. But I digress.)

Whether you fell victim to the siren song of a "new era," or whether you waited stoically for the inevitable crack-up (while doing Lifeboat Drills night and noon), we are now all in the same position. As professional advisors, we must craft from the wreckage a synthesis that enables us to guide our clients. We must answer, first to ourselves and then to people who rely on us, the question, "Where are we, and what do we do now?"

I certainly do not mean by this that we have to develop a viewpoint on the next moves in the economy and/or the markets. To the contrary, I think a market viewpoint is the last thing a long-term investor should have.

A financial plan, and the portfolio constructed to execute that plan, should be driven by only three basic issues: who the money is for, what the money is for, and when the money will be needed.

When we lose sight of this, and focus instead on questions such as whether the Labor Day panic lows will hold, or will Hong Kong devalue, or will the U.S. have a recession next year, we've put the portfolio ahead of the plan. And then, consciously or not, we're engaged in the madness of market timing, which isn't what our best clients want or need. They didn't hire us to guess the zigs and zags of the market; they hired us to help them reach their life goals. (If clients want meaningless market commentary from people who change their viewpoint more often than they change their underwear, let 'em watch CNBC.)

Rather, when I say that we have to form (or re-form) a coherent view of the world, I specifically mean that we have to ask what, if anything, has changed. Is the world at the autumn equinox a fundamentally different place from what it was in the spring?

Twenty years ago, Japan's economy was a beacon to the world, and ours was a slow-motion train wreck. Ten years ago, when the Nikkei was 30,000 and the Dow less than 3000, the grounds of the Imperial Palace in Tokyo were said to be worth as much as all of Los Angeles. Today the U.S. economy is the world's standard, while Japan's leaders (as the economist Paul Krugman observed) are like a guy who ran somebody over with his car, and then — mortified and vowing to undo the damage — backed his car over the victim again. These observations are surely true; the question is, what's changed?

204

In 10 years, Russia has gone from a totalitarian prison state to a brave experiment in free-market capitalism to total collapse. Mexico has boomed, busted, and boomed again. These are the facts; how ought we to change our course of action regarding our investments, based on these facts?

Here at home, the less important (though by no means unimportant) answer to the question of what's changed is that our stock market has experienced one of the greatest value rallies of the modern era. Rising stock prices extinguish value — particularly when that rise enters its bubble phase — while crashing markets are always value rallies. And this one's been a real beaut. To the point where an adult, for the first time in a long time, can actually buy stocks and not feel like he's trading tulip bulb futures.

When the stock of Merrill Lynch, perhaps the finest investment banking/brokerage franchise in the world, declines by half — that's a value rally. When Schlumberger, undoubtedly the premier oil field services company on the planet, goes from 94 to 44, I'm suffused with a warm glow. When PepsiCo stock — *after* they spin off those no-growth restaurants and acquire Tropicana, which is maybe the second most powerful consumer brand in America — cycles back to 1991 levels, I want to start off each day with a song. Earnings, schmearnings. These stocks aren't just selling on fear, they're selling on raw, mindless, screaming terror. Ain't life grand?

And yet the basic question — what's changed — still stands. Were we in a "new era" of Panglossian perfection six months ago? Are we in a "new era" of serial monetary meltdown now? For the definitive answer, let me refer you to the Archdruid of global finance, one Alan Greenspan.

On September 4, at UC Berkeley, the chairman gave what I believe was the speech of his life. Trouble is, no one was really listening. People just try to figure out what he's telling them about the next change in interest rates, so much so that they miss everything else he says. Then they complain they couldn't follow his syntax.

And that's too bad, because more than anyone else in American public life, Alan Greenspan actually thinks out loud. This particular evening, he was thinking about the topic, "Question: Is There a New Economy?" And what he said deserves to be read again and again — in its entirety — by anyone groping for a consistent viewpoint in this seemingly inconsistent world.

"We have relearned in recent weeks," Greenspan said, "that just as a bull market feels unending and secure as an economy and stock market move forward, so it can feel when markets contract that recovery is inconceivable. Both, of course, are wrong.

"But because of the difficulty of imagining a turnabout when such emotions take hold, periods of euphoria and distress tend to feed on themselves. Indeed, if this were not the case, the types of psychologically driven ebbs and flows of economic activity we have observed would be unlikely to exist."

Did you hear what the master said? "*Psychologically driven ebbs and flows of economic activity.*" He's not just talking about markets here, boys and girls. He's talking about the whole macroeconomic ball of wax! "As in the past," he said, "our advanced economy is primarily driven by how human psychology molds the value system that drives a competitive market economy. *And that process is inextricably linked to human nature, which appears essentially immutable and, thus, anchors the future to the past.*" (Italics mine.)

And so, finally, the answer to the question of what's changed is, of course: nothing of critical importance.

Economies and markets get too far ahead of themselves when human psychology goes into its manic phase, and investor expectations outrun not just reality but possibility. In a year like that, Russia can be the best-performing stock market in the world.

But then that greatest of all capitalist principles, Schumpeter's "creative destruction," smashes the sandcastle. This principle doesn't say, "You can't ever have capitalism in Russia"; it makes no predictive value judgments. It just says, you can't have a capitalism based on corruption, cronyism, thuggery, and a fictionalized currency. Start over again.

And the principle of creative destruction is, to be sure, an equal-opportunity sandcastle-smasher. It breaks up phony third-world economies, but also 40-to-1 leveraged hedge funds run by Masters of the Universe in Greenwich, Connecticut. It even crushes group-thinking yuppie fund managers who pay 50 times earnings for a company that makes fizzy caramel-colored sugar water, and then has trouble selling it to a world, much of which doesn't have enough money to buy food right now.

Then, when human psychology has been exposed to too much creative destruction too fast, investors go into their depressive state: "Sell everything! The U.S. is about to be engulfed by a tsunami of deflation!" (Sadly, because human nature feels instead of thinking, it fails to notice that deflation is, by orders of magnitude, the easiest macroeconomic problem to fix. You just print more dollars. But I digress.)

Do you not see that this is the most comforting, indeed the most liberating thing I could tell you? Because it means you never have to prepare yourself or your clients for new eras, new paradigms, or new anything elses.

In rising markets, you don't have to know much more than that trees do not grow all the way to the sky. In falling markets, you don't have to know much more than that the world does not end. "The sea changes colors," sings Fleetwood Mac, "but the sea does not change."

And so let us sit for just another moment at the feet of the Archdruid, and listen — really listen — before he withdraws once again into the mist:

"Perhaps, as some argue, history will be less of a guide than it has been in the past. Some of the future is always without historical precedent. New records are always being made. Having said all that, however, my experience of observing the American economy day by day over the past half century suggests that most, perhaps substantially most, of the future can be expected to rest on a continuum of the past. Human nature, as I indicated earlier, appears immutable over the generations and inextricably ties our future to our past."

.

COMES THE REVOLUTION

I don't know anyone who gets around this industry more than I do — brokerages, banks, financial planners, insurance companies — and everywhere I go, people solemnly assure me that the business is changing.

Even senior executives, who ought to be thinking strategically and even globally, but who apparently focus more on their own job security, tell me that yes, there's a lot of change taking place. But I always sense an unspoken conclusion, which I believe is: And after the dust settles, we'll be able to run our businesses pretty much on the same models.

These people remind me of French aristocrats, along about the late spring of 1789. I see them sitting around the old chateau, there, knocking back a little cognac, and talking about the news of the day. Yes, they all agree, things are changing.

People just won't stay in their place anymore, these chaps observe, and the restlessness is getting too big to ignore. So, one says, we're probably going to end up having to give them a little more bread. And, another notes, we may even have to let 'em have a bit of land of their own. One day, too, says a third, we may have to let them vote on some less important issues. And then, all the aristocrats agree, we'll be able to go back to running things, as nearly as possible, the way we always have.

Not all that much later, in the great scheme of things, these fellows are together again — standing in a cart, heading downtown. Once there, they've been reliably informed, something very bad is going to happen to them. Still, they're having a stimulating chat, this time on the topic: Where did we go wrong?

As the cart arrives at its destination, the most thoughtful of these noblemen announces that he's figured it out. And, just as someone starts helping him up the steps of the guillotine, he says:

"In our deep denial — because we had such a huge financial and emotional investment in the status quo — *we mistook revolutionary change for evolutionary change*. We saw things not as they are, but as we wanted them to remain." And then he doesn't get to say anything more.

Sic transit everyone who's telling me the business is changing. It's not doing anything of the kind. It's being entirely swept away, and replaced with a completely different business — one that is much healthier, and will be far more beneficial both to the American family and to the industry professionals who survive and transcend this revolution.

Like all revolutions, ours is one that builds for a long time. Until finally there's a single catalytic event that one can point to in retrospect as the flashpoint, after which there was no going back. And we've just seen ours.

Bastille Day in the financial services revolution was October 8, 1998. On that day, the nation's largest bank merged with a company comprised of one of the nation's largest stockbrokers and one of its largest insurance companies. And the government didn't fire a shot.

This marks the end of the old order. It is nothing less than the repeal of Glass-Steagall, *de facto* if not *de jure*, and nothing will ever be the same. In due time, after the politicians and regulators finish thrashing out their turf issues, formal legislation ratifying the revolution will follow. But be assured that the war's already over. And everybody won.

Under the old, sick Glass-Steagall synthesis, American families were forced to go to a bank for their saving and borrowing needs, to an insurance company for life/health/income protection and annuities, and to a securities dealer for investments. The result was that people owned financial products but had no overall plan, not least of all because each of their product providers was forever telling them that the other two sold cancer. This wasn't just different from the way it ought to be: It was the opposite.

As markets, investments, tax and estate laws, and life itself grow more complex — and as Americans are increasingly bombarded with data and facts instead of wisdom — what people need most is two-fold. First, a comprehensive, written financial/estate/investment plan. And second, a competent, caring, empathetic professional to serve as the steward of that plan, and to keep everybody and everything moving in the right direction.

Under the guise of protecting people from abuses that occurred 70 years ago, the old order effectively prevented these desirable outcomes from happening. That's precisely why it's been swept away. As Dwight Eisenhower said about peace, people want a unified, coherent financial life so much that one day government would have to get out of the way and let them have it. October 8, 1998 was that day.

The news of the revolution will not reach all of America instantly, like a giant thunderclap. Rather, people will sort of stumble onto it, household by household. One day, someone will walk into her Citibank branch to inquire about refinancing her mortgage at the new low rates she's been reading about. And she'll leave, not just with a new loan, but with an appointment to have her will, her insurance, and her investments reviewed, coordinated, and rationalized. Which is just what she always wanted.

Or maybe the invitation to consider a comprehensive plan will come from her Equitable life agent, or her Merrill Lynch financial consultant. No matter whence the offer comes, realize that it is coming. And that rational families will welcome it with open arms.

Thus, this is truly a revolution — the convergence of all financial services, available under one roof, pursuant to one plan, from one Primary Financial Advisor. It is not, among other things, an evolution — the consolidation of similar entities within separate distribution channels (much as you might like it to be, *monsieur le comte*).

And, even to some of its most ardent partisans, the true nature of the revolution may still not be clear. It may look like the apotheosis of The Plan and the death of The Product. But I think the truth is more complex than that. Indeed, through the still-billowing smoke, I can see emblazoned on the revolution's banner its real slogan: The Plan *Is* The Product.

If you can't deliver that product, someone else will, and you will lose first your clients and then your business. It won't matter how good an investment advisor or insurance expert you are, if that's all you can do. You can't negotiate a truce with a revolution, nor get it to cut you some slack because you're narrowly competent or even a nice person. Revolutions don't make those distinctions. (After Thermidor, it didn't matter how kind you'd been to your peasants. If you had a "de" in front of your surname, your head went into a basket.) Your practice can either provide a comprehensive plan, or you can plan to become history.

Yet one must also not lose sight of the inarguable fact that the plan is a product. And, like all products, it isn't bought but sold. Indeed, since time immemorial, the death song of the American financial planner has been, "I found all the facts; I created a magnificent plan; I explained it to the prospects in exquisite detail. And I never heard from them again."

More now than ever, a balance of technical competence and sales skills will be required of all of us. (The notion that these two strengths are somehow contradictory exists solely in the perfervid imaginations of journalists, who possess neither.)

Plans are rational; human nature is non-rational. Trust and empathy are the bridge. No plan is so brilliant that it sells itself. It has to be sold and re-sold, again and again, as bear markets or hot-fund advertising or just plain boredom and entropy try to derail it.

Planning is by its nature focused on the great goals of life — indeed, of *lives*, since planning is almost always multigenerational. Investment advisors in particular will find this a difficult transition, since their agenda has usually been set in terms of markets and investments, rather than in terms of life. (SIA members, take careful note, because you are starting from very deep in your own end zone on this one. While the life insurance industry is starting from no worse than midfield.)

Whoever you are, you'd probably better assume that you won't be where you need to go until you become skilled at asking these six threshold questions — and until you can provide a plan for helping people find all the right answers to the questions:

(1) What will happen to your family if you die tomorrow? A year from now? Ten years from now?

(2) How will you build a retirement income that you and/or your spouse can't outlive, given that one or both of you may live 30 years in retirement?

(3) If your income will always suffice, you can plan to leave your principal to the people you love. How will you do that with a minimum of taxation?

(4) How will you educate your children, and/or how will your children educate your grandchildren?

(5) Half one's total lifetime medical expenses may come in the last five years of life. Who will provide for the last five years of your parents' lives? How will you provide for the last five years of yours?

(6) Consider the institutions that have intervened in your family's life. Would you wish to leave them meaningful legacies, if we could figure out highly tax-efficient ways for you to do so?

On these great questions are comprehensive plans built. And on comprehensive planning will the career of the post-revolutionary Primary Financial Advisor be built. Screening for low-expense-ratio mutual funds isn't going to cut it. Plan to serve the whole client, or to watch someone else do so. It's what the client needs. Even more important, it's what the client deserves. And now he can finally have it.

Vive la revolution!

Foreword To The Book Reviews

In early 1997 I read an astonishing book — surely the definitive history of the Greenspan Fed, and as such a terrific window into the monetary policies which made the past decade the miracle that it was. The book was called *Back From the Brink* by the well-regarded Fed watcher Steven Beckner.

That's when I made my mistake. I called my friend Barry Vinocur, the senior publisher at Dow Jones Financial Publishing, and offered to review the book for *Investment Advisor*. Well, no, Vinocur thought, it wasn't a fit for *IA*, but they might want to run it in their new magazine, the very erudite bi-monthly *Asset Management*.

I had forgotten — or perhaps had chosen to forget — that, when it comes to writers he likes, Vinocur is the tar baby. I handed him the book review, and got stuck to him.

Well, he opined helpfully, maybe if I gave him another book review with my other hand, I could push off. Tried that. Other hand got stuck.

Two years and 10 books into this mission, I find these reviews pound for pound the most challenging and stimulating work I do. It's one thing to toss off a 2,000 word rant each month on whatever's bothering me at the moment — 34 examples of which you've just been through. But to have to read a serious book closely and critically, and then try to do both the author and the reader justice in roughly the same number of words, is a very different kettle of fish.

Early on, I decided only to review books that I thought the magazine's audience really needed to read. This, together with an abiding sense that what goes around comes around, precluded my writing about books I hated.

Rightly or wrongly, this decision involved appointing myself a proxy for the audience as well as an arbiter of what it needed to know. Someone whose ego was under better control might have shrunk from this; no such petty cavil troubled me.

I felt — and feel — that the one quality in shortest supply in our industry is *perspective,* in all its many forms, and so this becomes the above-the-line common theme in all 10 books. (The below-the-line commonality is, of course, that they were all books I really wanted to read.)

For instance, if you truly understand the case for free trade, as you can after reading Melvyn Krauss' *How Nations Grow Rich* and some of Paul Krugman's essays in *The Accidental Theorist,* you're in much better shape to appreciate issues like China's Most-Favored-Nation status and the steel industry's recent campaign for protection against "dumping" by foreign competitors. Microsoft's anti-trust troubles are vastly more comprehensible by the light of Standard Oil's, as described in Ron Chernow's *Titan: The Life of John D. Rockefeller.*

The problematic role of the IMF in the financial difficulties of emerging economies will be much clearer to you after Charles Kindleberger's lucid examination of the lender-of-last-resort concept in his *Manias, Panics and Crashes.* So, too, of course, will be the great euphoria/panic shunt of 1998.

Speaking of which, what the Fed did right in the fall of 1998 is foreshadowed in Beckner's explanation of its brilliant handling of the crash of 1987, in *Back From the Brink.* In turn, an understanding of monetary actions in '87 will — as perhaps nothing else ever has — make you see exactly why the crash of 1929 turned into a great depression, while the more modern crash had no lasting effect.

Accepting that most readers probably won't get to all of these books, I've always tried to present a clear idea of each work's central themes and theses, in the hope that you can mine a nugget or two of useful perspective from the review alone. That effort is too often constrained by the very real limitations of my own understanding of the material. Still, I hope that this volume's extremely busy audience will find these 10 snapshots helpful in making sense of the world in which we must invest.

REFLECTING ON THE GREENSPAN YEARS

In the roughly three months between Alan Greenspan's "irrational exuberance" speech and the Fed's March 25 snugging of interest rates, the world's most powerful central banker came in for more criticism than he'd received in his previous nearly 10 years in office. Rarely, in fact, has someone who had gotten such good press for so long gotten so much bad press so fast. In part, this is simply the nature of celebrity in America: We build people up to cast them down, in roughly equal measure. Whom we lionize today we will demonize tomorrow.

It is particularly apt, then, that Steven Beckner of Market News Service — "as knowledgeable a 'Fed watcher' as we have in the land," according to no less an authority than Bill Seidman — has written a book that only he could write.

A fan of Greenspan since his college days (and since Greenspan's days as a disciple of Ayn Rand), Beckner has compiled an encyclopedic, virtually day-to-day account of the Fed chairman's stewardship. After reading this indispensable book, you will be hard-pressed to argue with Beckner's conclusion that the Greenspan years have been "the most difficult time to make monetary policy in the central bank's 83-year history," and that the Greenspan Fed has triumphed on a scale that is almost beyond comprehension.

The victory, in Beckner's view, is not just that Greenspan has guided the economy through an Odyssean series of crises: the '87 crash, the '90 recession, a virtual meltdown of the banking system, the liquidation of the S&Ls and the ensuing credit crunch, wildly swinging exchange rates, and accumulating trade deficits. Nor is it that the Greenspan Fed has engineered a long period of steady if unspectacular growth, low inflation, and low interest rates — paving the way for the greatest run in the history of the American stock market. To Beckner, the true miracle is that Greenspan has orchestrated all of this in the face of a cataclysmic breakdown of fiscal policy and indeed the complete abdication of their fiscal responsibilities by Congress and the White House. In fiscal 1987, the national debt was $2.35 trillion or 51.67% of GDP. Seven years later, despite two major tax hikes, it was $5 trillion and 70% of GDP.

And therein lies the real crux of *Back From the Brink: The Greenspan Years* (John Wiley & Sons, 1996, 423 pp., $29.95); it isn't just a chronicle, it's a dire warning. Beckner wants us not just to understand fully how very fortunate we've been to have Greenspan at the helm of an otherwise rudderless ship. He says "... it is a very bad sign when our central bank has come to occupy a spot of such central importance, when the name of Greenspan has become a household word. It should not be that way.

"We as a nation," Beckner concludes, "must get a grip on our finances and stop putting the onus on the Fed to manage our economy and stave off financial disasters — or financial disaster we shall surely have."

This book — at 423 pages of very densely packed material — is not an easy read; it takes work. But at a time when meaningful perspective is in very short supply, *Back From the Brink* is simply must reading for financial advisors and money managers. If you get nothing out of this book but a deep understanding of the financial and market near-disasters of 1987 and 1990, you'll have been richly rewarded for your investment of time and effort in reading it.

Beckner begins not with a history of the Fed, but rather an intellectual tour of Greenspan's development — which tells you where the real focus of the book is going to be. (If you're interested, the United States functioned without a central bank after Andrew Jackson paid off the national debt in its entirety and then killed the Bank of the United States in the 1830s. A new central bank, the Federal Reserve, was not put in place until 1913. Part of the reason for its establishment was that in the panic of 1907, with President Teddy Roosevelt incommunicado hunting in the Louisiana canebrakes, J.P. Morgan saved the country — for the second time. Much as the heirs of Jefferson and Jackson still resisted the idea of a central bank, they preferred it to having the nation's economic fate in the hands of one Wall Street banker.)

Greenspan didn't set out to be a central banker, nor even an economist. He studied clarinet and saxophone at the prestigious Juilliard School and toured professionally with a well-known swing band. Fatefully, one of his fellow band members (who had no more future in music than did Greenspan) was Leonard Garment, who would later become a top aide to Richard Nixon. Realizing that he was never going to be a successful musician, Greenspan began reading economics and fell in love with it. He earned a bachelor's degree summa cum laude from New York University in 1948 and a master's from the same institution in 1950. He then went on to advanced studies at Columbia, where he met his first great mentor, Arthur Burns, who was later a Fed chairman himself in the 1970s.

Greenspan soon came into the orbit of Ayn Rand, the Russian-born novelist and philosopher. (Rand, whose family had fled the Red revolution, was a radical libertarian and advocate of laissez-faire capitalism.) In 1954, he formed Townsend-Greenspan Associates and, after his partner died in 1958, built it into a powerhouse economic consulting firm that made him a multimillionaire.

In 1968, Greenspan entered the political arena, becoming director of domestic policy research for the Nixon campaign. In 1974, when Herbert Stein retired as chairman of the Council of Economic Advisors, Greenspan took the job after Burns assured him it would be a great platform from which to fight Greenspan's most hated enemy — inflation. By the time the Senate took up Greenspan's nomination, Nixon was gone, but President Ford affirmed the nomination.

Beckner is vivid on the vigor and skill with which Greenspan pursued his political advantages and connections. (Though slight in build and given to fainting spells, he has driven himself to become an accomplished tennis player and golfer.) Even after returning to his consulting practice in 1977, he stayed in close touch with the corridors of power and became Ronald Reagan's chief economic advisor in his successful campaign to unseat Jimmy Carter. In 1987, when Paul Volcker indicated that he didn't want another term at the Fed, the job — after much consummate politicking — was Greenspan's. In a very real sense, as Beckner makes clear, it was the job Greenspan had been preparing for all his life.

Beckner gives Volcker relatively short shrift. Part of this is because *Back From the Brink* is about Alan Greenspan. Still, what praise there is for Volcker — who single-handedly broke the back of hyperinflation in the early years of his 1979-87 run as chairman — comes in this book from Greenspan's mouth rather than from Beckner's pen. It was Greenspan who said, upon arriving at the Fed in August of '87, "the big job had been done."

As recently as 1995, Greenspan said that had it not been for "Paul and his colleagues ... the issue we would be talking about today would not be the deficit, which is a relatively civilized concept, but we'd be talking about the stability of our society." As someone to whom Volcker is a great hero, I wholeheartedly concur. Indeed, I believe — Reagan revolution or no Reagan revolution — it was Volcker who made Greenspan possible.

Greenspan was confirmed as Federal Reserve chairman by the Senate on August 3, 1987 — and 77 days later he was facing the imminent meltdown of the U.S. (and probably the global) economy, triggered by the greatest stock market crash of the century. Greenspan's superb generalship of that crisis — orchestrating a worldwide liquefaction of the financial system, just the opposite of what the Fed had done in 1929 — turned the cataclysm into a non-event. This section of the book — including the author's hypothetical extrapolation of the 1929 response, had someone of Greenspan's vision not been there — is Beckner at his very best. It is not just grippingly written, but, like the rest of the book, exquisitely sourced. (Beckner's Rolodex must contain the names of as many powerful people as Greenspan's. Indeed, at times you suspect he's using Greenspan's.)

Having captured the reader, Beckner now takes him on an extremely detailed journey through the economic/interest rate/exchange rate battles of the next few years. Among other ideas that he brings into very clear focus is the constant struggle Greenspan's Fed has had in maintaining course, given White House jawboning and Congressional threats to Fed independence. Beckner never met a President nor a Treasury secretary he didn't dislike, primarily because they've always been trying to get Greenspan to do things he felt were wrong — like lowering interest rates, no matter what the economy was doing, for political reasons.

What is truly frightening — and Beckner clearly wants to make sure you are sufficiently frightened — is the ongoing effort by Congress, that paragon of fiscal irresponsibility, to bring the monetary authority of the Fed under its control. As recently as 1992, major legislation was proposed that would have required presidents of the Fed's regional banks to be appointed by the President and confirmed by the Senate — thereby politicizing the process. There are also delicious (if horrifying) accounts of such advanced economic thinkers as Sen. Alphonse D'Amato (R-N.Y.) tongue-lashing Greenspan for not lowering interest rates. This stuff really makes your blood run cold.

The closest Beckner can come to suggesting the possibility of a major mistake during Greenspan's tenure is the tight-money policy pursued by the Fed going into the 1990-91 recession. Greenspan, it was and is widely argued, misjudged the severity of the credit crunch that followed on the bank/S&L crisis and didn't loosen credit until recession was upon us. But even here, Beckner is inclined to blame misguided banking legislation (FIRREA), the disastrous Bush tax hike, and finally the Gulf War for pushing the economy into recession. Would the economy have tipped over without Saddam's shock to the system? Beckner concludes that we'll never know — effectively (if fairly) exonerating Greenspan.

In addition to being economic history at its very best, *Back From the Brink* is a refresher course in macroeconomics, money and banking, and international trade (unless you never actually took those courses in college, in which case this book becomes all the more indispensable). The book is, however, marred by a lack of editing that has become, for me, a John Wiley trademark. Nevertheless, at least the editing lapses are consistent: erstwhile Drexel CEO Fred Joseph is always called "Josephs," and the adjective "loath" is always given as the verb "loathe." But when they start doing things such as identifying the star of the film *Bridge on the River Kwai* as "Alex" *(sic)* Guinness, it feels like somebody running his fingernails down a blackboard. This is a petty cavil, however. Nothing should be allowed to detract from my wholehearted recommendation that you read and re-read this extraordinary book.

DEBT ADDICTION

In 1916, the richest man in America, John D. Rockefeller, could have paid off the national debt all by himself. In 1997, Bill Gates and Warren Buffett together couldn't pay two months' interest on the debt without going broke.

This is precisely the sort of sparkling, delicious anecdote that makes business historian John Steele Gordon's book the delight that it is. *Hamilton's Blessing: The Extraordinary Life and Times of Our National Debt* (Walker and Company, 1997, 214 pp., $21) is an elegant entertainment, and that is the least of its accomplishments. Most important, this book is a complete history of the philosophy and practice of our indebtedness. By showing, with a professional historian's dispassion, how we slid into our current fix, Gordon provides a much needed dose of perspective.

He also — in a book expanded from an article first published in *American Heritage* magazine — enumerates the major theories on how we might extricate ourselves (or, more properly, our children and grandchildren) from our present fiscal pickle. The concluding chapter is lucid, if not particularly original. Its thesis — that the flat tax is the least unthinkable solution — is presented simply, clearly, and with a refreshing absence of rhetoric. Indeed, this final chapter, like Gordon's first, titled "The Hamiltonian Miracle," alone is worth the price of the book.

The United States, Gordon tells us, was quite literally born not merely in debt but in total fiscal chaos. By the end of the Revolution, Congress was no longer paying interest on its bonds held by its own citizens, had defaulted on all of its foreign debt, and was months in arrears in paying the army. But the national government, neutered by the Articles of Confederation, had no power to cope, not least of all because it had no power to tax.

223

Thus, to Gordon, the real impetus for what turned out to be the Constitutional Convention of 1787 was fiscal rather than philosophical or political. And it is in the Constitution that Gordon finds the seeds of fiscal mess. Congress was given the power "to borrow Money on the credit of the United States." This is one of the very few major powers in the Constitution which, Gordon notes, "has no checks and balances upon it whatever." Why?

"The British Parliament, necessarily the model the Founding Fathers used in creating Congress, had come into existence at the end of the thirteenth century precisely to be a check upon the extravagance of the king, and remained such a check 500 years later. Britain's richest men represented themselves in the House of Lords, while the merely affluent were represented in the Commons. The poor, having no money, weren't represented at all. So when Parliament voted to spend money, its members were, in a very real sense, voting to spend their own money. The Founding Fathers expected Congress to be no different, and, at least for a while, it wasn't," Gordon writes. The framers, in other words, could not have conceived of a professional political class that would spend money it could never collect merely in order to get re-elected.

Alexander Hamilton is Gordon's hero. Indeed, the book takes its name from a letter the young Hamilton wrote to his mentor, Robert Morris, in which he opined, "A national debt, if it is not excessive, will be to us a national blessing." Hamilton, virtually single-handedly and despite furious opposition from the bank-hating, government-fearing Jeffersonians, put the fledgling United States on a rock-solid financial foundation. First, he got Congress to establish a tariff on imports, which both fostered the development of domestic industry and provided the bulk of the federal government's revenues for the next century.

Next, Hamilton masterminded the refunding of the old government's debt, both to establish the new regime's credit and to create a larger and more flexible money supply (because banks could lend against government bonds as collateral). Hamilton ran into a wall, however, when he moved to have the new federal government assume the war debts of the states. Virginia and other Southern states had largely retired their debts and objected to assuming, in effect, part of the burdens of states that had not. Hamilton prevailed by doing a deal with the Virginians to move the nation's capital to the "muddy and fever-ridden banks of the Potomac." The resulting bond offering was a smashing success.

The last leg of Hamilton's grand plan was the establishment of a national bank. He got it done, but at the cost of the final split of the Revolutionary coalition into two warring political parties — the system that persists today. Still, Hamilton's program was quickly proven right. By 1794, the United States had the highest credit rating in Europe, and some of its bonds were selling at 10% over par. By 1801, Europeans held $33 million in U.S. debt (out of a total of about $81 million), and European capital was fueling the rapid growth of this, the mother of all "emerging markets."

A huge rise in imports (and, therefore, tariff revenues) in the new century led to a near halving of the national debt between 1800 and 1811; in all but one of those years the government ran large budget surpluses. The debt exploded in the War of 1812, but then began falling again — almost literally to zero — when Andrew Jackson, Jefferson's true heir, made it his mission to retire the debt and liquidate the national bank. Jackson succeeded, but by depositing federal funds in a large number of smaller banks around the country, he set in motion the events that would lead to our first great crash and depression: the Panic of 1837.

These "pet banks," enjoying federal deposits without any federal control, printed bank notes galore. In less than 18 months, the U.S. money supply increased by a whopping 50%. This caused an upsurge in inflation, stock prices, and (especially) land speculation. Appalled, Jackson issued the Specie Circular, ordering the government's Land Office to accept only gold and silver in payment for land (except for bona fide settlers buying 320 acres or less). Land prices crashed, setting off a wave of loan defaults and bank failures.

As federal revenues fell, deficits shot up again. They moderated in the early 1840s, but soared yet again to fund the Mexican War.

Boom times and big surpluses prevailed through most of the 1850s, and then the staggering deficits of the Civil War blew the national debt to a new plateau. From $3.3 million in 1837 and less than $29 million as late as 1857, the national debt peaked at nearly $2.8 billion in 1866. From then until the eve of World War I, the United States enjoyed a golden age that was nowhere more clearly reflected than in its fiscal health. By 1916, the year John D. Rockefeller could have paid it off single-handedly, the national debt stood at $1.2 billion and only 2.54% of GNP — two numbers it would never even remotely see again.

Gordon's narrative pauses here, in a chapter titled "Twilight of the Old Consensus," to review the two great watershed events of that era: the creation of the Federal Reserve and the imposition of the modern income tax. He is very succinct on the one (the government could no longer stand to have J.P. Morgan be the nation's *de facto* central banker) and quite vivid on the other. Along with the fiscal irresponsibility of Congress, Gordon sees our income tax system as the other root of all evil. He finds it arbitrary, regressive, inefficient, largely unenforceable, and ultimately just another repository of the hidden agendas of special interests and politicians. (Since the Tax Reform Act of 1986, Gordon points out, the tax code has been amended no fewer than 4,000 times or at a rate of more than once a day. The huge preponderance of these amendments, he asserts, were nothing more or less than political favors.)

Between the World Wars, Gordon identifies the rise of Keynesian economics, with its intellectual legitimization of deficit spending as an important tool for managing the economy, as the booze that ultimately made a fiscal alcoholic of the U.S. government. Though consistent with the currently fashionable demonization of Keynes, this is the one argument in the book that Gordon simply gets wrong.

It's a little like blaming Alfred Nobel, the inventor of dynamite, for modern war. Like Nobel, Keynes invented a tool. Used properly, it can be of great benefit; it becomes a disaster only if and when misused. Nobel never made anyone blow up his neighbor; Jack Daniels never forced anyone to get drunk; and Keynes just isn't a villain, much less *the* villain. (Still, the specter of Keynes seems to have the power to cloud Gordon's mind. In the only factual error I noted in this whole scrupulously researched book, Gordon calls Keynes' breakthrough book *The Economic Consequences of the War,* when its whole point, including its title, is the consequences of the peace.)

The United States ran its last budget surplus in fiscal 1969. By 1981, the year the Reagan revolution took effect, the national debt was still under a trillion dollars and, at 33.84% of GDP, was at its lowest point in half a century. And then the dam broke.

In his penultimate chapter, "The Debt Explodes," Gordon traces the tripling of the national debt in one short decade. (In the single year 1983, the budget deficit "reached an awesome $208 billion — a sum greater than the entire federal budget as recently as 1970.")

"Most of the spending increases during Reagan's administrations," Gordon admits, "came in the entitlements, such as Social Security, Medicare, and Medicaid, that were written into permanent law and thus did not cross the president's desk." Still, Reagan's massive military build-up, including the Star Wars initiative, was funded without any spending cuts elsewhere to pay for it. That trend, exacerbated by the $481 billion savings-and-loan bailout, ran the debt from $909 billion in 1980 to $3.2 trillion in 1990 (and from 34.5% of GDP to 58.2%).

Even after the total collapse of Communism — the last major external threat to our national security — the debt (if not the actual annual deficit) has continued to run amok, and this is finally what Gordon finds so ominous. This has simply never happened before. Staggering deficits in wartime are perfectly normal, and it can be argued that the Reaganites used them to win the Cold War by raising the ante so high that Soviet Communism had to fold or face a revolution from within.

But at each previous war's end, we moved back into surplus and made huge inroads into the debt, both absolutely and (especially) as a percentage of national income. Yet from fiscal 1990 through 1995, the national debt soared from $3.2 trillion to over $5 trillion, and from 58.2% of GDP to over 70%. To Gordon, this is not simply bad fiscal policy. It is the absence of any fiscal policy at all.

The culprits, in Gordon's view, are Congress and the tax system. He finds the former incapable of making unpopular decisions to cut spending and the latter incapable of collecting the revenue it should. Simplifying Gordon's fairly elegant antidotes, it can be said that he thinks term limits would go a long way toward solving the former problem, and a flat tax would go a long way toward fixing the latter.

The ultimate goal of fiscal irresponsibility is re-election, Gordon avers. By limiting the re-election motive, term limits might infuse legislators with some fiscal willpower. (Gordon also likes the line-item veto and perhaps a presidentially set limit on overall spending.) And, as mentioned earlier, Gordon makes an eloquent case for the flat tax (as opposed to a value-added tax or other consumption tax). He finds it the least unfair way of finally curing a fatally diseased tax system that has proven itself incapable of collecting more than about 19% of national income, year in and year out, regardless of tax rates.

Few people have any real perspective of the national debt; it is perhaps the ultimate issue that has been pulverized into nine-second sound bites. *Hamilton's Blessing* will give you not only all the perspective you need, but all you could ever want. It is complete, eminently readable, and ultimately indispensable.

A SHORT COURSE IN THE COMPLEXITIES OF EMERGING MARKETS

On June 17, *The Wall Street Journal*'s editorial page featured an analysis by Richard Burt, an assistant secretary of state under President Reagan and chief strategic arms negotiator for President Bush. Burt's piece, "Are We Losing Turkey?", examined the complex economic, military, and human rights issues surrounding our country's relations with that strategically vital ally.

A month earlier, Burt's article would have made my eyes glaze over. Much as I might have wanted to, I wouldn't have been able to follow it. But on the day it appeared, I understood it perfectly — just as, later that same month, I finally understood both sides of the debate over the renewal of China's Most Favored Nation (MFN) status.

The difference was that by then I had read Jeffrey Garten's book *The Big Ten: The Big Emerging Markets and How They Will Change Our Lives* (Basic Books, 1997, 255 pp., $24). Garten draws directly on his experience as undersecretary of commerce for international trade from 1993 to 1995. But he also brings to the table a multifaceted resumé as a government bureaucrat in the Nixon, Ford, and Carter administrations; then as an investment banker with The Blackstone Group in New York, Tokyo, and Hong Kong; and now as dean of the Yale School of Management.

Garten and his boss, Commerce Secretary Ron Brown, developed what remains today the U.S. government's basic strategy for commercial diplomacy: to engage what it sees as the 10 Big Emerging Markets (BEMs) — Mexico, Brazil, Argentina, South Africa, Poland, Turkey, India, Indonesia, China, and South Korea. (Why not Russia? "It was not far enough along with its economic reforms; its political leadership seemed too precarious ... ." And, finally, because of its enormous military and nuclear capability, Russia is in a high-level Washington category by itself.)

In this view, the BEMs — rather than Europe and Japan — are "the key swing factor in the future growth of world trade, global financial stability, and the transition to free-market economies in Asia, Central Europe, and Latin America."

But, along with new and gigantic economic opportunities for the United States, the BEMs present huge challenges. Over a billion people, mostly from the BEMs, will enter the global economy in the next 10 years. "They'll earn, say, $5 to $10 a day, compared to the $80 to $90 their U.S. counterparts will earn. With the diffusion of technology and the injection of Western or Japanese management techniques, they could be 85% as efficient as workers in the West."

"For America," says Garten, "the implications for commercial competition, employment, wages, the cohesion of communities, politics — virtually everything — are staggering." A billion people are far more than the current populations of the United States, Japan, and Western Europe combined.

Finally, and perhaps most difficult, "the BEMs do not share our values regarding human rights, child labor, corruption, or environmental degradation," Garten notes. As U.S. contact with these countries grows, our notions of fairness and our moral sensibilities are cruising for a major bruising. Whether it's China's piracy of our intellectual property rights, or 24% of Turkey's child population working for pitiful wages, or Indonesia's extermination of 200,000 East Timorese (one third of the population), we Americans are going to find ourselves between a whole bunch of rocks and some very hard places in dealing with the BEMs.

These and many other complex aspects of globalizing capitalism are not well understood by American investment advisors and asset managers because we tend to look at economics and markets in sort of a vacuum. And, even at that, we often get blindsided by very rapid shifts in the finances of the BEMs. Look at the Mexican crisis of 1995 that Garten says "took the world by surprise and shook the foundation of the international financial system."

The beauty of Garten's book is that it is a phenomenal crash course on all of the relevant economic facts and figures *plus* all of the critical social and political issues. In fact, you don't even have to read the whole book to complete the course, if you don't want to. The introductory 23 pages that state all the basic issues, plus the first six chapters (119 pages, or about half the book) will do nicely.

The second half of the book contains Garten's wide-ranging prescriptions for solving any and all of the issues at hand. And, to my mind, this second half is far less successful than the first and of much less practical use to this magazine's readers.

That said, one of the later chapters, "A Vigorous Commercial Diplomacy," is worth a good, hard look, if only because it successfully debunks the notion of government activism in the trade area as "corporate welfare." Governments in Western Europe and Japan are engaged in massive forays into the BEMs, Garten argues convincingly. And he says we ought to — and desperately need to — galvanize the power of our federal government to beat the daylights out of these competitors on their own terms.

Garten also is alarmed — quite properly, I think — with the turning inward of our national focus at precisely the time when we most need to develop a coherent, aggressive, outward-looking strategy toward the BEMs.

The end of the Cold War and the onset of a certain bitter aftertaste with respect to Desert Storm (which left the loser, Saddam Hussein, in place while his conquerors, President Bush and Lady Thatcher, went into the darkness) have left America disinclined to think much about "foreign entanglements." (And when it does, it thinks mostly in Perot/Buchanan sound bites about jobs.) In 1985, Garten notes, "24% of the articles in *Time* and 22% in *Newsweek* were devoted to international news, but in 1995, the percentages were 14 and 12, respectively."

Garten's experience of Washington politics — specifically, that government doesn't act, it only reacts to whatever the electorate is most concerned about — tells him that the resulting benign neglect could spell big trouble. Consider:

• Over the past four years, U.S. exports have grown about three times as fast as the overall economy, and sales to foreign countries have accounted for about one third of our economic growth.

• Over the last quarter century, trade as a percentage of our GDP has grown from 11% to 23%. Today, exports support some 11 million jobs, which typically pay about 15% more than the manufacturing wage.

• By the year 2000, over 16 million jobs are likely to depend on exports, and nearly 30% of U.S. GDP may depend on trade.

• At current trends, the BEMs will account for $1 trillion of incremental American exports between 1990 and 2010, according to the Commerce Department. And that just counts exported goods; it doesn't attempt to quantify the BEMs' purchases of banking, engineering, or legal services!

But, says Garten, we are in a war with the rest of the developed world for this business. And our competitors tend to take a much more pragmatic and far less moralistic approach to the conduct of that war than we do. Moreover, other nations see this war as a vital national imperative, which the American electorate — to put it mildly — doesn't. This is at the heart of what another reviewer called Garten's "constructive alarmism."

Readers of this magazine will find *The Big Ten* immensely helpful. That is not to say that it is, in any accepted sense, a good book. The writing and editing are pedestrian at best, and neither is always at its best. The author's policy-wonk prescriptions range from obvious to idealistic to loopy, and generally put far too much emphasis on government action, while placing too little faith in the private sector's competitive creativity.

And sometimes, you just don't know what Garten can be thinking of, as when he announces, straight-faced, that during his tenure, trade missions to other lands always "contained some representatives from small- and medium-sized firms, and also from minority-owned companies." This strikes one as a transcendently Clintonomic concept: the politically correct invisible hand.

But perhaps the book's oddest aspect is Garten's treatment of his boss and mentor/point man on the BEM strategy — Commerce Secretary Brown. Garten mentions Brown, always favorably, upwards of 20 times in *The Big Ten*. (Indeed, the closest thing to a warm, human anecdote in this quite charmless book concerns a meeting between Brown and the President of China, Jiang Zemin.) But if you do not already know that Brown is dead (he was killed when his plane crashed in Croatia in April 1996), you will not find it out in this book. Now, you can think what you will of Brown, but I believe it is generally agreed that he was a vigorous and effective advocate for American business around the globe. Indeed, he lost his life in service to that cause. And, as it slowly dawns on you that his deputy has written a book that isn't even going to mention Brown's death, much less reveal how the author felt about it, you get the feeling that you're reading a very strange guy.

Its many shortcomings aside, *The Big Ten* should be read by everyone who has a professional responsibility to invest globally. You don't have to like Garten's answers (nor even Garten) to see that he has framed a lot of really important questions correctly.

A LOVELY LITTLE JEWEL OF ECONOMIC HISTORY

"History is medicine," the documentary filmmaker Ken Burns *(The Civil War, Baseball)* said recently. "It has nothing to do with the past. It has everything to do with the present."

This observation struck me as particularly apt with respect to economic history, which can supply much of the perspective so sorely needed by today's investors and their advisors. Trouble is, a lot of the economic history that's being written today comes from academe, where a prose of Saharan aridity seems to be a requisite for publication. What a joy it is, then, to discover Ron Chernow's new book *The Death of the Banker: The Decline and Fall of the Great Financial Dynasties and the Triumph of the Small Investor* (Vintage Books, 1997, 130 pp., $12).

Chernow has a spectacular track record; his first book, *The House of Morgan*, won the National Book Award for nonfiction and the Ambassador Award for best book on American culture. His next, *The Warburgs*, was awarded the Columbia Business School's 1993 George S. Eccles Prize for Excellence in Economic Writing, and was named a notable book by *The New York Times* and one of the year's 12 best nonfiction books by the American Library Association.

The Death of the Banker is really a short history of the financier — the intermediary between the suppliers and the consumers of capital — from the painful rise of Mayer Amschel Rothschild in the late 18th century through the merger of Morgan Stanley and Dean Witter earlier this year. The title essay in the book (85 of the 130 pages) carries the main argument; it was expanded from the Barbara Frum memorial lecture that Chernow gave in Toronto in April 1997.

Chernow is primarily interested in the migration of financial power. At the turn of the century, one man — J. Pierpont Morgan — controlled a third of America's railroads, 70% of the steel industry, and three banks (his own, Bankers Trust, and Guaranty Trust). Today, Chernow observes, the hegemonic power in American finance (if not the world) is the small investor in mutual funds. How did either (much less both) of these things happen? (Chernow also might have asked — but doesn't — how Baring Brothers, the financier of the Louisiana Purchase and called one of the "six great powers in Europe" by Louis XVIII's prime minister, got taken down by one rogue yuppie derivatives trader.)

In measuring the shifts of financial power, Chernow suggests that we think of a simple graph with three bars. He says, "As the middleman ... the wholesale banker naturally occupies the center position. He is forever suspended between the providers of capital — whether individual or institutional investors — and the consumers of capital — whether individual, business, or governmental borrowers." As the reader watches the size of the bars changing in relation to one another over time, the shape of Chernow's argument becomes clear.

All banking is originally merchant banking, and "any successful business that engenders a large surplus is, potentially, an embryonic bank," Chernow writes. So he begins with the story of Mayer Amschel Rothschild, a legendary financial power and the sire of five gifted sons who fanned out across Europe in the early 19th century. (It is astonishing that the first-ever biography of Mayer Amschel was published only last year by the Israeli historian Amos Elon. I recommend it highly; in addition to important economic history, it provides a searing look at the roots of anti-Semitism.)

Mayer Amschel had one great patron, Wilhelm IX, the landgrave of Hesse; this rich nobleman used Rothschild, in effect, as a front. He felt he could not gouge his fellow noblemen with usurious loans, but that they would expect (and accept) hard bargaining from a grasping Jewish moneylender. At this point, looking at Chernow's bar graph, the power of the capital provider was total; his captive agent, as well as the impoverished nobles borrowing his capital, were at his mercy.

Against these overwhelming odds, Mayer Amschel managed to endow his sons with a patrimony which, together with their joint

236

and several geniuses, enabled them to become titans of state finance. Aiding this trend was the fact that the nation-states of the early 19th century grew up in the shadow of the guillotine. Earlier monarchies might have had no compunction about taxing their citizens into the ground, but after the French Revolution borrowing seemed to be the better part of valor. Ultimately, the fatal Rothschild mistake (one that its archrival Barings signally did not make) was eschewing that raucous, uncouth, debt-repudiating madhouse of an emerging market: the United States. Still, wherever one looked, the wholesale banker (the middle bar on the graph) was now at "the apogee of ... power vis-à-vis the state," Chernow finds.

But between the Civil War and World War I, the United States finally achieved a unified national currency, created the Federal Reserve System (after J.P. Morgan saved us from bankruptcy not once but twice), and initiated a federal income tax. Equipped with these powers, government reclaimed a large measure of power from its bankers.

At this point, a new phase of finance moved to center stage: first railroad financing and then more generalized industrial financing via equity as well as debt. Chernow identifies the public offering of stock in the Guinness brewing empire in 1886 as a major turning point in corporate finance. As closely held industrial concerns became publicly held, their bankers tucked away huge blocks of stock for themselves. This may seem purely selfish to us, until we remember that the investors were buying new stocks in a disclosure-free world. So, the bankers were the only advocates the investors had.

Bestriding industrial finance like a colossus was John Pierpont Morgan, born to a wealthy American family then resident in England and acting as a banker and a broker between American states and companies and their English investors. Pierpont's vision and his power were to rationalize the wild, often piratical, boom-and-bust railroad industry on behalf of its British investors. What we might regard today as oligopolistic (if not downright monopolistic) restraint of trade, Morgan saw as bringing order out of chaos. On the bar graph, the banker's bar once again soared as "the capital providers, the London investors ... ceded much of their power to the banker Pierpont Morgan, who now acted as their fire-breathing, head-knocking proxy."

Rationalization was really the genius and the spirit of that age. Rockefeller in oil, Carnegie in steel — the great impulse was to dominate, to consolidate, to cut costs relentlessly, and to expand demand for the product. Morgan would, if he thought about it at all, undoubtedly have said he was doing the same thing with capital. (It isn't just that Morgan is the only one who could have orchestrated and financed the creation of U.S. Steel in 1901, I think. It's that he is the only one to whom Andrew Carnegie could possibly have sold.)

But democracy is ever the enemy of concentrated economic power, no matter how "rational" that power. When Theodore Roosevelt became president, the government brought an antitrust suit against Morgan's greatest railroad consolidation, the Northern Securities Company. (Astonished that Teddy, with whose father Pierpont had founded the American Museum of Natural History, would turn traitor to his class, Morgan famously told him, "If we have done anything wrong, send your man to my man and they can fix it up." Roosevelt's "man" was, of course, the Attorney General of the United States.)

If the tide of economic concentration ebbed savagely in the trust-busting, muckraking run-up to World War I, the 1920s saw the rise of yet another agent of economic democratization, the small investor. Even at the top in 1929, however, there were still only between one and three million people in the market (estimates vary); had the crash not cascaded into the Depression, the whole society might not have risen up against the Wall Street bankers.

Glass-Steagall shattered the hegemony of the House of Morgan and its ilk by divorcing commercial banking from the underwriting of securities. The banker could no longer be the one exclusive relationship his corporate clients had.

But even more than Glass-Steagall, Chernow sees the Securities Act of 1933, with its strong disclosure requirements, as the force "that would make the postwar world safe for shareholder democracy." A large part of the banker's power had previously been implicit in a huge reservoir of what we now call "inside information" about his corporate clients. (Indeed, no less moral a force than Sir John Templeton has repeatedly said that at the start of his career, inside information was the only kind worth having.) Now that playing field had been leveled for good and all.

By the 1960s, the bar graph was undergoing startling changes, Chernow points out. "On one hand, the capital consumers — the Fortune 500 companies — had grown indescribably huge during the Pax Americana and no longer needed a bank's imprimatur. This was less astounding than what had happened to the capital providers through the stupendous growth of institutional investors from corporate pension funds to mutual funds."

Now the bulge-bracket bankers were increasingly under attack from upstart firms who would offer institutional clients a capability the bankers disdained — the trading of "huge, unwieldy blocks of stock." (Morgan Stanley, to its credit, saw the depredations of Salomon Brothers and Goldman Sachs as the wave of the future, and quickly moved to become a fully integrated underwriting and trading power. Its great rival Kuhn, Loeb did not, and went into the darkness.)

It remained only for corporate America to throw off the yoke of the investment banker. For Chernow the final showdown occurred in 1979. Needing to float a billion-dollar debt offering, IBM asked its traditional underwriter, Morgan Stanley, to co-manage with the parvenu Salomon Brothers. Morgan Stanley said no, certain that IBM would back down. Big Blue gave the whole deal to Salomon. "The magic spell was broken, the slaves freed from the plantation," Chernow writes. Relationship banking was dead. This set the stage for transaction banking, and the stock market-dominated world of the 1980s and 1990s.

Chernow pauses here to inquire why old-style banker tyranny has persisted (at least until now) in Germany and Japan. He concludes that these countries, far more and far longer than most, "had political cultures that were deeply conservative, with some frighteningly authoritarian tendencies." He adds, "In despotic societies, power tends to be concentrated at the top in both political and economic institutions."

Emerging from World War II with "an exaggerated need for stability" over such "expendable frills as corporate profitability and a high return on assets," these countries naturally accepted fiercely controlling banker cultures. But these "Jurassic Parks of the financial world," as Chernow calls them, will slowly give way to the "bracing vicissitudes" of a truly stock market-driven financial system.

Returning to the United States, Chernow finds the 1980s' hostile takeover (so long eschewed by the gentleman banker) further enhancing the primacy of shareholder value, and therefore enlarging that part of the bar graph represented by capital providers. Increasingly, capital comes from many very small investors through what Chernow calls the "new arbiters of the financial universe: the mutual funds."

Chernow sees (although it isn't clear that he completely understands) "tens of millions of Americans in the alternatively giddy and terrifying position of managing their own retirement money ... ." The death of the corporate pension plan and the rise of self-directed 401(k) plans reflect a desire to transfer the risk of retirement investing to the individual beneficiary, Chernow believes. But more decisive, I think, was the stampede by corporate America to get out from under ERISA's prudent-man liability, which Chernow doesn't mention.

At any rate, the hypergrowth of fund assets (which soon will exceed the total assets of about $4.6 trillion in America's 10,000 commercial banks) represents, for Chernow, the apotheosis of the little guy (indeed, the littlest guy imaginable) over the financial titan of yore. But whereas Fidelity and Vanguard may be the new Citicorp and Chase (which, in their day, were the new Morgan and Rothschild), they are not, to Chernow, the repositories of any great power.

"Fund managers," he says, "inhabit a fishbowl world where everything is quantified, objectified, and published. The power of a J.P. Morgan isn't vested in mutual fund managers, but parceled out among millions of small investors who ... transfer money, in an instant, from places of lower to higher returns. These impatient, unsentimental 'little people' are the true martinets of modern finance."

And this, finally, is endgame. The small investor now has the money, the power, and above all the information that were once the exclusive province of the banking dynasties. Whether he will know what to do with those attributes in a bear market remains to be seen. Chernow finds it difficult to be very optimistic on this point.

Particularly given the great length of his previous books, Chernow's ability to compress this panoramic analysis into so short an essay makes his accomplishment all the more remarkable. It's a book that, as another reviewer said, "wears its considerable learning very lightly." You could easily read it on a long, rainy Sunday afternoon. And if you read only one book of economic history between now and year-end, do by all means make it *The Death of the Banker.*

FRESH AS TODAY'S HEADLINES

Where has this transcendent book been all my life? Or, more properly — since it was first published in 1978 — where have I been all of its?

Throughout my career, I've been a devotee of Charles Mackay's 1841 classic *Extraordinary Popular Delusions and the Madness of Crowds.* That great and charming work discusses many of the zaniest financial manias/disasters of the 17th and 18th centuries (the Tulip Mania, the South Sea Bubble), but also examines other lunacies that have seized the minds of whole populations through the ages. (Alchemy and witchcraft are my personal favorites.)

And, I confess, I've always thought Mackay's not merely the best but simply the only great survey of financial manias. So, I'm both chagrined and delighted (as well as grateful to the guiding spirits at Wiley Investment Classics, who have also revived Gerald Loeb's *The Battle for Investment Survival)* finally to discover *Manias, Panics and Crashes: A History of Financial Crises* by Charles P. Kindleberger (John Wiley & Sons, Third Edition, 1996, 263 pp., $39.95).

Kindleberger was the Ford Professor of Economics at MIT for 33 years. His involvement in our national economic life has been far more than academic, though. Indeed, his charming memoir of the heady days of the Marshall Plan is must reading for students of that period. A prolific economic historian, Kindleberger has written more than two dozen books, but I suspect that none will be of more long-term value to readers of this magazine than the volume I am reviewing here.

Updated to incorporate such phenomena as the Japanese boom and bust of 1988-90, the stock market crash of 1987, and the peso crisis of 1994, this third edition of Kindleberger's book continues his search for an economic model of the mania/crash cycle. This is a far more ambitious book than its modest subtitle suggests. It isn't just a history at all, although it is as complete a history as one may ever hope to encounter, starting with the currency devaluation in the Holy Roman Empire in 1618 and taking us up through the 1994 peso crisis. Kindleberger is trying to work through the unique historical aspects of each different cataclysm in order to arrive at "the underlying economic model of a general financial crisis."

Kindleberger begins, of necessity, with an attack on the currently fashionable views of markets being perfectly efficient, and market participants (taken as a whole) being rational. (Lovers of Modern Portfolio Theory — the Newtonian physics of the investment management world — take careful note.) In particular, the author warms the heart of this reviewer by kicking the living, uh, stuffing out of Milton Friedman, whose "monetarist school ... holds that there is virtually no destabilizing speculation, that markets are rational, that governments make mistake after mistake." The facts, in Kindleberger's often droll and always delightful recounting of event after ludicrous event, say otherwise.

What the real Adam Smith described as "folly, negligence ... knavery and extravagance" are human — and intensely destructive — constants. But, this turns out to be the good news as well as the bad news. For if there is a constancy to the cycle of excessive speculation (and the credit expansion necessary to fund it), followed by revulsion and panic liquidation (inflamed by the withdrawal of credit), then there is also a system to it. And, if it can never really be regulated or otherwise eliminated, at least that system can be understood and therefore, *in extremis,* dealt with through a structure of a lender (or lenders) of last resort.

It is Kindleberger's struggle with the concept of the lender of last resort — and with what the author and economist Peter Bernstein calls "the ambiguous nature of the appropriate moment for this step" — that is the most intellectually stimulating section of this extraordinarily stimulating book. (And that's saying something.) Its discussion of this issue is also, of course, what makes this book suddenly and almost preternaturally timely, given the ongoing serial crises in Japan, Indonesia, South Korea, and elsewhere in the developing world.

There is, however, no pressing need to rush to the final chapters of the book in order to get to this discussion, and the reader would miss a feast of delights if he did so. Take time to enjoy, first of all, the author's model of "speculation, credit expansion, financial distress at the peak, and then crisis, ending in panic and crash." Did you know, for instance (as I certainly did not), that the whole Tulip Mania was a speculation in the *futures* of tulip bulbs? The mania set in "after September 1636, when bulbs were no longer available for examination, having been planted to bloom the following Spring ... The excited bidding of November and December 1636 and January 1637 was conducted *with no specimens in evidence.*" (The words are Kindleberger's; the italics, I gleefully admit, are mine.)

Ancient history, you say? Well, how about this gem? Between 1977 and 1982, we learn that stocks and real estate were "bought and sold on the Kuwaiti stock exchange with postdated checks running into billions of dinars." (Dear Professor Friedman: How does government control the money supply when the maniacs are trading pieces of paper that require neither bank deposits nor bank loans?)

In July 1982, the first big wave of checks came due, and of course there was no money to cover them. In the ensuing bust, $91 billion (that's dollars, not dinars) in worthless checks came home to roost. In a wonderful postscript, after the smoke cleared, the Kuwati government simply built a new stock exchange and started over!

(Dumb, you say? Sure, but was it that much dumber than the Brady Commission's execrable 350-point-close-the-market "circuit breakers," instituted after our 1987 crash, when 350 points was a 20% move? Then, what about not changing the point value of the trigger even after the market had damn near quintupled? Excuse me, but *that's* dumb. However, I digress). If you just take these two little anecdotal gems of folly and multiply them a hundred times, you get some sense of the sheer pleasure to be had from reading Kindleberger's book. (And I suggest that, no matter what other uses you may put the book to, it ought to be read through once just for fun.)

245

THE CRAFT OF ADVICE

Having spent about half the book building his model of the financial boom/panic cycle, Kindleberger turns to ways of dealing with the inevitably resulting crises or, in the first instance, not dealing with them at all. In a lovely chapter called "Letting It Burn Out, and Other Devices," the author examines the school of thought that panic, like a thunderstorm, clears the air, purifies the system, and ultimately restores things to their proper balance.

This hands-off view was best expressed by President Hoover's Treasury Secretary Andrew W. Mellon — unless it wasn't. Hoover, in his 1952 memoirs, says that Mellon said this, but there's no other evidence of that assertion:

"Mr. Mellon had only one formula: 'Liquidate labor, liquidate stocks, liquidate the farmers, liquidate real estate.' He insisted that, when the people get an inflationary brainstorm, the only way to get it out of their blood is to let it collapse. He held that even panic was not altogether a bad thing. He said, 'It will purge the rottenness out of the system. High costs of living and high living will come down. People will work harder, live a more moral life. Values will be adjusted, and enterprising people will pick up the wrecks from less competent people.'"

We don't necessarily have to agree with the historian Paul Johnson who said, "(This) was the only sensible advice Hoover received during his Presidency." But, we can see that it frames the critical issue: in extreme financial distress which spills over into a general economic crisis, the government can legitimately consider doing nothing — as market purists will insist it should. But if it chooses to do something, what should it do, and how should it signal the marketplace as to its intentions in this regard?

This raises the issue of the lender of last resort (along with the corollary issue: the international lender of last resort, which — as anyone at the International Monetary Fund can tell you these days — is most certainly not the same thing). Kindleberger's last two chapters (covering 50 of the 263 pages) are devoted to this question, and alone are worth the rather steep price of the book, which must be the highest cost-per-page volume I own.

Without even attempting to summarize these chapters, let me say that they are most interesting in their examination of whether the marketplace's knowledge of the presence of a lender of last resort is not inherently destabilizing. If a market, a bank, or even a country knows that it will get bailed out if worst comes to worst, why seriously attempt to avoid the worst?

Alan Greenspan went famously ballistic over the weekend of October 17-18, 1987, when another Fed governor told the press that the central bank would pump into the system on Monday any and all liquidity required to keep it from melting down. This was no more or less than plain fact; Greenspan's concern was that it sent a signal to the market that it need make no attempt to discipline, control, or correct itself. Before you applaud the IMF too loudly for pulling South Korea's chestnuts out of the fire, you might just want to read these 50 pages.

"History is particular, economics is general," Kindleberger insists, and in the end his book turns out to be, as Bernstein says in the foreword to this third edition, a "unique contribution of the literature of both disciplines." I suspect that this is one of those books I'll end up reading once a year whether I think I need to or not. And, I suggest you run, not walk, to your nearest bookstore to get yourself a copy of this marvelous tome.

THE TRIUMPH OF THE MARKET ... FOR NOW

On March 28, 1979 — a day when Britain was so paralyzed by labor strife that even the catering staff at the House of Commons was on strike — the Labour Party government fell on a vote of no confidence by just one vote.

In the general election that followed, the Conservatives returned to power, led by a new prime minister, Margaret Thatcher. In the words of one of her cabinet ministers, Mrs. Thatcher "believed in hard work, achievement, and that everything had to be paid for." A grocer's daughter, Mrs. Thatcher started the global economic revolution that has become the defining event of our age.

That same year, Paul Volcker assumed the chairmanship of the Federal Reserve, and Deng Xiaoping initiated economic reforms in China. The next year, Ronald Reagan was elected president. Five years later, Mikhail Gorbachev began the policies of glasnost and perestroika. Five years after that, communism collapsed in Eastern Europe. The following year, the Soviet Union disintegrated.

The guiding principle in all of these events, and indeed in virtually all world history of this period, has been the failure of big government as an economic arbiter. "The commanding heights" of the world economy (the phrase, deliciously, is Lenin's) have been stormed and conquered by the free-market idea, or so we learn in *The Commanding Heights: The Battle Between Government and the Marketplace That Is Remaking the Modern World* by Daniel Yergin and Joseph Stanislaw (Simon & Schuster, 1998, 391 pp., $26).

Yergin, one of the foremost economic historians of our time, also wrote *The Prize: The Epic Quest for Oil, Money, and Power,* which won a Pulitzer Prize. It is the definitive story of that most important commodity and one of my all-time favorite books.

In *Commanding Heights,* Yergin and his partner at Cambridge Energy Research Associates, Joseph Stanislaw, present the most thorough study yet of the world's economic transformation over the past 20 years. But they have done more than that: The authors have given us a critical understanding of how the world turned over economic primacy to government in the first place. And they have conducted a dispassionate and brilliant autopsy on the disasters that ensued around the globe.

Commanding Heights is a unique resource for readers of this magazine; we are not likely to see a study of the triumph of the marketplace which is at once so comprehensive and so readable. For, as he did in *The Prize,* Yergin (with Stanislaw) delivers an immensely entertaining story, as interesting for its anecdotes as for its development of ideas.

Here, for instance, is how Yergin and Stanislaw describe, after 40 years of the most stultifying statism, India's government-owned Hindustan Fertilizer Corporation in 1991:

"...[I]ts twelve hundred employees were clocking in every day, as they had since the plant had officially opened a dozen years earlier. The only problem was that the plant had failed to produce any fertilizer for sale. It had been built between 1971 and 1979, using considerable public funds, with machinery from Germany, Czechoslovakia, Poland, and a half-dozen other countries. The equipment had looked like a great bargain to the civil servants who made the basic decisions, because it could be financed with export credits. Alas, the machinery did not fit together and the plant could not operate. Everyone just pretended that it was operating."

Though perhaps the most grotesque, this is only one of hundreds of examples the authors use to depict the unraveling of the illusion that government knowledge is superior to market knowledge. But where had this notion come from in the first place?

Yergin and Stanislaw make clear that the rise of government to the commanding heights was very much a function of the perceived failure of the market idea. From America's "progressive" notions of "the curse of bigness" at the turn of the century to Russia's revolutionary rejection of centuries of Czarist serfdom, free-market capitalism was under attack in all parts of the world by the time it spectacularly came a cropper in the worldwide depression of the 1930s.

And whether it was government ownership of the means of production under communism, or a complex and suffocating regulatory regime in the United States, the state was held to be a better arbiter of economic activity than the market. A more or less constant war footing from 1914 to 1989 only exacerbated the flow of fiscal power toward government.

The idea of government regulation of the economy was systematized and sanctified, the authors find, by Keynesianism, with its promises of growth and full employment. And indeed the brilliant progress of the West's economies from the Marshall Plan until Vietnam seemed to bear Keynes out.

But, of course, Keynes only favored government deficits when the economy was in need of stimulation. The idea that deficits would be used as a permanent form of electioneering by a new class of career politicians appears not to have occurred to him — or to nearly anyone else. (Although as early as the 1830s, Tocqueville is supposed to have said, "A democracy will always vote itself more benefits than it is prepared to produce.")

But when Bretton Woods' magisterially fixed exchange rates began to come apart in the early 1970s, as the marketplace recognized the cancer of U.S. inflation even when politicians did not, the end was in sight. When OPEC pulled the trigger, stagflation began its long run and Keynesianism became an idea whose time had gone. Also, the dark side of the post-World War II commitment to full employment appeared in the greed, corruption, and featherbedding that ultimately destroyed the power of labor unions around the world.

Different parts of the globe experienced their own brands of disenchantment with governmental management of economics; the authors take us around the world several times and recount each

251

country's or region's conversion in vivid detail. The privatizing of state-owned companies (after radical downsizing of bloated workforces) is a constant theme, as is the grudging acceptance of entrepreneurship in all its myriad forms.

This brings us to the book's single failure — an important one. The heroes of *Commanding Heights* are economists, central bankers, finance ministers, and heads of state. Missing almost entirely are the entrepreneurs and financiers who actually made the markets work. We want to read much more about those who created, in the words of another reviewer, "the technologies that linked (markets), who made closed societies impossible, who in many cases — as in the creation of global foreign exchange markets — actually wrested power from governments."

The authors might counter that the contributions of a Bill Gates or an Andy Grove have been well-chronicled elsewhere, whereas those of Argentina's Domingo Cavallo, Russia's Yegor Gaidar, or Korea's Kim Jae-Ik (especially as they relate to each other) have not. Still, a history of the market revolution with virtually no attention to actual market participants is a lot less than complete. But while this is a serious criticism, it does not lessen my wholehearted recommendation of *Commanding Heights*.

Close readers of this book will get the most out of it if they see that it is not (or not just) an account of the triumph of a good idea over a bad idea. The transfer of faith from government knowledge to market knowledge, like the trend in the other direction which preceded it, must ultimately be seen as the movement of a pendulum; it can swing so far and then no further. "In virtually every country," as Kissinger Associates' David Rothkopf has written, "there is a backlash against the perceived inadequacies of the market as a custodian of social values."

As the world population ages (there will be 400 million Chinese age 65 and over in the year 2030 vs. 100 million today), the politics of retirement benefits can only become more bitter. Moreover, while technology and capital can move effortlessly and instantly around the globe, labor cannot. The social demands of those left behind by the market will be significant.

And so, in the end, *Commanding Heights* succeeds brilliantly in framing the essential questions; it does not answer them because no one can. What are the differences between human rights and property rights, and how will society reconcile those differences? The marketplace sees to the efficiency of the distribution of wealth, but who will define, and how will we ensure, the "justice" or "fairness" of the distribution?

The next time the pendulum swings back, it may not be pretty for those of us who own and manage capital. But at least thoughtful readers of *Commanding Heights* will be far better prepared than they might otherwise have been.

A CALL TO ARMS FOR UNIVERSAL FREE TRADE

While reading Melvyn Krauss' *How Nations Grow Rich: The Case For Free Trade* (Oxford University Press, 1997, 140 pp., $22.50), I recalled something that Abbie Hoffmann or Jerry Rubin (I couldn't tell them apart 30 years ago, and my memory surely hasn't improved since) said: "Just because you're paranoid doesn't mean they're not out to get you."

As the subtitle to Krauss' book warns, this is not primarily a dispassionate analysis but a polemic. And after working through Krauss' densely reasoned arguments, I concluded that just because a book is a sometimes bitter and slashing polemic doesn't mean it isn't intellectually rigorous or ultimately right. This book is both, and the readers of this magazine will gain much from reading it.

In barely 120 pages of text, Krauss offers us a *tour d'horizon* of the headline-grabbing trade debates and such pressing but often obscure issues as development policy, foreign aid, child labor, human rights trade linkages, immigration, the European Monetary Union, and "affirmative action" trade policy. All of these issues weigh heavily on managers of capital, and it can be difficult to filter through the political and journalistic rhetoric to find the real economics of a situation.

The unifying theme in Krauss' analyses of these often disparate debates is that in a market economy where the consumer is the ultimate arbiter, only a consumer-based equity standard is valid. As water seeks its own level, the marketplace will figure out how to bring goods and services to the consumer at the lowest cost ... which is all he really cares about.

No matter what artificial barriers are placed in the way of this impulse — in the service of no matter what market-distorting perceived social "good" — the market will simply work around it. But not before all sorts of unforeseen harm has been done in the country that is trying to protect itself, or to advance its social agenda, by means of the distortion.

Krauss cites the classic example of a 1991 incident in which the United States decided that Japan was "dumping" flat-panel displays, also known as liquid crystal display screens, that are used in the manufacture of laptop computers. So we slapped a 63% tariff on the importation of these displays, and, of course, the resulting cost increase made domestic manufacturers of laptops uncompetitive.

Apple Computer moved its production facilities to Ireland from Colorado. Toshiba, which had been manufacturing in the United States, moved back to Japan. And IBM, which had originally planned to assemble some of its laptop models at a plant in Raleigh, North Carolina, instead set up production in Japan. The net effect of the allegedly "protective" tariff was to throw large numbers of Americans out of work.

For Krauss, this incident is a microcosm of every attempt by government to protect one interest group — here, a nascent sector of the American computer industry — from the rigors of the marketplace. (Having done its damage, the tariff was quietly rescinded two years later.)

And what is "dumping," anyway? If an industry in one country has mismanaged itself so badly that it has large surpluses of its product to sell below cost, why shouldn't we be delighted to have our consumers buy those things below cost? Clearly, this is a windfall for Americans and no threat to our industry: The foreign producers can't go on losing money forever.

But what if the phenomenon isn't "dumping" at all? What if foreigners can make a profit selling below our cost of manufacturing? Then, says Krauss, they *should* produce the product. Economic common sense, as opposed to uneconomic protection of jobs that are dead ducks anyway, dictates that world wealth is best served by letting the consumer have whatever he wants as cheaply as he can get it. That way, he can either use his savings to buy something else, or he can invest them. Either choice adds to economic well-being;

"taxing" the whole society through higher (protected) prices to keep dying industries on life support subtracts from it.

Now, maybe this is obvious to you (I always have the sinking feeling that this magazine's readers are a whole lot smarter than I am) but it wasn't to me. And it wasn't to all those folks out there whose feedback to their elected representatives in Washington almost derailed NAFTA and did stop Fast Track. So if it isn't obvious to you — or if it is but you have trouble explaining it to clients — this book is a must.

The net cost of protection — in no matter what form it appears — is, to Krauss, always higher, and sometimes much higher, than its benefits to the protected few. In 1993, the Commerce Department imposed dumping duties of up to 109% on steel imports from 19 nations, as well as subsidy penalties of up to 73% on steel from 12 nations. It failed to notice that steel-using industries employ more than 30 *times* more Americans than do domestic steel manufacturers. And the steel price increases that resulted from the duties/penalties immediately began putting some of these people out of work. One way or another, Krauss concludes, protectionism exports more jobs than it can ever hope to "save."

Krauss also is unsympathetic to the argument that free trade unfairly harms labor whose skills and mobility are "sticky." This isn't an argument against free trade, he says, it's an argument against *all* change. It ignores the basic tenet of capitalism — what Schumpeter famously called "creative destruction" — and is, to Krauss, merely another manifestation of a culture of entitlement. Labor's insistence that the society protect uneconomic jobs is the demand for a "security" that does not exist in nature. (Should we have maintained a thermonuclear balance of terror which threatened the existence of the species, in order to protect jobs in the defense industry?)

Another of Krauss' favorite targets is the neo-mercantilist argument that trade surpluses are by their nature inherently good and trade "deficits" are bad. Generally speaking, a country with a high savings rate will export capital and run trade surpluses. A country with a relatively low savings rate will import capital and run trade deficits. Savings rates, rather than some "fair" or "unfair" trade policy, drive the creditor/debtor status of nations.

Moreover, if indeed the Japanese unfairly (and uneconomically) tax their consumers by foolish protectionist measures that make U.S. imports too expensive, how does it follow that we should retaliate by doing the same thing — by raising the price of Japanese goods to our consumers? That doesn't hurt the Japanese — they're already hurting themselves — it only hurts us, by unfairly taxing *our* consumers.

Finally, anyone who's watched Japan's economy crater and ours soar in the 1990s — while our trade "deficit" with Japan went from "bad" to "worse" — must know that a country's economic health and its current account balances may be all but unrelated to each other.

Krauss is also interesting when he discusses a couple of qualitative issues that are involved when the United States holds trade policies hostage to its social agenda.

We ought not to trade with countries whose pollution standards are not up to ours, one such argument goes, because they have an "unfair" advantage. Krauss argues that free trade causes the country of higher environmental standards to "export" its polluting industries to the country of the lower standard. The net amount of pollution in the world stays the same, and the global consumer gets the goods at the lower cost — increasing world wealth (as seen above) and presumably increasing the resources society can use to fight pollution.

Another highly emotional issue is child labor. We don't want to import things produced by children for low wages under what we consider foul working conditions — apparently not realizing that this may be the only way for them to escape poverty.

Krauss quotes a Guatemalan economist: "Depriving developing countries, even with the best of intentions, of capital and jobs needed to grow out of these centuries-old conditions of poverty will merely ensure the indefinite perpetuation of this misery." Singapore's founder Lee Kuan Yew, in arguing against Western interference in "Asian values," has also made the point that a national right to economic development in the long run may legitimately be permitted to supersede many individual rights in the short run.

These and many other issues that we may consider one-sided are patiently and carefully dissected by Krauss. Even when you don't agree with him, you will have a tough time making the countervailing argument; at the very least, this exercise will sharpen your understanding of the issues.

Having said all these positive things, it pains me to add that this is the worst-edited book I can remember reading. If it were some quickie paperback bio of Leonardo DiCaprio rushed into print by some cheesy publisher, I could understand. But this is a very erudite work, published by none other than Oxford University Press; the resulting lapses are both unforgivable and incomprehensible.

Plural subjects take singular verbs and vice versa; quotations open but never close; and parentheses close that never opened. One two-sentence quote has quotation marks at the beginning, at the end, and in the middle of the two sentences. The journalist Anna Quindlen's name is spelled wrong as often as right, and within two pages she's referred to as "Miss" and "Ms." Ralph Nader's surname is often (but not always) spelled as if it rhymes with radar, and the book can never decide whether the last word in the acronym NAFTA is Agreement or Area. And these are just the highlights. Krauss wrote an excellent book; he (and we) deserve better editing.

Still, the excellence of the argument and its importance to us as stewards of capital are what ultimately count. And no book dedicated by an author to his dog, as this one is, can be all bad.

WEALTH: WHERE AND WHY?

It takes a lot of damn gall, as my Texan friends say, to ask people as pressed for time as are this magazine's readers to read a 650-page book. But this is me, jumping up and down and telling you that David Landes' career-capping *The Wealth and Poverty of Nations: Why Some Are So Rich and Some So Poor* is the one book you have to read this summer.

In truth, this wonderfully written, brilliantly argued analysis of world economic history only contains 529 pages of text (including the Introduction). But then there are 41 pages of footnotes as wise, charming, and intellectually rigorous (especially when Landes points out scholarly conclusions that disagree with his) as the text itself, and as necessary. Moreover, just to get a feeling for the lifetime of scholarship that went into this book, you want to at least page through the 69-page bibliography.

David Landes is professor emeritus of both history and economics at Harvard, and has been a world-class scholar for upwards of half a century. His 1969 book, *The Unbound Prometheus,* may still be the single most widely read history of Western technology. That said, no amount of scholarship can account for Landes' sparkling writing, acerbic wit, or generosity of spirit, all of which the lay reader needs — and receives in abundance — to get through this huge book.

Professor Landes has spent his career studying the causes of economic growth, and indeed has watched dozens of theories come and go during his lifetime. Researching the wildly disparate performance of economies the world over, in all historical epochs, Landes — going Adam Smith one better — has sought both the sources of the wealth of some nations and the sources of the poverty of others.

Why was China so far ahead of Europe in mathematics, technology, and culture, only to regress into isolation and economic failure?

Why, within 100 years of the Prophet Muhammad's flight from Mecca, had Islam swept past Gibraltar to the Atlantic and through Spain into central France, only to retreat again into the desert? How did Spain discover and colonize a whole New World and then turn back into irrelevance? Why did the Industrial Revolution happen in Britain and not in Germany or even in Japan? Why is the 300-year-old economy of the United States hegemonic in a 5,000-year-old economic world?

David Landes knows, and makes his report in *The Wealth and Poverty of Nations: Why Some Are So Rich and Some So Poor* (W. W. Norton & Company, 1998, 650 pp., $30).

Professor Landes' book is not merely a dispassionate scholarly inquiry: knowing for its own sake. "We live in a world of inequality and diversity," he writes. "Now the big challenge and threat is the gap in wealth and health that separates rich and poor ... . Here is the greatest single problem and danger facing the world of the third millennium."

The mature, successful economies can only grow and prosper by trading and investing with those who are far less developed, closing the gap between them. In the long run, the brutal efficiency of the marketplace will surely see to this. But, as Keynes said, in the long run we are all dead. Might we not both accelerate and smooth out the process, Landes seems to be asking, if we understood and ran it, rather than letting it run us?

This is not to suggest that Landes is in any way an elitist apostle of "managing" markets. Indeed, he concludes a lovely little chapter called "The Invention of Invention" (celebrating four European technological breakthroughs: the water wheel, eyeglasses, the mechanical clock, and movable metal type) with a paean:

"In the last analysis, however, I would stress the market. Enterprise was free in Europe. Innovation worked and paid, and rulers and vested interests were limited in their ability to prevent or discourage innovation.

"Success bred imitation and emulation; also a sense of power that would in the long run raise men almost to the level of gods."

But an analysis that reduces the issues of economic growth to any one variable — even one as powerful as "the market" or "technology" — will never do. Landes begins his book by examining (and disposing of) one classic argument — that geography is destiny. True enough, temperate zones have developed more rapidly and fully than equatorial ones due to the debilitating effects of heat, tropical disease, wildly uneven rainfall, and murderous droughts and floods on marginally subsistent populations. But the advent of modern health and sanitation methods, vaccines, irrigation/damming/crop rotation, and even air conditioning have barely affected the third world (and all but missed the fourth). And climate fails to explain why Europe was "so slow to develop, thousands of years after Egypt and Sumer," Landes notes. No, we must look at something other than the thermometer for economic clues.

Nor will technology answer the case. "Witness the long list of Chinese inventions," Landes writes, "the wheelbarrow, the stirrup, the rigid horse collar (to prevent choking), the compass, paper, printing, gunpowder, porcelain." The Chinese had a water-driven machine for spinning hemp in the 12th century, 500 years before the Industrial Revolution saw water frames and mules in Britain. China used coal and coke in blast furnaces and smelted 125,000 tons of pig iron annually by the late 11th century, a figure not seen in Britain for 700 more years.

What went wrong? The terrible, top-down imperial totalitarianism of a system without institutionalized property rights. The Heavenly Kingdom saw only danger in trade with the outside world, and was forever seizing or manipulating enterprise, even moving whole populations to different regions at the emperor's whim. "Isolation became China," Landes concludes, and the world passed it by.

Through India, Japan, Spain and Portugal, Holland, and finally to Britain and its Industrial Revolution, Landes charts epic rises and falls, conquests and dead ends, opportunities seized and missed through the ages, and not just by recounting the exploits of kings, conquistadors, and merchant princes. Landes offers delightful, often personal vignettes throughout the text. At one point, to illuminate Japanese social and economic dynamics, he devotes several pages to the story of a Japanese orphan and her marriage into an upwardly mobile family straight out of an oriental Dickens.

From all of this, Landes derives a template for the ideal growth-and-development society. Its hallmarks are knowledge of how to operate, manage, build, and improve instruments of production; willingness and ability to impart this knowledge to the young through formal education and/or apprenticeship; employment on the basis of competence and relative merit, and promotion or demotion on the basis of performance; opportunity awarded to individual/collective enterprise, with rewards for initiative, competition, and emulation; and the ability of people to use and enjoy the fruits of their labor and enterprise.

"These standards," Landes notes, "imply corollaries." Gender equality, for instance, doubles the workforce; the tendency of Islam to keep women housebound "made it impossible to exploit textile machinery profitably in a factory setting." If you exile all the Jews and forbid your other citizens from attending universities in other countries, as Spain did in the 60 years after Columbus, all your exploration will be for naught. If you burn your Giordano Brunos (and don't burn your Galileos only because they repudiate their scientific discoveries), as the Italian Catholic Church did in the early 1600s, you can bring all science and most technology to a screeching halt. Growth is therefore the relative absence of irrationality (although, in one of the countless footnotes that endear him to me so, Landes cheerfully admits that superstition — horoscopes, etc. — is preferable to fatalism).

One reviewer — a fellow academic of Landes' — took a potshot at him in *The Wall Street Journal* for paying too little attention to the development of societal institutions as a force for economic growth. But in two pages Landes succinctly enumerates the political and social institutions most conducive to growth and development. I quote him here because it would be a sin to try to abridge them:

264

"1. Secure rights of private property, the better to encourage saving and investment.

2. Secure rights of personal liberty — secure them against both the abuses of tyranny and private disorder (crime and corruption).

3. Enforce rights of contract, explicit and implicit.

4. Provide stable government, not necessarily democratic, but itself governed by publicly known rules (a government of laws rather than men). If democratic, that is, based on periodic elections, the majority wins but does not violate the rights of the losers; while the losers accept their loss and look forward to another turn at the polls.

5. Provide responsive government, one that will hear complaint and make redress.

6. Provide honest government, such that economic actors are not moved to seek advantage and privilege inside or outside the marketplace. In economic jargon, there should be no rents to favor and position.

7. Provide moderate, efficient, ungreedy government. The effect should be to hold taxes down, reduce the government's claim on the social surplus, and avoid privilege."

In the end, the beauty and importance of this volume defeat any attempt to encapsulate it in the book review format. Reading it is a workout, a treat, and a most elegant entertainment. Enjoy, enjoy.

BOUND TO BE RICH

To understand the government's distress over the business hegemony of Microsoft and its co-founder, William Henry Gates III, you need more than a passing knowledge of computer operating systems. But to fathom our democracy's intense anxiety about "monopoly" power, you must go back to the days of Standard Oil and to its silent, mysterious, complex builder, John Davison Rockefeller, Sr.

How timely, then, that Ron Chernow's long-awaited biography of Rockefeller was published this spring to universally favorable (if often unperceptive) reviews. This National Book Award-winning biographer of the Morgans and the Warburgs (as well as the author of a small gem of economic history, *The Death of the Banker*, reviewed in this space in the November/December 1997 issue) enjoyed unprecedented access to the Rockefeller archives. Chernow has produced the definitive biography, *Titan: The Life of John D. Rockefeller, Sr.* (Random House, 1998, 774 pages, $30), which masters and reconciles the great man's economic ruthlessness with his very real religious conviction and his wise (and unparalleled) philanthropies.

John D. Rockefeller was born in 1839, the last of a group of titans who burst into the world almost simultaneously: Andrew Carnegie, Jay Gould, J. Pierpont Morgan, and Rockefeller were all born within 50 months. Rockefeller's warring selves were the product of his parents' strange marriage: a fiercely religious, frugal, controlled and controlling mother and a father who was a flimflam man — snake-oil salesman, itinerant quack doctor, and — most notably — a bigamist.

The father, an immensely charming rogue, would simply hit the road whenever the spirit moved him, leaving his wife and children to live on the credit of the local merchants — and in fear that they might be cut off at any time. The oldest child, John inevitably became the surrogate husband/father, and early portraits show a solemn, joyless, very old young man. He was forced to leave school at 16 when his father, Big Bill, decamped for good to marry again and start a whole new family.

His mother's all-pervading Baptist faith became John's own. A singularly democratic religion with no allegiance to a central church hierarchy, it taught that man was a free agent who could be redeemed by an act of the will. Such a belief system was perfect for a rising, iron-willed, self-made man.

Moreover, Rockefeller's faith held that money was a reward for righteous living and hard work. "I was trained from the beginning to work and save," he remembered. "I have always regarded it as a religious duty to get all I could honorably and to give all I could." Thus, his implacable acquisitiveness and extraordinary philanthropy become, in Chernow's skilled analysis, complementary — and perfectly consistent — rather than contradictory, much less hypocritical. So much so that, years later, when Rockefeller says, "God gave me my money," we know exactly what he means.

Rockefeller started in business as a bookkeeper. Quickly, he "betrayed a special affinity for accounting and an almost mystic faith in numbers," Chernow writes. These qualities would stand him in good stead when he began to focus on the business of refining the newly discovered Pennsylvania oil into kerosene.

Early developing a visionary belief in the future of oil, Rockefeller was appalled by the wild boom-and-bust cycles that were evident within a few years of Colonel Drake's 1859 discovery well at Titusville. At one moment, it would appear that the oil fields would soon run dry and prices would soar. Then the next huge discovery would send prices crashing to less than the cost of transportation, and even below production cost.

What astonished and horrified Rockefeller was that in times of glut and low prices, the producers wouldn't stop producing, nor the refiners stop refining. Often heavily burdened by debt, industry participants would sell product at any price to stave off bankruptcy for one more day.

A prolonged depression in oil prices beginning in the late 1860s gave Rockefeller his opportunity (although he always insisted that his brilliant partner Henry Flagler gave him the idea). Colluding with the railroads for secret rebates (a practice not yet illegal) that would give him an insuperable cost advantage, Rockefeller engineered the "Cleveland Massacre." In 1872 he approached virtually all the oil refiners in that city and told them they must be acquired by Standard Oil or be driven into bankruptcy. Overnight, Standard became the dominant oil refiner in the world, and Rockefeller never looked back.

The story of Standard Oil's hegemony over world oil for the balance of the 19th century is one of genius, vision, and the welding of a peerless managerial structure — together with political corruption, corporate espionage, and cutthroat competition with potential rivals. The trust's monopoly power did not peak until the mid-1890s, by which time Rockefeller was retiring from active involvement in the business to pursue his epic philanthropies, which already included the endowment of the University of Chicago.

At its zenith, Standard Oil "marketed 84% of all petroleum products sold in America and pumped a third of its crude oil," Chernow notes. But the combination of Royal Dutch and Shell overseas forestalled a global conquest by the company. And Standard missed the Texas oil boom entirely because its most piratical agent got Standard thrown out of the state just before the Spindletop well came in, in 1901.

Thus, while the oil business was on the threshold of its greatest success yet — because of the automobile — and while the bulk of Rockefeller's personal fortune was still to be made, Standard Oil's power was on the wane as the century turned.

It's therefore ironic that the hugely popular demonization of Rockefeller and of Standard Oil by the muckraking journalist Ida Tarbell in 1903, and the breakup of the trust by the government in 1911, were essentially a great slamming of the barn door after the horse had been stolen ... and long after Rockefeller himself was gone from the Standard Oil fortress at 26 Broadway.

THE CRAFT OF ADVICE

The law of unintended consequences is never more in evidence than when government interferes with markets. Surely the apotheosis of this phenomenon was the aftermath of the Supreme Court's May 1911 decision, after a titanic five-year legal battle, that Standard Oil be dissolved. No single event in the company's 41-year history produced more shareholder value faster than did the edict that broke it up. (Microsoft shorts, pay careful heed.) And typically, no one seems to have anticipated this outcome more clearly than did Rockefeller himself.

He was playing golf at Pocantico with Father J. P. Lennon of the Tarrytown Catholic church when he got the news of the Supreme Court's decision. Rockefeller asked, "Father Lennon, have you some money?" The priest answered no, but asked why. And John D. Rockefeller said, "Buy Standard Oil" — arguably the single best stock tip in the history of the Republic.

"When trading started on December 1, 1911," Chernow tells us, "the public exhibited an insatiable appetite for the new companies, especially after they declared dividends averaging 53% of the old value of Standard Oil stock.

"Between January and October 1912, Standard Oil of New Jersey zoomed from 360 to 595; Standard of New York went from 260 to 580; and Standard of Indiana from 3500 to 9500 ... . During the 10 years after Standard Oil's 1911 dismantling, the assets of its constituent companies quintupled in value," Chernow reports. And indeed, the creatures of the breakup — including today's Exxon, Mobil, Amoco, Chevron, ARCO, and Conoco — continue to be giants of the world economy.

Chernow's singular achievement in this biography, and the thing that makes it truly definitive, is an understanding not merely of Rockefeller's genius, nor even of his psychology, but of his soul. The "perfect fusion of capitalism and Christianity" that Chernow finds in Rockefeller allowed him to view Standard Oil as "the moral equivalent of the Baptist Church," using means that were fully justified by the ends of bringing salvation to the squalid chaos of the oil business and the blessing of affordable illumination and energy to mankind.

The one thing missing from this book that might have improved it greatly is a detailed financial analysis of Standard Oil's rise. Chernow makes the point that, even in the wildly gyrating oil price environments of the 1860s and '70s, the Rockefeller enterprise was always profitable. I wish I understood how. And during the Cleveland Massacre, Chernow says many refiners capitulated once they examined Rockefeller's books. Exactly what, I wonder, did they see there?

Finally, when Chernow relates the last great battle of Rockefeller's career — against Andrew Carnegie over the Mesabi Range — I would have welcomed the Rockefeller side of the heated debate over who got the better of whom in the subsequent peace pact. Chernow takes no position in the matter, saying simply, "The bargain (was) Carnegie's belated attempt to redress his own error." Indeed it was. But as Carnegie's biographer, the late Joseph Frazier Wall (a scrupulous scholar and no idolater of Andrew by any means), is at pains to demonstrate, in the final analysis the canny old Scot seems well and truly to have cleaned Rockefeller's clock.

Such financial detail might have made *Titan* a deeper *business* biography. But in the larger sense, it's hard to image what could have made this a better biography overall. And it is one of the best biographies *of* anyone *by* anyone that you'll ever read.

DROLL DISPATCHES FROM THE DISMAL SCIENCE

After my son Mark graduated from high school this year, he and I fulfilled a longtime dream by going to France for the final week of the quadrennial World Cup soccer tournament. Perusing the *International Herald Tribune* one morning, the lad was appalled to read about a village in Pakistan where the women sew soccer balls for 60 cents a day until they become too arthritic and/or lose their sight.

"If you aren't a liberal at 20," Winston Churchill said, "you have no heart." And so Mark, enraged at the villagers' plight, declared that we should all be willing to pay a few more bucks for a soccer ball to help these poor people.

"And if you're not a conservative at 40," Churchill went on, "you have no brain." So although it's been a while since I was 40, I said: not so fast.

First of all, I guessed that 60 cents was two to three times what they'd been earning when the village was just another sinkhole of rural poverty. Second, if Mark raised their wages to, say, two dollars a day, I suggested that within a few months another soccer ball manufacturer would come into another village just a few clicks up the road, pay 60 cents, have that wage eagerly accepted, and proceed to undersell Mark to death. Thus the inevitable result of my son's largesse would be that his villagers would shortly be back in the abyss, and he'd be bankrupt.

In this way, the idea that dreadful jobs are infinitely preferable to no jobs became Mark's first lesson in the critical and not-at-all obvious distinction between economics (the way things really work) and emotions (the way we would like things to work). This is a distinction that many more Americans — even some in high places — need to learn to make. But, generally speaking, economists themselves are no help. They write almost exclusively for each other, in a densely mathematical language unfathomable to the rest of us.

Enter Paul Krugman. His day job is as a professor of economics at MIT, a datum eerily undisclosed on the jacket of his recently published collection of short essays, *The Accidental Theorist and Other Dispatches From the Dismal Science* (W.W. Norton & Co., 1998, 204 pp., $25). Perhaps the publisher feared that the book's potential purchaser, seeing that its author was an economics professor, would hurl it down in revulsion and fear.

But Krugman is actually something quite special. Without admitting it in so many words (he obliquely raises the analogy in the book's introduction, but then lets it drop), Krugman is trying to be to economics what Carl Sagan was to astronomy: both a first-rate practitioner of the science and its explicator/popularizer to the lay audience.

To do both without slighting either is a lot harder than Krugman makes it look — for, as Keynes said, economics is "a difficult and technical subject, but no one will believe it." As this charming and thought-provoking book attests, Krugman succeeds much more often than not.

Our difficulties with economics, Krugman insists, are not just implicit in the pedantic obscurantism of its professional acolytes. He writes, "The biggest problem with many business people, political leaders, and others is that while they are willing to talk and read about economics ad nauseam, they are not willing to do anything that feels like going back to school. They would rather read five books by David Halberstam" (ouch; that hurts) "than one chapter in an undergraduate textbook."

This, to Krugman, is why you can find the lamentable Robert Reich, while he was still secretary of labor in the Clinton administration, seriously proposing tax subsidies for companies that refrain from eliminating clearly uneconomic jobs. You'll hear Ross Perot and Pat Buchanan railing against NAFTA because it will draw low-skill jobs south of the border — apparently not recognizing that those jobs are sooner or later inevitably going to migrate to *some* low-wage country. And you see a whole generation of "conservatives" — the supply-siders, who come in for Krugman's particular scorn — proposing the radical notion that so much growth will flow from tax cuts that one need not trouble commensurately to cut spending.

The fundamental issue, Krugman finds, is that such thinkers, while clearly smart people, are operating without the one thing every Econ 101 student is forced to live by: an economic model. "They think," he says, "that you do economics the way a lawyer prepares a brief for a client — first you decide on your opinion, then you marshal as many plausible arguments as you can in support.

"But that's not the way economics is done," Krugman asserts. "A real economist starts not with a policy view but with *a story about how the world works.* That story almost always takes the form of a model — a simplified representation of the world, which helps you cut through the complexities. Once you have a model, you can ask how well it fits the facts; if it fits them reasonably well, you can ask what sorts of magnitudes, what sort of tradeoffs, it implies. Your policy opinions then flow from the model, not the other way around."

One prominent example of the wrong approach, to Krugman, was a notion advanced by (among others) the former Lazard Frères rainmaker Felix Rohatyn when he was campaigning unsuccessfully for the vice-chairmanship of the Fed. Rohatyn argued that the economy could easily be made to grow at 4% per year without inflation — not the 2.5% that seemed to be the Fed's target.

One key reason given for this position was the so-called "productivity revolution," in which technology is deemed to have greatly increased the economy's potential, but in ways that somehow don't show up in the productivity estimates from the Bureau of Economic Analysis.

This astonishes Krugman, inasmuch as "the *same* numbers are used to estimate productivity growth and GDP growth. If you think that productivity is really growing at 3%, not the 1% the BEA reports," he concludes, "then you must also believe that GDP is really growing at 4%, not 2% — in other words, that the Fed is already giving us 4% growth, so what's the problem?"

The work that Krugman is doing in these essays is no mere intellectual exercise. It bears directly on many of the critical issues that you must understand and deal with in order to form a coherent investment viewpoint: jobs, free trade, technology, the interplay between interest rates and exchange rates, our alleged trade deficit with China, and the problems of Japan, to name just a few.

And Krugman is, refreshingly, an equal opportunity illusion-buster, skewering with even-handed élan the goofy theories of left and right alike. Indeed, this is his point: that ideologies can rarely stand the rigorous economic light of day.

But while he's equally pillorying Robert Reich and Jack Kemp, he does it with a wit and a clarity that are every bit as important as is the rigor of his modeling. And that's his other point: the Saganesque quest for comprehensibility, "a parable, a metaphor, a particular line of approach — that makes a seemingly abstruse piece of economics easily accessible."

All of that said, one need not — and I do not — accept everything that Krugman believes he's proven. And one may find somewhat distressing his tendency to conclude that everyone who disagrees with him is both wrong *and* lacking in economic rigor.

And here let me state my belief that book reviews should only be done by the authors of other books, if only because this imposes a certain sense of fairness on a process that makes it too easy to take potshots. Thus while observing the occasional mote in Krugman's eye, I must not fail to acknowledge the beam in my own.

For example, nowhere in these essays will you find a hint that Krugman (and Treasury undersecretary Lawrence Summers, and I, for that matter) were convinced, in the early to mid-'80s, that the Reagan budget deficits must lead to resurgent inflation. He and the rest of us had a very rigorous Keynesian model which dictated this outcome. But the Volcker/Greenspan Fed had quite another model ... and theirs was right. (OK, so we both got that one wrong.)

Indeed, the role of monetary policy in controlling inflation is something the supply-siders got mostly right, and Krugman is wrong to trivialize them as Johnny-one-note "cut taxes/full stop/message ends" straw men. (OK, so I don't run around reminding everyone that I once sold tax shelters.)

Finally, in some of these essays — dating back little more than two years — Krugman's models made him pretty darn certain that the nonaccelerating-inflation rate of unemployment (NAIRU) was 5% to 5 1/2%, and that the Fed neither could nor should get inflation much below 3% to 4%. You *can* be both historically and economically rigorous and still misjudge how far powerful trends can carry. (OK, so I thought — and wrote — that the stock market was smoking dope at Dow 4500. Krugman has no corner on misjudging the power of trends.)

Don't hold these things against him — or me, for that matter. Paul Krugman does more good economics more clearly and with more flair in these 204 easily digestible pages than you're likely to find in any book three times its size. And reading *The Accidental Theorist* straight through on your next cross-country plane flight (as you can, and I did) will make you a better investor, a better advisor, and a better student of the real world of modern global economics.

In a profession that's prepared to embrace the utterly crackpot theory that the sole determinant of American stock prices is the age of the population, these would be welcome improvements indeed.

. . . And One Final Word

Millbrook School in Millbrook, NY, is perhaps the finest small college preparatory school in America today. It is also, I believe, the future of secondary education. And, when you've toured its Trevor Teaching Zoo, or wandered among the treetops on its Forest Canopy Walkway, you know you've been to a genuinely magical place.

A portion of the proceeds from the sale of every copy of *The Craft of Advice* will be donated to Millbrook. And, if you'd like to help me help the school, it would be my pleasure to send you a personalized, autographed bookplate for your copy of this book. Just write a check for a minimum of $20 *(more if you like: it's tax-deductible)* to MILLBROOK SCHOOL, and send it to me at:

THE NICK MURRAY COMPANY, INC.
P.O. BOX 1554
MATTITUCK, NY 11952

NOTES